MENTOR IN A MANUAL
Climbing the Academic Ladder to Tenure

A. Clay Schoenfeld
Emeritus Professor and Dean, University of Wisconsin-Madison
Contributing Editor, *Academic Leader*

and

Robert Magnan
Senior Editor, Magna Publications

Foreword by

Allan W. Ostar, President Emeritus
American Association of State Colleges and Universities

With a Special Appendix:
What Do I Do if I Don't Make Tenure?

MAGNA PUBLICATIONS
2718 Dryden Drive
Madison WI 53704-3086
(608) 246-3580
1992

Mentor in a Manual: Climbing the Academic Ladder to Tenure

Library of Congress Cataloging-in-Publication Data

Schoenfeld, Clay,   1918 -
       Mentor in a manual : climbing the academic ladder to
   tenure/ A. Clay Schoenfeld and Robert Magnan : foreword by
   Allan W. Ostar.
              p.   cm.
       Includes bibliographical references.
       ISBN 0-912150-20-3 : $29.95
       1. College teachers—Tenure—United States—Handbooks,
   manuals, etc.   I. Magnan, Robert.   II. Title.
   LB23335.7.S36   1992
   378.1'22—dc20   92-80411
                                                     CIP

Printed in the United States of America

Library of Congress Catalog Card Number: 92-80411

ISBN: 0-912150-20-3

Magna Publications, Inc.
2718 Dryden Dr.
Madison, WI 53704
(608) 246-3580

CONTENTS

FOREWORD

An American institution of higher education is not so much a set of buildings and grounds, or a hierarchy of administrators, or even a body of students as it is a community of individual scholars, engaged in instruction, investigation, and interpretation in areas of their own academic expertise.

It is the perpetual task of each such community to recruit and nurture a steady flow of new members — and, yes, to screen out those acolytes lacking necessary qualities of mind and heart.

As a recent issue of the Pew Higher Education Research Program's *Policy Perspectives* notes: "The peer review process that lies at the heart of [academe] in this country has proven substantially more effective ... than the programs of self-assessment existing in other professions."

For each newly appointed assistant professor, then, the path to ultimate acceptance as a full-fledged member of a community of scholars — to that award known as tenure — can be daunting. Yet navigating it successfully is not only essential to the personal and professional well-being of the individual aspirant, but to the recharging of an institution's batteries, and in a larger sense as an assurance to society as a whole that its colleges and universities are in a constant state of renewal and reinvigoration.

So any sound, effective field manual or guidebook for campus new hires can be an invaluable resource, indeed. That is the objective of this book and, on the whole, it succeeds admirably. Because our institutions of higher education are so disparate in their traditions, missions, and aspirations, not everything in this book can be universally applicable or even acceptable. But, to the extent that it is possible, this guide to how to climb an academic ladder to tenure does its job tenaciously and with a minimum of cant.

I am particularly pleased that the authors not only present the essentials of acquiring a professorial state of mind but also deal in refreshing frankness with the pragmatic "politics" of assimilation into the basic unit of most institutions, the academic department.

Befitting the current national emphasis on strengthening undergraduate instruction, the authors offer a very strong chapter on the central role of a professor as teacher, outlining tested, student-focused strategies and tactics.

Solid chapters on research and on service sketch out the depth and breadth of a beginning professors's tripartite responsibilities.

To the extent that appearing periodically in appropriate journals is a measure of scholarly accomplishment, faculty seeking promotion to tenure will also find of special value the chapter titled "A Bottom Line: Getting Published."

A final chapter treats in a definitive manner how a candidate for tenure might best present his or her credentials for that final peer review.

An Appendix — "What Do I Do if I Don't Make Tenure?" — deals sympathetically and helpfully with ways to turn a major disappointment into a challenge.

Yet this is no oversimplified "cookbook." It raises a new assistant professor's sights above the building blocks of career planning and professional development to the higher elevations of institutional ethos and public expectations.

I have known the senior author for some 40 years, so I can testify personally to his sensitivity and acumen in and about the halls of academe. As the senior editor of manifold newsletters and books for personnel in higher education, the junior author is alike most qualified. Their writing is eminently readable and practical, with wit and style.

If I had a son or daughter about to embark on a career in higher education, this is a book I would recommend strongly. In fact, I'd probably buy a copy for ceremonial presentation.

Allan W. Ostar, President Emeritus,
American Association of State Colleges and Universities

PREFACE

What **is** academic tenure, anyway, and **why**?

Tenure is intended to preserve and enhance an institution of higher education's excellence and its function in developing the human intellect. Tenure contributes to this objective by giving a strong measure of security and protection to faculty members; it frees them to teach, inquire, create, publish, and serve with less concern for the immediate popularity or acceptability of their efforts than would be the case if termination of employment were a constant possibility.

The granting of academic tenure represents a long-term commitment of institutional resources which requires proof of excellence in past performance and a forecast that an individual faculty member's intellectual vitality and future contributions will continue to be of high quality for many years to come. There is no entitlement to tenure based upon a record that is merely competent and satisfactory for a prescribed period of time.

Most institutions grant tenure in part through an evaluation of the candidate by his or her colleagues — called "peer review" — not by arbitrary administrative decisions or through outside influence.

Academic tenure has evolved from the right of students to learn, untrammeled by constraints on professional teaching and research that may stem from internal or external political pressures; from the right of the public to an effective campus faculty quality-control mechanism; from the need of faculty for a level of economic security; and from the need of an institution for a striving, stable staff.

In the political and economic security it provides its recipients, academic tenure is somewhat analogous to seniority in a union labor force; to no-fire status in municipal, state, or federal civil service; or to a commission as a "regular" in the armed forces. But academic tenure is qualitatively different in that it cannot be earned by mere time-serving, by passing a single exam, by attending a particular academy, or by raising one's right arm. It is the culmination of a dynamic process of trial and assessment.

Academic tenure has a tenuous basis at best in statutory civil law and has only limited protection in case law, but its inscription in institutional rules and regulations gives it powerful credibility. It is "policed," if that's the right word, by the academic community through the moral suasion of the American Association of University Professors and the practice of that society to "blacklist" institutions violating tenure principles, although the courts as well are increasingly willing to look at instances of an apparent breakdown in institutional due process.

The policing system has some holes. There's scarcely an issue of *The Chronicle of Higher Education* but what you can read in its **Faculty Notes** section about reports that "five professors say their college violated their rights by dismissing them for 'insubordination,'" that "six professors have filed a $100,000 lawsuit charging they were forced out of their contracts by conservative political activists," that "faculty-union members have voted no confidence in the university president because he failed to address faculty evaluation concerns," or that "a state legislature is contemplating a law that would permit independent panels of experts from other institutions to handle grievances based on sex or race discrimination."

Academic tenure is not immutable. An individual professor can abrogate the "contract" through gross incompetence or moral turpitude, and an institution can void tenure under dire fiscal exigency. That such situations have been rare does not make their arising in the future any less likely.

Nor is tenure automatically transferable from one institution to another. It is campus-specific; indeed, on any particular campus, it is usually department- or division-specific.

To be sure, not everyone is a tenure fan. A 1986 Carnegie Foundation for the Advancement of Teaching national survey identified significant pockets of vocal campus disenchantment with the tenure system. More recently, a distinguished historian/provost emeritus has called for "a more humane and sensible system of tenure [before it] inflicts what may turn out to be fatal wounds on higher education."

Such reservations notwithstanding, academic tenure is among the most prized and honored of professional awards by both campus citizens and the public at large. It is the ultimate rite of passage from acolyte to academe, pursued with gem-hard diligence by legions of assistant professors seeking promotion to associate professor and concomitant anointment as "tenured."

How does an assistant professor "make tenure"? Answering that question is the mission of this book.

Given the wide variance among institutions of higher education in the United States, the authors have had to be something less than utterly specific in trying to provide answers. But the azimuths they offer should be applicable in most situations, if read and applied with the judgment that has gone into the framing. Since both authors have "been through the wars," so to speak, and have conducted extensive conversations on the subject with faculty and administrators of all ranks country-wide, what they say is at least as concrete and practical as it is possible to render what is essentially intangible.

For very helpful assistance and/or review, the authors are greatly indebted to these colleagues around the country:

James Bell, Virginia Polytechnic Institute and State University
John Disinger, Ohio State University
Mavis Donahue, University of Illinois at Chicago
Ralph Frasca, University of Northern Iowa
William Feyerharm, Kansas State University
Laurie Golson, professional independent textbook developer, Evanston IL
Robert J. Griffin, Marquestte University
John C. Hendee, University of Idaho
Susan M. Johnson, Memphis State University
Sally Sieloff Magnan, University of Wisconsin-Madison
Ann McElaney-Johnson, Ripon College
Robert F. Meier, Iowa State University
Dayle Molen, California State University-Fresno
Robert M. O'Neil, University of Virginia
Allan W. Ostar, American Association of State Colleges and Universities
Laurence Porter, Michigan State University
Carl Reidel, University of Vermont
Carolyn Saarni, Sonoma State University
Harland Samson, University of Wisconsin-Madison
Alan T. Seagren, University of Nebraska
Sheryl Stateler Smith, Madison WI

But for any lapses in omission or commission, the authors take full responsibility.

ACS
RM

Madison, Wisconsin
January 1992

I
ACQUIRING A PROFESSIONAL FRAME OF MIND

> *We must focus our passion for this university as a fuel for change. I am excited by faculty members for whom teaching does not end after 48 minutes, by students whose learning does not end with the ringing of a bell, by staff whose time-clock is only the needs of those served and the quality and urgency of the task at hand, by alumni whose affection for this place is not diminished by the passing years.*
>
> *Our future rests in the passion of the pursuit. I see a university enlivened by such a commitment, and a university that rewards such spirit.*
>
> — Ohio State University President E. Gordon Gee in *The Ohio Alumni Magazine*, April 1991.

You might expect we'd begin this manual with some practical tips on that bottom-line requirement — publishing in lieu of perishing. No, that comes later — in spades. Initially here we propose to confront you with a sort of philosophical issue: **Do you really understand what being a professor is all about? Are you sure you're deeply committed to pursuing a career in academia?** Only *you* can know deep in your heart whether you're a worthy candidate to enter the professoriate.

For a decade or so, on this campus or that, as student and perhaps as junior staff, you've been exposed to a process of socialization. That you have chosen to strive to join the elect **may** be an indication of your devotion to a life in higher education. But are you in fact of a suitable frame of mind?

A PITFALL AND A PRESCRIPTION

Most newly appointed assistant professors have a general idea what being a professor is all about, or at least what they think it entails. But since there's no West Point for professors, real training **for** the assignment comes from being **in** the assignment. So they learn from role models and from making their own mistakes.

The focus of assistant-professor training is quite properly on what a professor **does**. Unfortunately in some cases that's where it tends to stop — just this side of what new faculty need to know each morning to get the day's job done. But you must go on from there to thinking and learning about what a professor **is** and **should be**.

Do you have a clear sense of yourself as an academic person with opportunities and responsibilities that are unique in American life? Or do you plod along day to day, working hard and developing essential skills, yet missing a critical step: developing a feeling for how your growing confidence and competence relate to the essence of what a professor is meant to be?

An antidote: To gain a vision of yourself to be, to acquire a much richer image of yourself as a member of the professoriate, steep yourself in the literature of higher learning in America — classic histories and interpretations, chronicles of more recent developments, the current crop of somewhat acerbic commentators on the academic scene. (*See "Suggested Readings" at end of chapter.*)

And, of course, perform a weekly scan of *The Chronicle of Higher Education* and a periodic look at such national periodicals as *Change, Academe,* AAHE *Bulletin, Academic Leader,* and *The Teaching Professor*.

WEIGHING THE PROFESSORIATE IN THE BALANCE

From your readings in the literature of higher education, you'll gain insights that will broaden your perspective. For one thing, you'll appreciate anew that while we're sometimes inclined to speak of America's "system" of higher education, there is in fact no system, unless a kaleidoscope can be said to constitute a system, so diverse are our colleges and universities in their traditions, circumstances, and aspirations. Nor are they, individually or collectively, so self-assured about the nature of their functions and policies as their promotional brochures might suggest.

So, diverse issues — pervasive, perennial, or passing — are constantly surfacing on the agenda of the professoriate.

The point being that, as with any profession, the professoriate is neither so complete in all respects, without defect or omission, sound, nor flawless that you need swallow it whole. Make it your objective, rather, to search out those institutional attributes that are admirable, that command your respect, and give them your wholehearted support — and to identify those characteristics less than admirable and seek to help bring about constructive change.

To paraphrase Carl Schurz, 19th-century German immigrant become American educator/soldier/statesman: "My profession, right or wrong. When right, to be kept right. When wrong, to be set right."

In short, whenever, wherever you join, you will find the professoriate, like any calling, a mixed bag.

As a group, and at their best, colleges and universities play a critical, and probably unique, role in establishing the quality of American life.

Institutions of higher learning serve as one of the key storehouses of knowledge, understanding, and cultural values in our society, and they carry responsibility for transmitting information, perceptions, and values between generations. They also have responsibility for developing new knowledge and providing the intellectual leadership needed for the rigorous examination of existing learning so that even better understanding may be achieved. ...

Teaching and research programs serve society in several ways. In providing education (including advanced research training), they are society's servants. In continuously looking for new and better ways of doing things, they are society's critics. In addition, academic institutions also serve as a "conscience" for society and as a stimulus for appropriate change.

— *The Commission on College Retirement, Pension and Retirement Policies in Colleges and Universities* (San Francisco: Jossey-Bass, 1990), pp. 281-282.

FORTUNATE ATTRIBUTES

The professoriate is at home in an enterprise unalterably dedicated as are few others to *the public weal.* In exchange for an outpouring of appropriations, higher education in America seeks to be a servant, not a master.

As individuals, professors represent scholarly attainment and love of learning. *Merit,* not *"pull,"* governs their promotions. Creativity and curiosity, not aggrandizement, motivate them.

The professoriate is devoted to *the life of the mind,* pledged to defend a climate in which free thought and unconstrained inquiry can flourish, to the everlasting benefit of students in particular and humanity in general.

To a degree the lay public doesn't appreciate, the professoriate on any particular campus is *a self-governing body.* Chief executive officers of institutions of higher education tend to be relatively powerless who haven't translated their thoughts into faculty thoughts and faculty sentiments into their own acts. No campus reform can sustain itself with which the tenor of the faculty isn't in sympathy.

No more rewarding *challenge* blesses any profession than to hold in its hands, as does the professoriate, the young minds of the country — to fill, to shape, to stimulate, to *teach* — and in turn to be challenged. And no other profession gets such an automatic annual recharge of new enthusiasm with each fresh influx of bright, questioning students, undergraduate and graduate — a veritable fountain of youth.

The *intellectual resources* of the professoriate are tremendous. Like a seed whose germination requires only favorable soil and water, professors ask only for an environment that will foster the growth of their understanding and the application of their skills and insights — plus a living wage.

The professoriate is marked, as are few other callings, by *high standards* of initiative and honor. The academic life is a good life. The qualities it demands are fortitude, integrity, self-restraint, personal loyalty to others, compassion, and altruism.

The power and the glory of a college or university are in its faculty, and the most distinguished institutions are distinguished precisely because of the quality of the men and women they have been able to recruit and retain on their professional staffs — able teachers in juxtaposition with eager students, together each spring bringing new life and enthusiasm to the citizenry of the country; probing investigators enlarging our knowledge, renewing our culture, and producing profound insights to help conquer disease, promote technological progress, husband the environment, overcome social problems; outreach specialists carrying light and learning to every corner of a commonwealth, linking soil and seminar.

This is *good company*. You can spend your life in it with sure satisfaction.

The performance of public duty is not the whole of what makes good life, of course; there is also the pursuit of private excellence. Both are to be found for the seeking in the academic life.

It gives much and takes more, enriching freely anyone prepared to give more than he or she can get, at least in terms of monetary rewards.

To paraphrase Stanford's professor of public service, John W. Gardner, a career in higher education isn't a mountain that has a summit. Nor is it a game that has a final score. A career in higher education is *an endless unfolding* and — if you wish it to be — an endless process of self-discovery, an endless and unpredictable dialogue between your own potentialities and the life situations in which you find yourself.

By "potentialities" he means "not just intellectual gifts but the full range of your capacities for learning, teaching, sensing, wondering, investigating, serving, loving, inspiring."

All this is not to say the professoriate is a roundtable of white knights and ladies. Like any profession, it has its flip side.

America's colleges and universities ... have rested far too long on our well-earned laurels .... Our self-satisfaction is exceeded only by our slowness to recognize that we have neglected the most central aspects of our enterprise, we have ignored our obligations to our most important clients .... We are coming to "the end of sanctuary" for higher education, the end of a time in which American colleges and universities were sheltered from the cold winds that buffeted other institutions. Today, American higher education can expect to be subjected to the same critical scrutiny and demands for accountability that all other institutions face.
— University of Maryland System Chancellor Donald N. Langenberg in his July 1991 inaugural address.

FLAWED CHARACTERISTICS

Some professors seemingly have an innate tendency toward *mental eccentricity and exhibitionism*. As higher education critic Carl Becker once remarked, "A professor is a person who thinks otherwise." All this is well and good provided it doesn't lead to an attitude of indifference to the fact that professors can't divorce themselves from their association with an institution. As a Yale Committee of Ten told their colleagues, "The public is bound to look upon you *as* the university," for good and ill.

Some professors as well have a bent toward *jousting with windmills*, "for an endless capacity for nonsense on stilts," as a recent *New York Times* editorial put it; too inclined to fight at the drop of a hat over fancied restrictions on their freedom or invasions of their privacy — meanwhile imposing on their students a level of restraint on speech and conduct the professors would never tolerate for themselves (3, 6).

No matter how liberal and progressive some professors may be as individuals, collectively they lean toward *conservatism*. It's been well said it's easier to move a cemetery than a faculty curriculum committee. After trying to get fellow scholars excited about switching to research on consequences of global environmental change, Professor Richard A. Berk, UCLA sociology chair, recently complained they were "too slow-moving and timid." As former Modern Language Association executive director William D. Schaefer writes in *Education without Compromise*, "The faculties of most colleges and universities have an extraordinary capacity to resist [curricular] change. [They] love to play at the margins, ... making only minor cosmetic adjustments."

In too many cases, *over-specialization* is a curse of the professoriate — to be consumed by highly differentiated subject matter, to be absorbed in departmental concerns, to place the interests of a divisional unit ruthlessly above the interests of the campus as a whole — all at the expense of a more inclusive frame of mind. In his current book, *Killing the Spirit: Higher Education in America*, the noted American historian and emeritus provost of the University of California at Santa Cruz, Page Smith, criticizes over-specialization by summoning testimony: "As disciplines become increasingly technical, they tend to devolve into competing sub-groups scarcely able to communicate with each other"; "Members of a modern college faculty sometimes strike one, in an Emersonian phrase, as a collection of 'infinitely repellent particles.' " Witness the short, unhappy life, for example, of the American Association for the Advancement of the Humanities. Even with nearly 60,000 faculty members teaching humanities courses in colleges and universities, the AAAH was able to attract only 3,000 dues-paying members, and folded after just three years (1979-1982) because, as its founder and chairman admitted, "individual humanists have failed to develop a sense of their collective interest." In his *The Moral Collapse of the University*, Bruce Wilshire describes a "balkanized" university formed around disciplines that won't — indeed, can't — communicate with each other: "the only thing holding the university together is the central heating system."

For an unwillingness to assume responsibility for *lack of attention to the teaching problems* in their fields, Ernest L. Boyer, president of the Carnegie Foundation for the Advancement of Teaching, has recently called on professors to redefine scholarship to include "the integration, application, and teaching" of knowledge as well as its "discovery" — and that the faculty reward system be reformed thereby. Schaefer admits that the humanists, for one group, "continue to stress the less important — dissemination in print, over the most important — dissemination in the classroom."

Then there are some of what distinguished bacteriologist become university president E.B. Fred called *"pebble-pickers" in research* — those who become so immersed in details and methods that they identify them for productive scholarship itself, who mistake volume of data for true achievement. Smith concurs: "The vast majority of so-called research turned out in the modern university is worthless .... It is dispiriting; it depresses the whole academic enterprise .... It robs the student ... of the thoughtful and considerate attention of a teacher ... unequivocally committed to teaching." In some instances, professors have even learned — in graduate school, no less — to fudge their data (1).

Add the *"bean counters"* who try always to assess the degree to which things "count" toward salary raises and promotions. How does chairing a divisional committee count, compared with completing a research paper? Does it count to handle the local arrangements for a professional meeting? Does it count to offer to teach the course of an ill colleague? Faculty who are continually engaged in a utilitarian calculus for everything they do — who always ask, "What's in it for me?" — display the very antithesis of a professional orientation in which one does what one does because that's what professors do, not in order to impress a chair or a dean.

Collegiality is not necessarily a hallmark of professors. Despite a recent movement to encourage the "mentoring" of new hires by senior staff, three psychologists examining mentoring in actual practice have found that many departments continue to apply a form of *social Darwinism:* "Let's throw the kids off the end of the pier and see whether they can swim or not. **We** didn't get any survival advice; why should **they**?" (6). As Schaefer confesses from his experience as a vice chancellor, "Otherwise well-intentioned members of a campus personnel committee can reach tenure decisions without having seen, much less talked to, the candidate. If we were to begin feeding deep, deep upon their peerless eyes, trusting, at times, to our intuition in appraising an individual's worth, we might have to rely, or rely less frequently, on the printed word."

Besides ignoring their colleagues, there are some professors who not only *dodge the knife-and-fork circuit* but belittle those willing to act as ambassadors to the public — performing the essential and never-ending task of explaining the need of our institutions of higher education for "funds, freedom, and freshmen," to use the alliterative phrase of Professor Scott Cutlip, personification of university public relations.

The professoriate by and large acquiesces in the institutional struggle to raise ever more money for new programs, research, scholarships, named chairs, new buildings — a struggle that can force colleges and universities to *adapt to priorities* established by foundations, government agencies, corporations, and private donors. At many a site you have to add "campus" to President Eisenhower's "military-industrial complex." Far from living in an ivory tower, the professoriate is influenced too much rather than too little by the outside world, says President Emeritus Derek Bok of Harvard in his current book,

Universities and the Future of America, and it is "precisely this influence that accounts for failure of academia to respond better to urgent societal needs."

According to at least one critic, and an in-house one at that, the professoriate is to blame for inventing and nurturing *a system of academic tenure* that has "inflicted what may turn out to be fatal wounds on higher education": the mandatory research criterion "does not result in any measurable benefit to anybody or anything"; the requisite "debilitating" promotion and tenure committee reviews "take literally uncounted faculty hours" and stress the nerves of candidates and families "filled with dread or resignation"; resulting decisions are often "highly questionable or blatantly unfair." Unsuccessful candidates are cast out in disgrace and fractured self-esteem, and, once safe in the tenure womb, associate professors can revert to a fetal position, never to be heard from again except for an occasional tremor, to paraphrase Smith.

Today the most serious flaw of the professoriate may be the safe harbor it can offer buccaneers who pledge allegiance only to an international guild of academic pirates or to the sources of their research money, who talk to their colleagues only en route to airports, meanwhile turning over their classes to teaching assistants who've never had so much as an hour of pedagogical training. It's these *peripatetic professors* who can leave open a campus door to a breed of amoral administrators who play fast and loose with the ethics of higher education. A recent result has been what national wire service education writer Anthony Flint calls "a crisis in public confidence — the ivory tower under siege," in consequence of a concatenation of flagrant abuses of public trust by personnel at some of America's most prestigious institutions (4).

THE CONSUMMATE CANDIDATE

In your continuing socialization as a candidate for tenure, you are free as in few other professions to adopt or reject qualities of your calling, to mold your own vision of the professional you can be — provided you give your vision a 360-degree traverse.

You're not a castaway on an island. You come not in entire forgetfulness, and not in utter nakedness, but trailing clouds of tradition. Put yourself in context of higher education in general and of your institution in particular — rooted in the past, responding to the present, revealing the future. Appreciate your responsibilities for reinforcing such internal emphases as teaching and research, and understand your obligations to be in touch with the needs of the larger community through public service.

Match the demands of today against the lessons of yesterday and the potentials of tomorrow. Seek both a diversity of culture and a "university" of thought.

Above all, see your institution as an integrated organism, with a spirit and a heart and a will that transcend the purposes of its separate parts and link it to the world, an institution that needs only a caring professoriate to enter new frontiers of educational excellence and public support as American life and American learning proceed together toward broader lands and fairer days.

Now if all that sounds to you like what they used to call "corny," so be it. Read on, please.

PREPARING TO BE A PROFESSIONAL

PERVASIVE ISSUES FACING THE PROFESSORIATE

Academicians like to make "problems" out of problems. As Robert M. Hutchins, then chancellor of the University of Chicago, defined the distinction: "A real problem is a confusion about the aim and destiny of the institution. A 'problem' is a difficulty in the material order."

Put another way, a strategist asks, "Where should I go?" while a tactician asks, "How do I get there?" Hence government agencies speak of "goals" and "objectives."

An example: In 1862, the Congress of the United States made a monumental strategic, **what-where** decision, that higher education was not to be solely for the well-to-do or for those going into the learned professions but for "the industrial and agricultural classes" as well, and in the enabling Morrill Act allocated grants of public domain lands to each of the states to fund the establishment of (hence) land-grant colleges. The **how** was left up to the states. The result changed the face of higher learning in America.

Problems and "problems" are still with us, and any dichotomy is not always clear; in fact, they tend to be mutually supporting or contradictory, as the case may be.

From your background reading, in your selection of role models, as you acquire a broader perspective, and as you cogitate about the dimensions of your chosen profession, you'll recognize the professor you will become will perforce have to grapple with a congeries — a "collection of things or parts mixed together" — of problems and "problems," of academic issues not limited to your discipline alone but endemic to higher education in the broad.

How better to prepare for the professoriate than to begin to confront some of those issues now?

*(In researching what issues to pose here, we've drawn on the
thoughts of a professor of higher education in a large state
university, the president of a foundation for the advancement of education, an emeritus president of an Ivy League
university, the chair of social studies in a community college,
a lawyer specializing in the ethics of higher education, an
education writer for a premier daily newspaper, a professor
and dean of a graduate school in a fine arts institute, a national campus trends survey conducted by a leading
academic organization, current articles in a higher education weekly, a distinguished scientist, a recent recipient of an
award for excellent teaching, a director of outreach for a midsize institution, a trustee, a West Coast historian/provost, a
business executive, a congressional aide, and our own experience and observations. The resulting list is indeed a congeries; we've run all the questions together in the thought you
may find it fun to try to decipher who phrased what.)*

Questions to ponder:

How can adequate financial support be ensured in an era of
uncertain economic conditions?

If fiscal resources decline, how can we recruit and retain
quality faculty, particularly in competitive disciplines?

Is the quality of undergraduate instruction as inferior as
some commentators maintain? If so, what's to be done?

How can facilities renovation and renewal needs be met
simultaneously with constructing new buildings?

Can or should we address the growing enrollment differences between public and independent institutions?

Can we maintain a desirable diversity among colleges and
universities without perpetuating undesirable inequality and
hierarchy? What is the public interest in private education?

To what extent do administratively imposed measures of accountability and productivity represent a bona fide threat to
cherished faculty autonomy?

To what extent is the total quality management (TQM) concept applicable to higher education?

How can the commitments of higher education to fairness
and equality best be reconciled with requirements for efficiency,
quality control, and value judgments?

Is it morally permitted or required for colleges and universities to go beyond race-blind and sex-blind standards in encouraging the prospects of minorities and women? If so, which
"quotas" are permissible and which are not?

What should be the faculty role in achieving academic respectability and fiscal honesty in intercollegiate athletic
programs?

How are we in academe to recapture our moral and intellectual equilibrium from the academic fundamentalists and their schemes of orthodoxies?

Will the teachers teach? If they will, can they? What will they teach?

Can a flood of mediocre monographs-for-the-sake-of-promotion be dammed; of journals for the same purpose be reduced to some manageable, rational number?

Can a more humane and sensible system of tenure be worked out? Or should the whole system be abandoned?

What theories of human nature and the human mind will guide higher education in the future?

Can we truly think critically and self-critically? To what end?

How will we balance a sense of community and our heterogeneities?

Can we correct historic injustices without witlessly creating new ones?

Why are our campuses slow to research and teach their own ethical behavior in the face of national press coverage of falsification of scientific research data, renewed racism on campus, expressions of bigotry by student publications, a seemingly endless chain of sanctions by the NCAA for major rule infractions, tuition and price-fixing, allegations of admissions quotas for Asian-Americans, actual or perceived abuse of institutional resources by presidents for personal gain, collusion on setting limits on financial aid, cavalier handling of federal research dollars, and so on? What is an individual professor to make of or do about all this?

How can departments implement the recommendations of the Association of American Colleges that the undergraduate advising system undergo major reforms, as outlined in the 1991 report, "Liberal Learning and the Arts and Sciences Major"?

How can institutions engage more closely the outside world and not succumb to its blandishments, its distractions, its corrupting entanglements?

Why is it that what Rachel Carson did for risks to the environment, Ralph Nader for consumer protection, Michael Harrington for problems of poverty, Betty Friedan for women's rights, they did as independent critics, not as members of a faculty? Why was it that the seminal work on the plight of blacks in America was written by a Swedish social scientist, not by an American professor?

Is there an optimum balance within the trilogy of teaching/research/service? Who is to decide? What level of voice should be granted to faculty, students, alumni, trustees, administrators, governments?

What should be the focus of undergraduate instruction —
the liberal arts that cultivate a learning life, or professional courses that impart skills in how to earn a living? Whatever the
decision, what are the relative merits of a required core curriculum versus a cafeteria of electives?

How should the need to develop fully the talents of the most
able students be weighed against the claims of less able and disadvantaged students for special support?

What are a college's optimum strategies for preparing students for useful roles in the constituent community, as well as
for roles in an increasingly global marketplace?

Should university research emphasize investigating basic
phenomena or applying research to solving practical problems?
Or is it this an unreal dichotomy? To what extent do federal and
foundation funds skew the support of productive scholarship in
the sciences, the social studies, the humanities?

Should the faculty reward system reflect a graduate school
focus on the discovery of new knowledge or can it recognize as
well the integrators and interpreters of knowledge? In that
reward system, should an emphasis be on *equality* (treating
everyone the same) or on *equity* (treating everyone fairly but differently)? In the reward system as well, how can newer fields of
interdisciplinary study be accommodated among traditionally
defined disciplines?

What level of institutional resources and skills is properly allocated to serving the needs of adult citizens in community or
commonwealth?

What relationship should exist between the contributions of
higher education to the economic well-being of the country and
to its non-economic aims?

---

*The University is for the students .... We have to
get the undergraduate back into the center of things.*
— University of Texas President Logan Wilson in his first
public statement Sept. 21, 1952.

To this list you can undoubtedly add problems and "problems" that have surfaced since these lines were composed —
agenda-setting for the professoriate being a very dynamic
process.

Whichever of these ideas seem to be the more relevant to
you, begin confronting them now, as we've suggested. The more
time you devote to profound academic issues, the more sure
your professional sense of direction becomes.

On the other hand, if macro-issues appear intimidating at this stage of your career, you can identify micro-issues that will intrigue you.

PERSONAL DISCIPLINARY ISSUES

Whatever else you're doing in academia, you'll be doing at least some teaching, and, given the current focus on undergraduate teaching problems and opportunities, you won't be able to duck issues pertaining to college teaching.

Professor Peter Frederick of Wabash College (IN) has compiled a list of challenging "questions for collegial conversations about teaching":

> What are the essential questions of your discipline? What are the irreducibly most significant basic facts, ideas, concepts, themes, and requisite skills your students must know? What in your course do they **have** to know as distinct from what they can live without?

> What are your teaching goals? What's primary and what secondary? What do you want your students to know? to think? to be able to do? what knowledge, skills, and attitudes to have?

> What do you know about your students? Can you describe them? How do they learn? What kind of learning styles and cultural diversity exist in your class? What do your students already know about your course subject? How do you acknowledge their prior knowledge and experience?

> What do you know about yourself? your teaching style? What are your thoughts? How do you teach best? In what ways do you want to stretch yourself and expand your strategies as a teacher?

> Where are you in your course right now? What did you do last week? yesterday? How did it go? What are your students learning? What are they having trouble with? How do you know?

> What about tomorrow's class? What are you going to do, and why? How can you connect your goals for tomorrow to what you know is already in your students' heads and hearts? How can you connect the epistemology of your field to a strategy for teaching the topic, text, or content for tomorrow's class?

> What does your class have to do with the departmental mission? the institutional mission? What kind of persons do you and your institution want your students, your graduates, to be? What does your course have to do with the kind of person/professional **you** want to be?

> Given all this, what are you going to do in class tomorrow, and why?

Academic issues, you see, are all around you for the confronting. It's the mark of the professional to face them head on.

AND NOW LET'S TALK HARD-BALL DOLLARS AND SENSE

The moment you make tenure, society (in the guise of a state legislature or an institutional endowment fund) sets aside an interest-bearing annuity of some three-quarters to a million dollars with which to fund your annual salary and fringe benefits for a 35- to 40-year period of active duty plus another 10 to 15 in retirement. That's no small change.

To qualify for society's investment on that scale in your academic career of a lifetime, you ought to be willing to make an appropriate financial investment of your own now:

- A professional library of books and serials.
- Computer hardware and software.
- Travel to conferences, and fees and accommodations there.
- Travel to and lodging at research sites.
- Summers spent working in laboratory, library, or field in lieu of vacation.
- Physical work space and facilities at home.
- A certain level of obligatory entertaining.
- Learned society dues.
- Frequent transportation to and from campus.
- Parking and/or shuttle bus fees.

And so on and on. The "laundry list" can be extensive — and shocking to an erstwhile graduate student used to a comparatively free ride.

"When my wife was starting on the tenure trail," the junior author (**RM**) recalls, "we had to get used to spending for association dues, journal subscriptions, travel, conference registration, and so forth — really tough after grad school years. But it's now a different game, with different rules and different rewards."

A not-so-minor reward is the fact that expenses that can be legitimately and directly attributable to the requirements of professional advancement are tax-deductible, provided you keep detailed records and use the long IRS form. For a savvy guide on the subject, consult *Tax Guide for College Teachers and Other College Personnel* (College Park MD: Academic Information Service, published annually).

But the massive payoff for your commitment of time, talent, energy, and money as a candidate for tenure is that massive lifetime annuity at the end of the rainbow.

(And yet if your obsession with work is so overwhelming

that you lose a slice of life and love in the bargain, it won't be worth it.)

AND SO, ON TO THE RACES

"All right," we can hear you saying, "enough of this frame-of-mind stuff. You may have helped raise my sights, but you haven't intimidated me. I'm still set on climbing the ladder to tenure and becoming all I can be as a professor. So let's get on with it."

OK, for starters, here's a once-over-lightly socialization guide for your next six years (5):

YOUR FOUR LEARNING OBJECTIVES

1. Knowledge.

Information, data, theories, concepts, facts. Answers the question: "What should I know?" May be achieved through many learning methods. Highly perishable in this age of information/research.

2. Skills.

Abilities that can be developed and manifested in performance, not merely in potential. Answers the question: "What should I be able to do?" Includes technical, scientific, communication, information retrieval, analysis, and synthesis skills.

3. Insights.

Ideas and thoughts derived internally from an ability to see and understand clearly the nature of things. A necessary part of making judgments, of "putting it all together," of "being aware" of wisdom, farsightedness. Answers the questions: "What does this mean? What is important in this situation?" Can't be taught directly, but can be induced by qualified mentors and by learning from mistakes.

4. Values.

Convictions, fundamental beliefs, standards governing behavior. Includes attitudes toward professional hallmarks such as duty, integrity, loyalty, public service, objectivity. Answers the questions: "What do I believe? Where and when do I draw the line?" Values, like insights, can only be derived by *you* if they're to have any meaning.

OBITER DICTA

In preparing to be a professional, harken to these complimentary words of counsel from two senior professors, each of whom has served as a dean:

First — "This is a generic manual; that is, one not unique to a specific institution. While what you will be reading summarizes the common wisdom on, and general pitfalls associated with, the achievement of tenure, any assistant professor who

actually thinks that any general prescription might assure him
or her tenure is probably too naive to survive in academia. The
generic suggestions herein may not apply in all situations.
There are other items of required reading as well — department, college, and university tenure and promotion documents;
the faculty handbook; the annual report of the faculty grievance
committee; the texts of recent statements about tenure and
promotion by deans and the provost — indigenous sources that
address the specific decision, and decision-makers, on a particular candidate. The best use of this manual is probably as a
'text' for interactions between the assistant professor and his or
her local mentor — a senior professor who is willing to work
with and capable of advising that new colleague. Too much
stress can't be placed on the value of a faculty mentor."

Second — "Tenure decisions are much more than adding up
teaching, research, and service points and how much each of
these is measured and evaluated. The slavish reader could let
this manual take the texture out of the process and smooth
everything too much. The process is much rougher than the
manual may suggest. The process is a tough one not just because the consequences are so important for the candidate. They
are also important for the institution in all its divisions. That is
one reason why tenure and promotion documents are vague.
The actual decision involves more of a *gestalt* than just the sum
total of individual costs and benefits on a curriculum vitae.
Tenure is a single outcome that tries to capture a multiplicity of
considerations."

References

1. Braxton, John H., "The Influence of Graduate Department Quality on the Sanction-
   ing of Scientific Misconduct," *The Journal of Higher Education*, January-
   February 1991, pp. 87-108.
2. Frederick, Peter, "Questions for Collegial Conversations About Teaching," *The
   Department Advisor*, Spring 1991, p. 5.
3. Leo, John, "Our Misguided Thought Police," *U.S. News & World Report*, April 8,
   1991, p. 25.
4. May, William W., Ed. *Ethics and Higher Education* (New York: American Council
   on Education/Macmillan, 1990), p. 1.
5. Nye, Roger H., *The Challenge of Command* (Wayne NJ: Avery, 1986), pp. 47-48.
6. Sands, Robert G., L. Alayne Parson, and Josann Duane, "Faculty Monitoring Faculty in a Public University," *The Journal of Higher Education*, March/April 1991,
   pp. 174-193.
7. Simpson, Catherine B., "New Politically Correct Metaphors Insult History and Our
   University," *The Chronicle of Higher Education*, May 29, 1991, p. B 48.
8. "Undergraduates at Large Universities Found to Be Increasingly Dissatisfied," *The
   Chronicle of Higher Education*, Jan. 9, 1991, p. A 1.

SUGGESTED READINGS

A DOZEN CLASSIC REFERENCES

Arnold, Matthew, "Literature and Science," in Robert H. Super, Ed., *The Complete Prose Works of Matthew Arnold*, Vol. 10 (Ann Arbor: University of Michigan Press, 1974; originally published 1884).

Brown, Elmer E., *The Origin of American State Universities* (Berkeley: University of California Press, 1903).

Butts, R. Freeman, *The College Charts Its Course* (New York: McGraw-Hill, 1939).

Flexner, Abraham, *Universities, American, English, German* (New York: Oxford University Press, 1930).

Jordan, David Starr, *The Trend of the American University* (Stanford CA: Stanford University Press, 1929).

Kelly, Fred J., The American Arts College; A Limited Survey (New York: Macmillan, 1925).

Meiklejohn, Alexander, *The Experimental College* (New York: Harper & Row, 1932).

Newman, John H., *The Idea of a University* (New York: Holt, Rinehart, & Winston, 1960; originally published 1852).

President's Commission on Higher Education, *Higher Education for American Democracy* (Washington DC: GPO, 1947).

Russell, John Dale, *American Universities and Colleges* (Washington DC: GPO, 1952).

Slosson, Edwin E., *Great American Universities* (New York: Macmillan, 1910).

Van Hise, Charles R., "Inaugural Address," in *The Jubilee of the University of Wisconsin* (Madison: Jubilee Committee, 1905).

A DOZEN-AND-A-HALF INTERIM READINGS

Astin, Alexander W., *Four Critical Years* (San Francisco: Jossey-Bass, 1977).

Baldridge, J. Victor, *Power and Conflict in the University* (London: Wiley, 1971).

Baskin, Samuel, *Higher Education: Some Newer Developments* (New York: McGraw-Hill, 1965).

Bowen, Robert O., *The New Professors* (New York: Holt, Rinehart, & Winston, 1960).

Burch, Glen, *Challenge to the University: An Inquiry into the University's Responsibility for Adult Education* (Chicago: Center for the Study of Liberal Education for Adults, 1961).

Clapp, Margaret, Ed., *The Modern University* (Ithaca NY: Cornell University Press, 1950).

Eddy, Edward D., *Colleges for Our Land and Time: The Land -Grant Idea in American Education* (New York: Harper, 1957).

Fowlkes, John Guy, Ed., *Higher Education for American Society* (Madison: University of Wisconsin Press, 1949).

Kerr, Clark, *The Uses of the University* (New York: Harper & Row, 1966).

Liveright, Alexander A., *Adult Education in Colleges and Universities* (Chicago: Center for the Study of Liberal Education for Adults, 1960).

Miller, Richard I., *The Assessment of College Performance* (San Francisco: Jossey-Bass, 1979).

Millett, John D., *The Academic Community* (New York: McGraw-Hill, 1962).

National Association of State Universities and Land Grant Colleges, *Scope Report* (Washington DC, 1958).

Sanford, Nevitt, *The American College* (New York: John Wiley, 1962).

_____, *College and Character* (New York: John Wiley, 1964).

Schoenfeld, Clay, and Donald N. Zillman, *The American University in Summer* (Madison: University of Wisconsin Press, 1967).

Shannon, Theodore J., and Clarence A. Schoenfeld, *University Extension* (New York: Center for Applied Research in Education, 1965).

Veysey, Laurence R., *The Emergence of the American University* (Chicago: University of Chicago Press, 1965).

TWO DOZEN CURRENT COMMENTARIES

Barzun, Jacques, The Culture We Deserve (Middletown CT: Wesleyan University Press, 1989).

Bennett, William J., *To Reclaim a Legacy: Report on the Humanities in Higher Education* (Washington DC: National Endowment for the Humanities, 1984).

Bloom, Allan, *The Closing of the American Mind* (New York: Simon and Schuster, 1987).

Bok, Derek, *Universities and the Future of America* (Durham NC: Duke University Press, 1990).

Boyer, Ernest L., *Scholarship Reconsidered: Priorities of the Professoriate* (Princeton NJ: Carnegie Foundation for the Advancement of Teaching, 1991).

Cahn, Steven, *Morality, Responsibility, and the University* (Philadelphia: Temple University Press, 1990).

Clark, Burton R., *The Academic Life: Small Worlds, Different Worlds* (Lawrenceville NJ: Princeton University Press, 1987).

Creswell, John W., et al., *The Academic Chairperson's Handbook* (Lincoln: University of Nebraska Press, 1990).

D'Souza, Dinesh, *Illiberal Education: The Politics of Race and Sex on Campus* (New York: Free Press, 1991).

Eaton, Judith S., *The Unfinished Agenda: Higher Edcucation and the 1980's* (New York: ACE/Macmillan, 1991).

Gilley, J. Wade, *Thinking About Higher Education: The 1990s and Beyond* (New York: ACE/Macmillan, 1992).

Johnson, Paul, *Intellectuals* (New York: Harper & Row, 1990).

Kadish, Mortimer R., *Toward an Ethic of Higher Education* (Stanford CA: Stanford University Press, 1991).

Levine, Arthur and associates, *Shaping Higher Education's Future: Demographic Realities and Opportunites, 1990-2000* (San Francisco: Jossey-Bass, 1989).

Millard, Richard M., *Today's Myths and Tomorrow's Realities* (San Francisco: Jossey-Bass, 1991).

Neumann, William F., *Persistence in the Community College* , Ph.D. Dissertation, Syracuse University, 1985 (Ann Arbor: University Microfilms).

Orem, Sue Don, and Deborah Brue, Eds., *Practical Programming in Continuing Professional Higher Education* (Washington DC: American Association for Adult Continuing Education, 1991).

Pascarella, Ernest T., and Patrick T. Terenzini, *How College Affects Students: Findings and Insights From Twenty Years of Research* (San Francisco: Jossey-Bass, 1991).

Riesman, David, *On Higher Education: The Academic Enterprise in an Era of Rising Student Consumerism* (San Francisco: Jossey-Bass, 1980).

Santovec, Mary Lou, Ed., *Building Diversity* (Madison WI: Magna Publications, 1990).

Schaefer, William D., *Education Without Compromise: From Chaos to Coherence in Higher Education* (San Francisco: Jossey-Bass, 1990).

Schuster, Jack H., Daniel W. Wheeler, and Associates, *Enhancing Faculty Careers: Strategies for Development and Renewal* (San Francisco: Jossey-Bass, 1990).

Shaw, Peter, *The War Against the Intellect: Episodes in the Decline of Discourse* (Iowa City: University of Iowa Press, 1989).

Slaughter, Sheila, The Higher Learning and High Technology: Dynamics of Higher Education Policy Formation (Albany: SUNY Press, 1990).

Smith, Page, *Killing the Spirit: Higher Education in America* (New York: Viking, 1990).

Tinto, Vincent O., *Leaving College: Rethinking the Causes and Cures of Student Attrition* (Chicago: University of Chicago Press, 1987).

Wilshire, Bruce, *The Moral Collapse of the University: Professionalism, Purity, and Aleination* (Albany: State University of New York Press, 1990).

II
GETTING TO KNOW YOUR TERRITORY

As he recalls in recent addresses to newly commissioned lieutenants, when Gen. Colin Powell, head of the Joint Chiefs of Staff, was a fresh "shavetail" being shuffled from Army post to post between wars, at each new station he was always at pains to locate promptly his chaplain, the pay officer, the PX, the medics, the quartermaster, and his first sergeant — in reverse order.

A newly minted assistant professor has different priorities, of course, invariably including the reference room shelving annual directories of grant-making agencies, the center for teaching support services, or the outreach office. But the principle's the same: as the traveling salesman sang in *The Music Man*, "You've got to know the territory!" And your No. 1 question is, "What do I have to do around here to get promoted?"

Gen. Powell says something else pertinent: "There are no secrets to success. Don't waste time looking for them. Success is the result of perfection, hard work, learning from failure."(16)

No, there's no magic formula for making tenure, either. The whole process is both simple and complicated — involving something less and yet something much more than the contents of this manual.

Simple, because promotion to tenure is but the epitome of your professional career — translating Greek poems, chairing a curriculum committee, analyzing mysterious chemical substances, evaluating community development efforts, studying socioeconomic processes in Zambia, isolating a new germ plasm in corn, bringing history alive for a roomful of sophomores. Simple.

But the process is also made up of the stuff of which you'll read here. Complicated. Because it involves institutions and persons beyond your control.

Yet if there are no recipes, there are clues to success, like getting to know your territory.

THE SACRED TRIAD

A representative American institution of higher education springs to a greater or lesser degree from three principal roots. First, the crown academy, with its focus on instructing an undergraduate elite in the classics as preparation for professional careers. Second, the German institute, with its emphasis on scientists tutoring selected graduate students in the discovery of new knowledge. And third, that peculiarly American invention, the land-grant university, with its emphasis on a utilitarian curriculum for an egalitarian citizenry, both on and off campus.

While a particular college or university may emphasize one departure or another today, each will likely engage in some manner in each function. In like manner, an individual professor will usually be asked to display in his or her career path a certain level of adeptness at teaching, at research, and at service.

For example, take this paraphrase of a typical *Chronicle of Higher Education* want ad:

MIDLAND UNIVERSITY

ASSISTANT PROFESSOR OF BOTANY AND APPLIED ECOLOGY

COLLEGE OF LETTERS AND SCIENCE

Responsibilities: (1) Help develop courses for new master's program in biological conservation/sustainable development; teach standard intro botany courses; offer appropriate post-master's research seminar. (2) Advise undergraduate and graduate students; assist students with research design, prospectus writing, and thesis/dissertation studies. (3) Establish and maintain service to the University, community, and professional organizations. (4) Develop and maintain a record of scholarly productivity commensurate with the expectations of faculty at Midland; published research in support of this goal is expected.

As that **Midland University** ad suggests, at the outset you can assume that your institution, like most others, says it's engaged in three primary complementary activities — teaching, research, and service. But the extent to which your college or university places emphasis on which of the three in what order is up to you to discern; or, better stated, which expectations apply to **you** in your particular niche in the big picture?

Don't even assume that all institutions seemingly in the same category have **identical** characteristics. For example, one land-grant university, occupying a "crown jewel" position in its state, can mingle a large extension apparatus with a strong liberal arts college and a graduate school/research establishment adept at competing for federal and foundation dollars, while in the state next door a second-class-citizen land-grant university can be relatively poverty-stricken in all three regards. Liberal arts colleges can be just as diverse. (21)

The various organizational echelons **within** an institution, befitting their particular missions, can vary widely in their adherence to any all-campus standard. For example, a school of business may have quite different priorities from a department of English or a college of life sciences. And yet all three can reflect markedly the stance dictated by the institution's traditions, present ethos, and future aspirations.

VARIATIONS ON A CENTRAL THEME

Peter Seldin, professor of management at Pace University-Pleasantville (NY) and author of the book *How Administrators Can Improve Teaching* (San Francisco: Jossey-Bass, 1990), has visited over 200 colleges and universities of varying size, shape, and mission in his capacity as a consultant, and continues to be impressed how different institutions can be, despite professed similarities in their pledge of allegiance to the triad. For example, "At one institution the department chair may wield considerable power [in enforcing faculty adherence to institutional norms], at another the chair may be almost impotent. At one institution the faculty may be pressed to do extensive research and publication, while at another such involvement may be casually regarded. One institution may encourage and support faculty outreach, another not."

"It's absolutely essential," writes a colleague, "that a new hire ask these questions: What is the mission of the institution? Is the mission changing? Where has the school been and where is it going? Some traditionally teaching-oriented colleges now want their faculty to do research. (A former grad student of mine who is in her first year at East Tennessee State was told in her interview that professional presentations and publications were necessary for getting tenure.) On the other hand, traditionally research-oriented schools are now stressing teaching (for example, Stanford). What exactly are the expectations here?"

FACULTY HETEROGENEITY

What's more, the individual faculty colleagues and administrators who will preside over your fate can be as varied in their own ways as are institutions in theirs. By design or luck of the draw, some will be grindstone researchers all but oblivious to any life outside their laboratories or carrels; some will take sheer delight in teaching both their specialties and introductory courses and in counseling undergraduate advisees, but will not have contributed much to the storehouse of knowledge since their dissertations; others will play public, institutional, and professional service roles with great zest, subordinating other duties; still others will manage to perform adequately, if not with distinction, in each area of the trinity of institutional missions.

Peer Traits

Some of your peers will take suggestions readily, others will revolt or sulk. Some will conform to all but the most ridiculous

restrictions; others will revel in a maverick independence. Some
will abhor even minor administrative chores; others will have
their eye on the prize of an ever-higher administrative post.
Some will be homesteaders; others will constantly seek offers to
move. Some will happily share their insights; others will guard
their privacy.

In like vein, some will be monastic, some gregarious, some
cavalier. Some will sail through their careers with nary a distraction; some will be haunted by repeated tragedy; some will
move in and out of alternating tranquility and travail.

The one thing all your judges will have in common: each will
see it as his or her profound duty to academia to ensure that
your career replicates and ratifies his or her own mode. The
overwhelming biological desire of a species to reproduce itself is
alive and well in academe today: no mutants need apply. Former
UCLA Vice Chancellor William D. Schaefer describes the phenomenon thus: "Having devoted their lives to a particular kind
of study, ... [professors] want to see their position filled by someone who will continue to do whatever it was they were doing —
a perverse if understandable form of academic immortality."

One senior commentator states frankly:

"The academy tells us that tenure and promotion should be
governed (if not determined totally) by universalistic rather
than particularistic criteria — criteria summarized by, but not
necessarily identical to, those mentioned in tenure and promotion documents. But we all know certain truths about the
process:

- "Particularistic criteria are as important as universalistic criteria, at least in some cases.
- "Some disgruntled faculty seem quick these days to consult attorneys, or say they are going to.
- "Some tenured faculty even in good departments are
  generally fearful of denying tenure; they'd rather live
  with a less than adequate colleague than risk offending
  one with a negative vote."

A jaundiced opinion, perhaps, but not unique.

Peer Opinions

But don't take our word for it that all professors are not so
many peas in a pod. Look at the results of the latest poll of professorial opinions reported in May 1991 by the Higher Education Research Institute at the University of California at Los
Angeles. (2)

Typical spreads in attitudes:

Political views — 37% said "liberal," 25% said "conservative."
Right to ban speakers with extreme views — 27% said "yes,"

12% "no."

A lot of racial tensions at their institutions — 22% "yes," 11% "no."

Essential professional goal — 98% included "be a good teacher," 58% included "engage in research."

Satisfactory aspect of job — 82% included "autonomy and independence," 76% included "undergraduate teaching assignments."

Source of stress — 84% listed "time pressures," 29% "subtle discrimination."

Attribute of institution — 34% said "it's easy for students to see faculty," 10% that "faculty are rewarded for being good teachers."

Institutional priority — 76% included "promoting the intellectual development of students," 45% included "conducting basic and applied research."

Of course some of these responses may reflect as much the type of institution as the leanings of individual faculty, but the net lesson is clear: there's no peer uniformity out there.

A SETTING FOR THIS MANUAL

So diverse are the territories in which you may find yourself, we've decided to fabricate a journeyman's institution to lend verisimilitude — "the appearance of truth" — to all the possible permutations attendant to this discussion of your grasping generic institutional expectations for making tenure and appreciating the practical politics of your professional path.

THE INSTITUTION

If our hypothetical institution were actually to be listed in a Higher Education Publications *HEP Directory*, its profile would look like this:

Midland University

PO Box 412, Midland, ST 53102
County: Pontiac
Telephone 606/263-2331
FAX # 606/263-6299
Established: 1881
Annual Undergrad Tuition & Fees
Enrollment: 21,627

Con Dist 06
FICI #: 003986
Entity #: 1-38-700-6942-78
Calendar System: Quarter
(as a private normal school for teachers)
$2,907
Coed

Affiliation or Control: Independent Non-Profit
Highest Offering: Doctorate
Program: Comprehensive
Accreditation: NH, ARCH, BUS, CYPSY, ENG, LIB, MBA, MT, MUS, NSC, NUR, OT, SP, SW, TED
01 President
05 Vice President for Academic Affairs

Principal Divisions
Allied Health Professions
Architecture and Urban Planning
Business Administration
Education
Engineering and Applied Science
Fine Arts
Forestry and Environmental Studies
Graduate School/Research
Letters and Science (the "mother" college)
Library and Information Science
Outreach and Continuing Education
Social Welfare

THE COMMUNITY
Socioeconomics

With a population of 300,000-plus, Midland is the metropolis of its heartland state — a transportation hub. Diversified mix of heavy industry, high-tech light industry, agribusiness, banking, and insurance. A relatively stable economy, yet with its vicissitudes. A growing gulf between the "haves" and the "have-nots": the former clustered around Burr Oaks Country Club (private) in a suburb, the latter in sub-standard housing literally on the other side of the Northwestern tracks. A reasonable array of cultural and recreational amenities, news media, churches, and service organizations. The only military-industrial complex is a small U.S. Air Force base on a prairie 10 miles to the south.

Town-Gown Relations

The Midland faculty used to be concentrated in College Heights near the campus but is now widely dispersed, although an enclave seems to be developing in Starlight Hills 12 miles westward. Community support for "its" university varies with the times, but in general would be rated comparatively solid, Midland alumni being well represented in the city power structure.

In no sense, however, is the university subservient to municipal interests, its increasing national stature giving it a prestige and independence much envied by the local community college and Baptist seminary.

Nonetheless, Midland University lives politically in the shadow of the sprawling state university 77 miles down the turnpike in Carthage, the state capital; State faculty steer clear of any entangling alliances, except when grant monies dictate a measure of collaboration.

An assistant president for university relations, a director of development, and an outreach dean work hard at cultivating Midland's publics. The graduate school/research dean has a

part-time representative in Washington soliciting federal
monies; a career development center under the chief academic
officer (CAO) offers support services to faculty who seek them.

All told, the two Midlands are a microcosm of U.S. academia
and its environs.

YOUR *ALTER EGO*

Your *alter ego* at Midland University is a new assistant
professor in the Department of Botany and Applied Ecology in
the College of Letters and Science. His full name is August Wilmot Campion. Growing up in the South, as he did, his boyhood
nickname naturally was A.W., but in a later hitch in the Naval
Reserve he acquired the appellation Bill, which he now prefers,
although, because his middle name is that of a grandfather
professor of linguistics and because it has a nice academic ring
to it, he signs his research papers A. Wilmot. From now on we'll
refer to him as just plain Bill.

Bill comes highly credentialed from the Eugene Odum
program at the University of Georgia plus a two-year post-doc
assignment with the Chesapeake Bay Commission under a Midland botany Ph.D. One of his former Georgia professors is now
the Dean of the Midland School of Forestry and Environmental
Studies, a Georgia grad student peer has just joined the zoology
department next door, and Bill's wife is a State native.

THE DEPARTMENT
Background, Development

The department traces its lineage to one of the original
Midland chairs, that of natural history. It was one of the first to
offer a Ph.D. (originally joint with zoology).

Stemming from its heavy teaching role in offering service
courses to satisfy university science requirements and prerequisites for majors in related professional disciplines, the department is large, having a faculty complement presently of 31, and
a healthy roster of graduate students supported by teaching as-
sistantships. The number of undergraduate majors was limping
until the addition of the "applied ecology" moniker in 1972,
responding to student demands for programs "relevant" to the
environmental era (and to the threat of the rise of environmental studies in what had been a conservative forestry school
across campus).

The department's research stature jumped during WWII
when its faculty participated strongly in the national search for
a penicillin mold that could be mass-produced. Combining his
background in bacteriology with serendipity, Professor E.
Ronald Pendarvis identified a mutant strain found on rotting
melon rinds and cultivated it into a major source of the

life-saving antibiotic. A grateful Department of Defense built the laboratory wing where Professor Pendarvis still keeps office hours at the age of 87.

Based on that reputation, the department "took off" in the 1960s by staffing up to meet the almost bewildering requirements of modern botany in a university setting.

A Mason-Dixon Line

Today the department is less a department than a loose confederacy of two rival factions — the field or applied botany (taxonomy, dendrology, pathology, economic, agronomy, horticulture, and a revitalized ecology) and the laboratory or basic botany (genetics, molecular, morphology, cytology, histology, and bio-technology to include gene-splitting).

The two cultures are archrivals for funds, freshmen, and favors. The department chair position alternates between the two. At the moment it is a plant pathologist in her first year of a five-year term, so her proclivities are unknown and untested. The college dean does his best to help preserve civility by sponsoring departmental curriculum committees and so on. (Actually from his perspective the department is no more split than a number of others in his domain.)

Bill's Challenge

Bill's assignment is to help beef up a new applied ecology master's program over the dead bodies of the more theory-minded botanists, a development that the dean of the college very much favors and that has a decent chance to rate support from state and federal environmental protection agencies and public conservation organizations.

Along with teaching his share of introductory courses, establishing a research program, attracting Ph.D. acolytes, and playing a service role, Bill is to design and offer a key course in "Biological Aspects of Environmental Impact Analysis" for graduate students.

All in all, Bill has his work cut out for him — as do you wherever you are.

TEACHING POINT

You'll recognize our Midland scenario as a common teaching technique — reducing a set of variables to a common denominator — and as a recommended essay-writing principle focusing on a representative situation or character.

In so doing, of course, we mask certain differences among the wide range of American institutions of higher education, from community colleges and teachers colleges, through church-related colleges, and on to private and public comprehensive universities.

For example, at not all institutions will you find Midland's generous use of teaching assistants (TAs). As one commentator recalls, "The university was very reluctant to fund TA-ships. As a result, faculty had to teach many basic courses because enrollments in graduate seminars were so low. I was in effect teaching at a college rather than a university."

Again, at not all universities will faculty enjoy free choice of residence: "Church-related schools and some other four-year colleges may expect their faculty to live contiguous to the campus so as to be readily available to students. One friend of mine had to rent an apartment in a college town rather than commute from the home of her husband and children 40 miles away. Even so, she was considered unserious and disloyal, and did not receive tenure."

The point is, take all coming Midland data as "for instances" only. Under no (repeat **no**) circumstances assume that what's true at Midland necessarily applies at your institution. Midland mores are an example, not a prescription. On the other hand, they're a useful guide as you do considerable local reconnoitering to learn your own territory.

To help you further, we're about to suggest some essential elements of information to gather, and some available sources of that information.

> *(Incidentally, the excerpts from Midland documents we'll present from time to time we didn't just dream up. They're actual quotations from the literature of real institutions — which we choose to use without attribution — to protect the innocent or the guilty, as the case may be.)*

GRASPING GENERIC INSTITUTIONAL EXPECTATIONS

Contrasting life at "research-intensive" institutions vs. life at "teaching-intensive" institutions, a 1990 Carnegie Foundation for the Advancement of Teaching study of colleges and universities conferring the baccalaureate (6) makes it crystal-clear why it's so important that you learn what's expected of **you** at **your** institution.

For example:

> At research institutions, the three most widely used indicators for tenure decisions are numbers of publications, caliber of publications, and recommendations from outside scholars; at teaching institutions, on the other hand, the three most widely used indicators are student evaluation of courses taught, service within the university community, and number of publications.

> Tenure-decision indicators having the least common use at

research institutions are recommendations from current and former students, observations of teaching by colleagues and/or administrators, and service within the university community; at teaching institutions, research grants received by the scholar, recommendations from outside scholars, and reputations of presses or journals publishing any books or articles.

At research institutions, research salary outlay as a percent of educational and general salaries runs 20.8%, at teaching institutions, less than 1%.

Considering mean hours per week spent in preparation for teaching, professors at high-intensity research institutions spend 8.4, at high-intensity teaching institutions, 13.1.

Mean hours per week spent on research runs 22 for researching professors, 9 for teaching professors.

Mean enrollment in typical introductory undergraduate courses at research institutions is 82, at teaching institutions, 29.

It's two different worlds out there.

Befitting its position in the mainstream of higher education, Midland University invests 14% of all salary funds on research salaries, Midland professors spend 11.5 hours a week on teaching prep and 15 on research, and enrollment in introductory courses runs 46.

Say the CFAT report writers:

The type of performance needed for career success varies markedly, depending on where the institution fits on the research-intensive vs. teaching-intensive continuum. Where the institution is heavily oriented toward research, the professor must concentrate intently on impressing peers beyond the local campus with his or her scholarly creativity. Publishing in competitive outlets is therefore mandatory. It matters little what is happening in the classroom. In teaching-intensive institutions, what is happening in the classroom is all-important for career success. Scholarly creativity in the classroom is the prime objective. Impressing peers around the country can take a back seat.

Obviously the writers are describing polar positions; most colleges and universities fall in between the two extremes in one way or another. To discern where your institution fits, you have to ask some penetrating questions and develop solid answers.

ESSENTIAL ELEMENTS OF INFORMATION
How Long Do I Have to Make Tenure?

While the testing or gauntlet period at some institutions is seven years, at Midland University it's six in which to either go up or go out, and that's the national norm. (Although in the sense that, if you're terminated at the end of your sixth year, you'll typically be granted a seventh, severance year of duty with pay in which to seek other opportunities, you could be set for seven years, if you want to look at it that way.)

From another perspective, as one reviewer points out, "you really have only four to five years in which to accumulate a tenure dossier, in that it takes time for work to be published, and the tenure process itself may take most of a year."

But don't panic. If they're on your side, evaluation committees will be understanding. If not, there may be greener pastures.

During your projected six years you're in various stages of probationary status. At Midland your quarter-system schedule would look like this:

Annual Reviews

Submit Goals and Objectives Report	Aug. 1
Counseling session with department Chair	Aug and Sept
Submit Faculty Activities Report	April 1
Review session with Chair	May and June

Tenure Progress Review (second year)

Preliminary Screening Committee appointed	April 1
PSC Report to department Promotion and Tenure Committee	May 1
P&T Committee Report to Chair	May 15
Tenure Progress Report to candidate	June 1

Tenure Candidacy Review (fourth year)

PSC appointed	Aug. 15
PSC Report to P&T Committee	Nov. 1
P&T Report to Chair	Nov. 21
Chair's recommendation to Dean, copy to candidate	Dec. 1

Tenure and Promotion Review (sixth year)

PSC appointed	Aug. 15
Preparation of P&T packet	Oct. 15
PSC Report to P&T Committee	Nov. 1
P&T Committee vote and recommendation to Chair	Dec. 1
Chair letter of recommendation to Dean	Jan. 1
Review by College P&T Committee	Feb. 1
Dean's letter of recommendation to Vice President for Academic Affairs	March 1
Review by University P&T Committee	April 1
VPAA recommendation to President and Trustees	May 1
Trustee action	June 30

It's not unheard of that a particularly outstanding young assistant professor would be put up for promotion in his or her fourth or fifth year, the most likely circumstance being to forestall the raid of a star by a rival institution. And it's not without precedent that the promotion to tenure would come through. But by and large departments refrain from pushing an early promotion, for fear that if the appeal fails the candidate is stuck with a "blackball" on the record that might color future chances. So don't expect your department to jump the gun.

Be sure and read the tea leaves carefully in any periodic counseling sessions and tenure progress reports. Unless you're blind, deaf, and dumb, from them you ought to be able to get a very clear perception of how you're doing.

For example, if your second-year progress report leaves a lot to be desired, either hitch up your bootstraps or start sending out résumés; in fact, if it's really bad you can be told you'll be terminated at the end of your third year. On the other hand, if your second-year report is glowing, while that doesn't mean you're "in," it does suggest that if you maintain your present pace, you have a favorable future — unless you start resting on your laurels.

While a favorable fourth-year report isn't a sure harbinger of promotion, it does mean you're definitely in the zone of consideration. But an unenthusiastic fourth-year report should strongly suggest that you get on your horse to other climes, even if your department chair doesn't so counsel openly.

That's because there's practically no way you're going to get promoted to tenure in the face of an unfavorable review at the departmental level. On the other hand, even the most ecstatic departmental recommendation can fail to pass muster at higher echelons. We discuss those hurdles a bit later.

When Does My Tenure Clock Tick?

If you're starting out from scratch as an assistant professor with no prior service anywhere at the rank of instructor or above, your six-year clock starts from the date of your letter of appointment or thereabouts.

On the other hand, if you've had such prior service, it may or may not be included in your probationary period, depending on what's mutually agreed to at the time of your appointment. It's a judgment call on the part of both you and the institution. If you're bringing along an impressive record and prefer to spend as little more time as possible untenured, you may opt to count your prior service, particularly if it was at an institution with recognized standards. Your new department may concur, or it may prefer to give you and the department the maximum number of years in which to make sure you're a mutual match, in which case it will waive the prior service and put you on a fresh six-year track. Midland habitually prefers the latter option.

The one thing to double-check: make sure the department has the autonomy to render such a decision. At Midland only the dean of the college has the authority to decide when to start a tenure-track clock.

Once started, can you stop your clock temporarily? You can't of your own free will, but your institution can if it has such a policy. For instance, if you go on an approved research leave for a semester, your institution can say it'll stop your clock for the period. There are other circumstances, as well. Witness this exemplary statement in the Midland *Faculty Handbook* (II, A, 9):

> Ordinarily the probationary period will provide sufficient time for the faculty member to demonstrate his or her qualifications for tenure. On occasion, special circumstances may occur that would interfere significantly with the faculty member's opportunity to develop qualifications necessary for tenure in the ordinary time allowed. (The assumption of parental responsibilities or a major change in assigned job description might be two such circumstances.) Under such conditions the faculty member may request to be transferred temporarily from a regular-term appointment to an adjunct appointment for a specific term not to exceed two years, during which time the person's probationary term is suspended and no time toward tenure is accrued. When transferred back to a regular appointment, the faculty member will resume the probationary period at the point suspended.

Comments one colleague:

> The 'parental responsibility' element takes on heightened salience today. At the University of Illinois, the original 'stop the clock' policy came from a Chancellor's Committee on Women's Status, specifically to lengthen tenure periods for new parents (mothers being the primary candidates).

How Tough Is It Going to Be to Make Tenure?

It's a rule-of-thumb that the higher the academic ranking of your institution, the tougher it is to get promoted. For example, Harvard is extremely careful in its national and international search for persons for tenured positions — with the president personally participating in every search and every appointment ("Is this the best person in the world available to us?"). It is determined to keep a numerical balance among the younger and older faculty members, with a rapid turnover of junior fellows competing for tenure. At UC-Berkeley, the elected Academic Senate plays a central role in ensuring high-quality additions to the tenured faculty, with common oversight of **all** departments and **all** professional schools and colleges. Similarly, at UW-Madison elected faculty divisional committees exercise practically immutable quality control over **all** promotions to tenure, irrespective of department, school, college, or extension.

Outside of the "top 10," screening processes and procedures may be not quite so rigid. For example, at 55-ranked Midland, the tenure hurdles are somewhat less rigorous.

But that doesn't mean it's going to be a snap at the Midlands of the country. For example, the Midland *Faculty Handbook* states (IV, B, 9):

> Superior intellectual attainment is the crucial qualification for tenure, promotion, and salary increases at Midland University. This standard of continuing performance is essential for faculty in a quality university dedicated to the discovery and transmission of knowledge.
>
> The University pledges to establish a climate that facilitates professional growth, stimulates cooperation and innovation, and promotes quality in all academic endeavors. But the ultimate responsibility for professional development and advancement rests with the individual faculty member.

For assistant professors at Midland, the batting average in making tenure is about .600. That's superior in baseball, but in academia it suggests pretty tough competition.

What the batting average is at your institution is a key element of information to ferret out. Of course, the situation can vary significantly among campus units, depending on recruiting standards, departmental mentoring, and the vagaries of decision-making at higher echelons in response to changing institutional needs and external pressures.

Against profound pronouncements of rigid quality control at Midland, there is this interesting paragraph to be found in its *Faculty Handbook* (III, B, 2):

> In evaluating the candidate's qualifications within the areas of teaching, research or other creative work, and service to department/college/university/public service related to academic expertise, reasonable flexibility shall be exercised — balancing, where the case requires, heavier commitments and responsibilities in one area against lighter commitments and responsibilities in another. Each candidate is expected to engage in a program of work that is both sound and productive. As the University enters new fields of endeavor and places new emphasis on its continuing activities, instances will arise in which the proper work of faculty members may depart from established academic patterns. In such cases care must be taken to apply normal criteria with sufficient flexibility.
>
> Still, in all instances, superior intellectual attainment is the crucial qualification for promotion to tenured positions at Midland.

The lords giveth and the lords taketh away.

What's My Ultimate Measuring Rod?

A really essential element of information: the ultimate standard against which you'll be judged for promotion to tenure. Is it departmental? School/college? Institutional? National/professional? Constituency feedback? All or some of the above? The answer may lie under a rock.

Various tenure grievances and lawsuits over the past decade or two show that written "job descriptions" or "P&T guidelines" don't and can't cover every situation. Rather, faculty working toward tenure must contend with preconceptions, perceptions, personalities, and practical politics. While you keep your shoulder to the wheel, keep your ear to the ground. Detect comments about why tenure was granted to one applicant but not to another, about changes in procedures, about the nuances in departmental/institutional character you can find outlined in subsequent sections of this chapter.

Who Promotes Me?

As we've suggested, promotion-to-tenure procedures can vary a good deal from campus to campus. As a guide to what to investigate at your institution, here's a run-down on the various **Midland** steeplechase barriers in ascending order of rank (but not necessarily of their crucial nature).

<u>Department</u>. As at most institutions, the botany department at Midland holds the primary fate of your *alter ego* Bill in its hands. After that series of annual reviews, in the penultimate year the chair appoints a Preliminary Screening Committee to work with the candidate in developing a Promotion and Tenure Packet of documentation (which the young faculty member should have been assembling continuously throughout the probationary years). Theoretically any faculty member can serve on the Screening Committee, but the chair usually opts to exclude fellow untenured peers.

Samples of the candidate's work the PSC will send to distinguished people in the candidate's field outside Midland, with a request for written appraisals. The panel can include persons the candidate suggests and persons the PSC selects independently. All responses — positive, lukewarm, or negative — enter the P&T packet for later appraisal by reviewing authorities, along with brief profiles of the respondents.

Once it's assembled all documentation, the PSC evaluates the case and prepares a report recommending for or against tenure. Voting in the PSC is by written ballot prepared and distributed by the department chair. All members must vote and a simple majority will prevail. The report then goes to the department P&T Committee, consisting of all tenured members of the department, which may or may not gather further documentation.

Voting in the P&T Committee is by secret ballot, with absentee ballots mailed to any faculty on leave. The department secretary and the chair of the P&T Committee tabulate all votes. A positive recommendation requires a simple majority. The committee chair then formulates a letter to the department chair, highlighting the candidate's strengths and weaknesses and recording the vote. Any dissenting faculty members can submit written demurs. These letters and the whole P&T Packet go forward to the chair.

The department chair, following critical review and assessment of the materials plus additional information he or she chooses to collect, prepares a letter of recommendation, positive or negative, for the dean of the college. (While the chair can overrule the P&T Committee, the chances of his or her decision carrying the day in such a case are remote, unless the dean has a like agenda.)

A commentator points out that so precise a departmental review as is in place at Midland may not exist at a small college: "The faculty member on his or her own may have to go to the dean for input. At my institution, a third-year review has just been instituted. Until now, it was up to the assistant professor to figure things out. The dean is happy to meet at any time, but it's up to the assistant professor to initiate the conference — unless, of course, there are real problems in tow."

<u>The College</u>. Midland has no formal college procedure for the dean to consult with anybody but the stars, but he or she normally has a standing college P&T Committee of rotating tenured faculty members from various college departments, which in fact could include at the time a member of the candidate's department, who in turn would normally bow out of the discussion, or at least out of the vote.

Depending on college tradition, the college P&T Committee makes either a detailed, routine, or perfunctory review of the P&T Packet in question, checking largely to see that the candidate's record does no damage to written and unwritten college standards of faculty quality. It then renders a report to the dean, who may or may not pay much attention to it. If, however, the dean would overrule the committee, he or she would have to document that decision to the Vice President for Academic Affairs when forwarding the P&T Packet.

Midland University's college-level protocol may or may not be representative. For example, as one commentator writes:

In some institutions, a departmental P&T recommendation goes directly to a provost, bypassing any intermediate dean.

In others, the departmental faculty has no role; the chair
sends his or her recommendation to a college-wide committee. At some institutions every assistant professor must be
formally considered for promotion every year, with the candidate formally presenting himself or herself before the committee.

What the drill is at your institution is a top item on your
agenda of essential elements of information.

The President and Staff. While at Midland the President
(CEO) technically is the sign-off official on any promotion-to-tenure
recommendations going forward to the Trustees, in practice he or
she delegates such decisions to the Vice President for Academic Affairs (CAO). Again at Midland there's no formal policy that the
CAO consult anybody but his or her immediate staff, but habitually he or she employs a standing all-University P&T Committee consisting of appointed rotating tenured faculty members from each of
the institution's principal divisions. In deference to faculty sentiments, Midland currently gives considerable weight to the P&T
packet review performed by the committee, and its subsequent
recommendation. It's not unheard of that the all-University panel
would reject the college decision, but if it were to do so, it could anticipate a vigorous appeal by the college dean and the department
chair, assuming that the CAO goes along, the CAO reserving the
right to be the ultimate arbiter. The CAO formulates a recommendation to the CEO, who would normally accept it and forward it to
the Trustees, although he or she can under duress exercise independent judgment.

The Trustees. Technically, all promotions-to-tenure at Midland and other institutions are the prerogative of the governing
board, but if the board were to go counter to the manifest
desires of faculty and administrators with respect to the appointment and promotion of personnel, it would set off seismic rever-
berations on a scale of at least 7.0. Except for one circumstance:
because promotion-to-tenure normally carries with it a substantial salary raise, in a day of fiscal constraints the board might
have imposed a ceiling on the number of promotions-to-tenure
in any given year, whereupon the President and his or her
lieutenants would have to go back to the drawing-boards and
perform triage on its list of recommended candidates — a grim
assignment, indeed.

Midland has no written policy about what to do with any
also-rans in such a situation, but the present CEO has made it
known informally that any candidate denied tenure because of
budgetary strictures would be reappointed until the money
problems mellow — but as an assistant professor on indefinite
hold — and the Trustees have unofficially concurred. Were the

fiscal shortfall to continue indefinitely, nobody knows what would happen, except that there is this daunting sentence on the Trustee books:

> A chronic shortfall of income *vis-à-vis* expenditures might so jeopardize the University as to require the termination of faculty, even of tenured faculty, on the basis of fiscal-exigency decisions made by the President on the advice of the Committee on Faculty of the Faculty Assembly.

To ease any concerns that sentence may cause, let it be recorded there are no precedents for such draconian measures at any institution of Midland's comparable stature, but we suppose there's always a "first," in which case you can hope for an adequate alert as to when it's prudent to leave a sinking ship before it founders.

In your favor is the fact that, to stay afloat in the next 20 years, America's institutions of higher education will have to replace three-fourths of their faculty plus adding staff to serve rising enrollments, so the odds are all in your favor — barring a total collapse of the system. The trick, of course, is to be at the right institution at the right time, but it has been ever thus.

<u>People</u>. Regardless of the organizational echelon involved in your promotion to tenure, in the final analysis it's **people** who are the key.

After all the student ratings are tabulated and assessed, after all the publications are counted and evaluated, after all the service records are weighed in the balance, after all the outside letters are read, the final decision is *qualitative,* not *quantitative* — arrived at by individual faculty personalities asking, "Does this person meet our standards?"

Despite what institutional documents may state precisely, there is inevitably a strong element of vagueness about those standards, stemming from the varied interpretations of faculty member to faculty member — relating to perceived importance of teaching, research, and outreach, and personal assessments of the potential of the candidate to "be a good colleague."

Individual recommendations of "up or out," in other words, are as gross as the ultimate decision itself. There can be no ambiguity about "tenure" or "not to tenure." Mixed evidence — decent research but nothing outstanding, excellent teaching, a bastard to work with on committees, offended my spouse at last year's Christmas party, connected big on a grant, journeyman outreach performance — must be reconciled at a general, not a specific, level by heterogenous evaluators.

So, while we can tell junior faculty they have to be excellent at research, teaching, and outreach, and have grant potential for future productivity, we cannot tell them (a) exactly how to do it, (b) if their voting colleagues will recognize excellence when confronted with it, or (c) that the same balancing act used by evaluators one year will be in effect the next.

Recognize, too, that, as one commentator points out, "some institutions are in greater flux than others, and some departments are in paradigm shifts. Look for indicators that 'uh-oh, the rules are changing.' "

Go to a savvy mentor for tips. If you need a guarantee, go to Sears or Chrysler.

Professional goals noted as essential or very important by college and university faculty members, 1989-90:

Engage in research	58.5%
Engage in outside activities	52.5%
Provide services to the community	43.4%
Participate in committee or other administrative work	29.2%
Be a good colleague	80.0%
Be a good teacher	98.2%

— "The American College Teacher: National Norms for the 1989-90 HERI Survey," University of California at Los Angeles Higher Education Research Institute, *The Chronicle for Higher Education*, Aug. 28, 1991, p. 32.

What's With Teaching Here?

"If there is any one undoubted principle in higher education, it is this: instruction ranks every other consideration." John Bascom said that in the 1870s, and other college and university presidents have been saying it ever since. But on some campuses today an emphasis on undergraduate teaching consists largely of publicity brochure pieties and commencement oratory; in the classroom itself, devotion to effective teaching sits in the back row.

Or so you've heard in song and story. However — and it's a big however — you yourself may very well have just joined the faculty of a growing number of institutions with a decent respect — and rewards — for good teaching. In that case, better shape up your instructional capabilities. Even if you're on a research-oriented campus, you could help energize there the powerful national trend toward what Ernest L. Boyer of the Carnegie Foundation for the Advancement of Teaching has called "the 1990s as the decade of undergraduate education."

Whether or not your institution subscribes, you can draw a personal azimuth from Page Smith's dictum in *Killing the Spirit:* "There is no decent, adequate, respectable education ...

without personal involvement by a teacher with the needs or concerns, academic and personal, of his/her students; all the rest is 'instruction,' 'information transferral,' 'communication technique,' or some other impersonal or antiseptic phrase, but it is not teaching."

Your Midland University *alter ego* got a pretty clear signal about the importance of teaching at that institution in the form of this memo from his Letters and Science Dean, E. Howard Harrier:

> Let me commend to you two recent statements by professors turned administrators:
>
> "When the graduate school's definition of scholarship makes its presence felt within the work of the college teacher, it can fundamentally distort the commitment of the undergraduate curriculum to the aims of general education." — JAROSLAV PELICAN of Yale.
>
> "I pray that academicians will reconsider the extraordinary emphasis they currently place on publication of scholarly drivel — an obsession that has diminished the classroom experience and has cheated generations of unsuspecting students." — WILLIAM D. SCHAEFER of UCLA.

Whether the Midland faculty reward system will actually reflect that memo is another question.

If you're under a Midland-type Dean Harrier, you can at least be sure you wouldn't get a memo like that unless the dean subscribed to the Page Smith dictum that the primacy of undergraduate instruction needs restoring in our institutions as a badge of professorial performance.

To make his point about atrophy of faculty interest in teaching, Smith once narrated this little anecdote:

He met a young colleague on campus and greeted her with a perfunctory, "How are things going?" The reply: "Oh, just fine, very fine. You see, I'm not teaching this semester!"

(For more on teaching, see Chapter III.)

What's My Teaching Load?

In the six years that Howard Mancing served as head of the department of foreign languages and literature at Purdue University, he conducted a large-scale recruiting program, hiring over 20 new faculty members. Virtually every candidate asked some variant of the same question — having nothing to do with salary, fringe benefits, or even what it's like to live among cornfields. No, the single universal query was, "What will my teaching load be?"

It's a natural question. Your teaching load inevitably dictates the amount of other time you have to devote to research, service, and personal life. Right or wrong, too, a light teaching load has come to signify some form of peer accolade, sort of like a Distinguished Service Cross.

But if you look on teaching only as what you do when you aren't doing anything "significant," forget it. Particularly in this era of public insistence on improvement in undergraduate education, your teaching scorecard could turn out to be a crucial asset or liability.

Here's what the latest Midland University Faculty Development Committee Report has to say on the subject:

> Every Midland faculty member is expected to excel in teaching. They exhibit their command of the subject matter in classroom discussions and lectures, and they present material to their students in an objective, organized way that promotes the learning process. They outline the subject matter with logic and conviction, and awaken in students an awareness of the relationship of their subject to other classes, fields of knowledge, and cultures. They display concern and respect for their students, guiding and inspiring. They strive continuously to broaden and deepen their knowledge and understanding of their discipline, seek to improve the methods of teaching their subject, keep informed about new developments in their field, use appropriate instructional technologies, and prepare educational materials that are up-to-date and well-written. Their influence and reputation as teachers is demonstrated further by student and peer evaluation, by authoring textbooks, by lectures and publications on pedagogy, by the publication of such instructional materials as laboratory manuals and videotapes, and by significant contributions to professional associations that seek to improve teaching.

> Excellence in academic advising serves to augment excellence in teaching, as faculty interact constructively with their advisees. Faculty are knowledgeable about scheduling and about curricular and extracurricular matters, keep informed of current policies and procedures, and aid students in making use of University resources to enhance their educational and personal development. They assist students in learning to make intelligent decisions for themselves. They demonstrate excellence in advising by student and peer evaluation, advising awards, active participation in local and national advising conferences and seminars, by writing and presenting advising papers, and by preparing institutional advising guidelines.

That's quite a mouthful, but that's the growing standard in academia today at other than ultra research-intensive campuses, and even there zephyrs of change are blowing.

Want a standard reference for a teaching load? The American Association of University Professors decreed in 1968 that "faculty members should spend no more than 12 hours a week per semester in the classroom. If there is an expectation of ongoing research, they should not be required to teach more than 9 hours per week. Institutions that require faculty members to publish for tenure and promotion should lower teaching loads, especially for junior faculty members."

At many institutions those loads would be considered excessive today. In the Midland department of botany and applied ecology, for example, the chair tries to limit each faculty member to a course a quarter, but current personnel shortages dictate that every third term each professor must teach two.

Whatever your teaching assignment, you'll just have to build the rest of your work load around it.

How Will My Teaching Be Evaluated?

In one of her first memos to the faculty of the Midland University department of botany and applied ecology, Chair Amanda Perkins wrote:

> On the advice of the department committee on instructional improvement, we will emphasize two objective means of measuring undergraduate teaching performance.
>
> The first is **classroom visitation.** Through a series of visits to classes, a duly appointed panel of peers will acquire firsthand knowledge of just exactly how proficient each of us is in practicing the teaching techniques that should mark undergraduate instruction. Admittedly, such a procedure may be somewhat alien to what some consider as academic freedom, yet so long as the panel confines itself to an objective assessment of how effectively a subject is being taught, using those standards which have long been refined by schools of education, the claim cannot be substantiated that inspection is any sort of damper on freedom to teach. Indeed, classroom inspection may be said to be an essential mechanism for protecting the other side of the academic-freedom coin — the freedom of students to learn — to learn from practitioners who are technically qualified.
>
> The second method we will employ to measure teaching performance objectively is **student ratings.** While some professors may have been opposed to this administrative technique on the grounds that it somehow invades their privacy without contributing anything valid to the measurement of professional proficiency, student evaluation sheets have been used too long on too many campuses and subjected to too many tests for them to be dismissed as dangerous or invalid. Undergraduate ratings of teachers have been shown to have a marked correlation with alumni assessments, and a negative correlation with the subject matter itself and with grades received. Such ratings are in fact relatively accurate guides to the effectiveness of teaching at the

undergraduate level.

Classroom visitations and student ratings can identify those qualities of effective teaching that must continue to mark this department:

Define the major aims of your courses and keep them before your students.

Develop adequate outlines for your courses and revise them frequently.

Discover early the extent to which your students have the basic skills and information for successful course work and adapt accordingly.

Recommend an excellent basic textbook for each course or assemble a custom "text."

Make certain that reference books and readings are readily available.

Assign outside work in such a manner that it will be challenging to your students' interests and efforts.

Afford your students adequate opportunities to raise questions on points about which they want additional information or explanations.

Cultivate an interest in humorous incidents in your classes and make judicious use of humor in your teaching.

Exhibit a genuine enthusiasm for the values and worth of your courses.

Exhibit marked faith in the potential success of your students and show a noticeable degree of patience in dealing with individuals.

Recognize the genuine value of a spirit of good will and friendliness in your classes.

Experiment with teaching techniques and seek continually better methods of teaching, using your classroom visitation reports and student ratings as clues.

Share with your students your own joy in learning, and present materials objectively, rather than seeking to impose personal opinions or prejudices.

The department committee and I are personally committed to placing the department of botany and applied ecology in a lead role in Midland University's renewed devotion to the improvement of undergraduate instruction. Please join us in this important mission.

With that memo in hand, your Midland *alter ego* Bill has no doubt about how his teaching is to be evaluated. If you have no such written guidance, ask. *(See Chapter III.)*

Regardless of prescribed means of measuring teaching effectiveness, you can assume that your personal goal might well be to "knock 'em in the aisles," to warrant the accolade Willa Cather had a colleague pronounce in her profile of *The Professor's House:*

> I wish to pay my tribute to the lecturer's clarity. I have seldom listened to a lecture that explained so difficult a subject in such simple language. I'm left with the feeling that the most inexperienced student in this hall must have learned as much as I have today.

Tips from Student Evaluation Forms. We have before us three typical Student Evaluation of Instruction forms, one in use at a large public research university, one at a small comprehensive university, one at a college. Interestingly enough, the first question on each one in turn is:

- "How effective was the instructor in making clear the goals and objectives of this course?"
- "How clear were the goals, aims, and requirements of the course?"
- "How well organized was the instructor?"

To make a good impression of organization, you can start off the first day with the organization and style of your handout materials. Pitch them to your student audience, not to a faculty committee.

Here's a handy outline for a student-oriented course syllabus:

    YOUR COURSE PROFILE
     What This Course Is
     What It Does
     For Whom
     How
     Why
     Where and When
     By Whom
    YOUR PROGRAM OF INSTRUCTION
     First Week
     Second Week
      and so on
    YOUR COURSE REQUIREMENTS
     Text(s)
     Main Readings
     Reading Report(s)
     Class Discussions
     Practical Work

Exam(s)

Grading

GUIDE TO YOUR PRACTICAL WORK PROJECTS

SUPPLEMENTARY READING LIST

To Be Supplied by Instructor

To Be Found by Student

It Could Be the Company You Keep. After many interviews with entry-level faculty hires at two large universities over their first two years, psychology professor Robert Boice has a bit of advice for you:

1. Some tyro professors uniformly rate lousy student teaching evaluations, don't seem to know what to do about it, rarely seek or get collegial help, feel isolated, say they have too little time for research.

2. On the bright side, some beginners are off and running right away on their own as effective teachers, productive scholars, and happy campers.

3. Those who volunteer for a faculty development program find their level of classroom comfort and time management improves. (4)

You take it from there. In doing so, remember that you're not alone. You have in your memory a kit of role models — the best sort of company. Good teaching, you know, is like what a Supreme Court Justice said about pornography: "You know what it is when you see it." You've seen it in your own undergraduate days. Conjure up now in your mind's eye an incandescent image of one of your own excellent teachers.

Perhaps it is of a botany professor, striding up and down in the well of an auditorium, saying again and again, "I want you to see this now," as she postponed the classification of angiosperms to open a door to the marvelous evolution of the scientific method. Or a medieval historian who clarified why the glorious days of Charlemagne were really not so glorious. Maybe an instructor of English literature making the connection between Tennyson's "Ulysses" and you. Or a physics TA unraveling the mysterious workings of the atom. It could be a Socratic philosophy professor never tired of asking the questions that ended up blowing your mind, revealing you to you and you to him. Perhaps a Billy Graham type of economics professor who could construct a whole sermon on state socialism out of a *U.S. vs. Schechter Poultry Company* text. Or a poli sci professor reducing the whole of a course in American government to a single question on a two-hour final exam: "Discuss the U.S. Constitution as a conservative document."

And, yes, a venerable geology professor addicted to reading

from shopworn notes, lecturing one day on soil erosion and reading, "Every year the Mississippi River carries with it to the Gulf
of Mexico millions and millions of dirt." The bright young sopho-
more in the front row raising her hand to ask, "Professor, do you
mean millions and millions of tons or cubic feet?" The professor
glancing down at his notes and then looking up sheepishly, "It
doesn't say."

These memories are now not to be dismissed. You can put
them to good use as teaching models, good or bad.

What's Par for the Research Course?

When it comes to research/publishing, you may well ask
what's par for the course. According to U.S. Department of
Education data garnered in a 1988 national faculty survey, each
of the nation's estimated 489,000 full-time faculty members
produced an average of two refereed-journal articles and 0.6
scholarly books, chapters in edited volumes, monographs, or
textbooks during the previous two years. Professors at research
universities averaged twice as many publications; those at two-
year colleges published far fewer.

(If each professor were the sole author of each publication,
his or her efforts would add up to nearly a million refereed-
journal articles and 300,000 books, chapters, monographs, and
texts over two years!)

Education Department data did not include the thousands
of book reviews, articles in general-interest publications, technical reports, extension manuals, and conference presentations
also produced by faculty.

So it's a researching/writing world you're in. The box score
for your particular department/institution? Learning the answer
to that question is a key aspect of learning your territory. The
Midland University expectation: a 1.5 published professional
paper average per year.

The Midland Graduate School/Research dean has just issued guidelines to the all-University P&T Committee under
which it's to evaluate the research/publishing of candidates for
tenure. They read like this:

> Research, scholarship, and artistry are the vehicles by
> which Midland University, though its faculty, contributes to
> the discovery of new knowledge. This is a primary mission
> of the University. Research and scholarly activity enhance
> undergraduate, graduate, and outreach teaching by ensur-
> ing the currency of the information being transmitted and
> by exposing students to the excitement of learning at the
> cutting edge of new knowledge.
>
> In evaluating research productivity, quality as well as quan-
> tity should be considered. The primary guardian and

arbiter of research quality is the peer review system. Therefore it is essential that faculty at all levels submit their intellectual products for rigorous review by peers. Such review is most often accomplished by submitting manuscripts to quality professional journals and research proposals to review panels for outside funding agencies. A record of peer acceptance establishes the academic and professional credentials of the faculty member; provides credibility to his or her non-refereed publications, presentations, and teaching; and is the academic foundation for the titles of Associate Professor and Professor.

Because faculty members in the University vary considerably in their research and scholarship interests, flexibility must be maintained in evaluating the quantity and quality of production. In all cases, however, reviewers should look for evidence that the faculty member/candidate has established a program or direction of research and produced scholarly works that make a significant contribution to the field.

Neither superior teaching nor extensive outreach can replace a lack of evidence of an active mind at work at Midland University.

Your own institution may or may not be quite that arbitrary. To be on the safe side, get going on a sustained regimen of publishing.

(For more on research, see Chapters IV and VI.)

Does Service Really Count?

The "service" component of the triad may be the most difficult for an assistant professor to grasp. As a graduate student he or she has been abundantly familiar with the teaching and research activities of professors, but their service roles can have been largely invisible.

Yet the answer to the question posed in the heading is, "Definitely yes."

For the flavor of what service can connote to a P&T Committee, here is what the Midland College of Letters and Science "Promotion-to-Tenure Criteria" document has to say:

While service contributions cannot be the sole basis for promotion to tenure, every faculty member is expected to be involved.

Since the faculty plays a vital role in the administration of the University at all levels and in the formulation of policies, scholars are expected to participate effectively and imaginatively in faculty government and particularly in departmental affairs in the case of assistant professors.

Faculty should seize opportunities to utilize their professional expertise to disseminate information to help improve

the knowledge and skills of lay clientele or the environment
in which they live and work.

Service in and for technical, professional, scholarly, or arts
societies and organizations related to the candidate's academic expertise is a required mark of the faculty member's
local, state-wide, regional, national, or international
academic citizenship.

At the outset, it's important to find out what *counts* as service, even in terms of institutional service. For instance, one
commentator reports that, at a small liberal arts college, "service on faculty-appointed or -elected committees counts for more
than service on president- or dean-appointed committees, and
much more than voluntary work — for P&T, that is."

A tactical question: Do you spread yourself over the service
continuum or do you concentrate on one or two activities? A possible answer: Try to develop quick visibility in (a) a role in faculty governance, say on a departmental committee, (b) an outreach or consulting activity, and (c) a professional association
chore.

Consider service activities that could be mutually supporting. For example, our Midland botany professor could volunteer
for membership on the department's public service committee,
render counsel to a local prairie restoration project, and get appointed to the State Endangered Species Commission.

NOTE: To count as "service" for promotion to tenure, your
extra-campus activities must be related directly to your
academic expertise. Teaching a Sunday School class, leading a scout troop, or chairing a parents-and-teachers committee doesn't qualify (unless you're in a school of education). On the other hand, were your department chair's
child one of your troopers and were to go home glowing
about your camping-trip prowess, it couldn't hurt!

In summary, does service **really** count? To answer that question pragmatically, answer this question: "As an assistant professor, can I afford to leave in the lurch the colleagues who will be
voting on my case?" Without faculty at all ranks performing service
chores, important institutional tasks don't get done. A large department may be able to afford a few brilliant researchers who don't
pull their weight in other areas, or one or two "teacher only and nothing else" types, but most department members cherish well-balanced
colleagues adept at the full range of expectations.

Does a One-or-Two-Out-of-Three Rule of Thumb Apply?

It's the conventional wisdom in some circles that any devotion to the sacred triad is observed more in the breach than in
the application in some situations. There is evidence to that
effect.

For example, the Midland University College of Letters and Science guidelines for promotion to tenure state unequivocally:

> Each faculty member, regardless of funding source, is expected to perform over the full range of responsibilities: teaching, research, and service. Performance in each of these areas will be given due weight when reviewing individual faculty members for salary adjustments, promotion in rank, and tenure.

Across campus in the Midland School of Architecture and Urban Planning, however, the guidelines equivocate:

> Evaluation of a faculty member for promotion and/or tenure shall be based on criteria related to the individual's appointment responsibilities and activities, domestic and/or international, in the following four areas: (1) teaching, (2) research, scholarship, or artistic activities, (3) outreach or professional practice, and (4) service. To be promoted and/or tenured, a faculty member must exhibit a strong sense of professional ethics.

> Competence means performance of tasks and responsibilities in an appropriate and proficient fashion as opposed to inept, unacceptable performance. Excellence refers to performance that exceeds what is expected or required.

Why the difference in nuance between the two guidelines? One befits the mission of a comprehensive college, the other of a professional school. Make it a priority to determine which sort of guideline applies to you in **your** situation in **your** institution.

Am I in Any Kind of Special Situation?

There are several types of tenure-track appointments that can present special problems — and opportunities.

Extension. There are two general forms of extension (or outreach) appointments.

If you're in a land-grant university (there's one in every state, founded under the 1862 Morrill Act), your appointment might be in whole or in part in the Cooperative Extension Service of a college of agriculture as an assistant professor of extension in one of the college's departments ("cooperative" because the enabling 1914 Smith-Lever Act called for tripartite funding — federal, state, and county). In such a case the institutional expectations will be unique. You will teach largely non-degree certificate youths and adults in on-campus short courses and off-campus institutes and workshops or in one-on-one consultations. Your research activities will be applied, constituency-oriented, problem-focused, synthetic. Your service role will be on college and university committees and in state and national organizations (any extension teaching and research work not counting for you as conventional public service). If your tenure-track hurdles are within your department and college, colleagues and administrators sympathetic to the extension mission will understand your career contributions. But if your university employs any form of all-campus quality control, some faculty members on a review panel may find it hard to understand why, for example, a wildlife management extension professor should be given productive-scholarship credit for an extension bulletin on how to build and install back-yard bird houses in lieu of a paper in an appropriate scholarly journal on the changing ecology of the mallard *(Anas platyrhynchos platyrhynchos)* in the Mississippi Flyway.

As departments and divisional units go more and more to outside evaluations for promotion to tenure, the plight of the extension faculty member darkens. While outside assessments apply well to judging quality of research in a subspecialty of a decentralized discipline, and for determining the extent to which the candidate is making a reputation as a scholar, outside evaluations don't fit neatly the extension mission. Extension is local, usually visible only to immediate clients, and seldom to extension specialists in other climes who are potential letter-writers. To the extent that extension faculty A has an out-of-state "name," his or her status may rise among researcher evaluators but fall among extension evaluators who see the candidate neglecting the home garden plot.

Some institutions also maintain general or urban extension divisions, with faculty distinct from "residence" faculty. If your appointment is in such a configuration, your tenure-track problems will be much the same as those of an ag co-op professor, except that your mission will appear even less distinct to any all-campus P&T committee, general outreach faculty not being protected by the massive historic and funding traditions enjoyed by ag extension faculty in what is generally recognized as the finest lay education enterprise in the world.

But take heart. Any institution with tenure-track extension or outreach appointments should have all the kinks worked out by now in how to get qualified extension faculty promoted even in a climate of orthodox teaching, research, and service.

Split Appointment. If your appointment is joint in two departments, you will in effect have to run two tenure-track races. If the two departments are in the same school or college, you will at least report to only one dean; but if your departments are in different colleges, you'll be subject to two different expectations. If joint appointments are common at your institution, P&T committees will be understanding; but if split appointments are irregular, you face a tougher hurdle. The best protection: make sure your appointment is not a 50-50 split but more like

60-40, so that one department feels particularly responsible for you and takes the initiative in helping forward your tenure-track progress.

Interdisciplinary Studies. To the delight of some faculty and the consternation of others, the 1960s saw the emergence on college and university campuses nationwide of such interdisciplinary programs as women's studies, environmental studies, and various forms of ethnic and geographic studies. If your appointment is in such a department, particularly one so new it has no established track record of promotional criteria, you could have problems. For one thing, universities tend to be more atomistic than holistic in their approach to knowledge, so interdisciplinary programs do not exist under a particularly benign reward system; thus assistant professors in cobbled-together programs live dangerously. Secondly, faced with a threat to their ordained territories, established departments can muster awesome retaliatory power. The scalps of some of yesterday's interdisciplinary programs are dangling from the belts of defensive disciplines. Finally, fiscal shortfalls can starve out campus configurations lacking fixed budget lines and well-cultivated constituencies, especially in the absence of nurturing government and foundation grants. The best defense: try to wangle a joint appointment in an orthodox department so that you look more respectable to suspicious deans and provosts, and break your back to amass an extra-impressive CV.

Professional School. An appointment in a professional department, school, or college can present problems, since some such units tend to be "schizo" about their proper stance, and hence can be ambivalent about their expectations for new hires — skills vs. scholarship, in other words.

A common internal dichotomy in a professional unit, for example, pits theory-and-methodology researchers against practitioners, as between oncologists and internists in a medical school.

Mature professional units in effect tend to employ two tenure tracks — one for avowed researchers and one for applied people. In such a situation your one essential element of information is, "Do the unit and I agree what track I'm on?"

The real trouble can arise when a professional unit is in transition, with the two camps vying for ascendancy, tugged one way or another by changing divisional agendas. Internal tensions can then reach flash-point proportions, with new hires — and students — caught in the cross-fire.

In a school of mass communication, for example, an assistant professor with a brand new Ph.D. from the Excelsior School of Communication, who can quote sociologists Melvin L.

DeFleur and Sandra Ball-Rokeach *ad infinitum* on "theories of mass communications" yet who has had not one day of practical experience in a newspaper newsroom, can wind up assigned to teach "Reporting and Newswriting 101" to unsuspecting sophomores.

Similarly, an experienced senior TV investigative reporter turned assistant professor without a Ph.D. can do a polished job on that teaching assignment yet find his or her track to tenure blocked in a professional unit seeking to raise its scholarly credentials.

Timing can be everything. The senior author (**ACS**), who doesn't have a Ph.D., could not now be appointed an assistant professor in a journalism school that welcomed him with open arms in 1953 as a young M.A. with an impressive professional portfolio and promoted him without hesitation in 1958, that school today being heavily oriented to research as a survival strategy in its research university.

A colleague of ours emphasizes strongly that the two-track tenure system "is not always honored" in a professional school: "The Ph.D. becomes the union card that allows you to remain a faculty member. An alternative to rejection for tenure for lack of a Ph.D. may be to enroll in a doctoral program. I know of at least two cases where the dean said there would be no tenure without a Ph.D. One person, who already had two M.A.s, finally got the Ph.D. The other did not, but found a teaching post at an institution more appreciative of his professional experience."

Even though a botany department is not normally thought of as a professional unit, your *alter ego* Bill at Midland is feeling the effects of tension between researchers and practitioners as that department seeks to fashion an applied-ecology thrust. Fortunately, Bill seems to have his own tenure track well defined.

The ABD Situation. Some departments in some institutions will appoint as a tenure-track assistant professor a person who has completed all his or her terminal-degree course work but who has yet to finish a Ph.D. thesis (hence ABD — **all but dis-**sertation). Such a person is obviously in a double bind — trying to meet degree and tenure requirements simultaneously.

Institutions hiring ABDs may adjust the term of appointment. For example, it was the experience of one commentator that at his state university:

"If you were appointed ABD and you completed the degree in one year, you could be reappointed for two years, then again for three years. If reappointed a third time, then you received tenure. If you completed the degree in two years, you could be twice reappointed for two years each time.

"Retirement benefits and departmental voting rights began

only after you received the degree or after the two years of service, whichever came first. Promotion to associate before the probationary period ended carried tenure.

"When I came in, my dissertation sat on the end of my dining-room table for two years. I taught as many as four different preparations from 8 a.m. till 5 p.m., all over campus. That alone took 50 hours a week."

In other words, entering academia as an ABD is to live dangerously.

The variability in roles, missions, and performance among the institutions of higher education is enormous. Some institutions are tied to public employment, others are not. Some faculty are represented by labor unions, others are not. Some institutions function on a merit-based system of faculty salaries, others do not. Some sustain a deep commitment to scholarship, while others see their primary mission as teaching. For some institutions, mobility of faculty is a constant consideration, for others it is less so. Some perform very well, others do not. Corresponding to these differences are important differences in the working conditions, aspirations, institutional and professional loyalties, and governance responsibilities of the faculty ....

Notwithstanding the diversity, one compelling constant characterizes higher education in America — the maintenance of academic freedom and a system of academic tenure as a means to assure such freedom.
— *The Commission on College Retirement, Pension and Retirement Policies in Colleges and Universities* (San Francisco: Jossey-Bass, 1990), pp. 282-283.

What's the Status of My Position?

First, why the vacancy? Did somebody retire, leaving a slot the dean didn't recapture? Or is it a new position?

If the latter, you'll want to consult the department budget to see whether you're a firm line-item or funded temporarily on "soft money" from college discretionary funds or a grant.

You can't change the facts in any case, but they'll give you a clue to how your colleagues view the situation in terms of its — and your — longevity.

Why Me?

If you can find them, there's nothing like consulting the minutes of the search-and-screen committee that recommended you — for determining your department's expectations for you *vis-à-vis* the attributes of your erstwhile competition.

Your *alter ego* Bill at Midland found those minutes that pertained to him. Out of an invitation-and-application list of 16, the committee picked a "wish list" of six and proposed to interview all of them, but the dean would allocate travel funds for only four.

One was a generalist with two years of a superior teaching record at a fine four-year college in Iowa but no research publications worthy of the Midland name. A second was a combination geneticist/pathologist, one of the last of James Crow's grad students at the University of Wisconsin-Madison, with his name already on a multiple-inventor patent covering a potential cure for oak wilt. A third was a taxonomist from Cal Tech with extensive Peace Corps experience in South American rain forests and a strong desire to energize campus concern for their fate. The fourth, of course, was Bill.

The minutes reveal a heated all-department debate between the two botany "camps," the one side promoting the UW-Madison candidate, the other Bill with his experience as both a TA and RA under Eugene Odum at Georgia and his promise as a first baseman for the proposed new master's program in applied ecology. It's a wonder the Cal Tech candidate hadn't won out as a compromise. The vote had been close, and wounds there were, assuaged only by a sudden appearance at the decisive faculty meeting by Emeritus Professor Pendarvis, pleading for "civility," plus covert word from the college dean that he would "make things up" with new instrumentation for the lab people.

That reading, of course, gave Bill a pretty clear indication of how the land lies at Midland. He either makes peace somehow with the malcontents, meanwhile driving ahead to fulfill his potential for the ecology faction, or he's in trouble.

If you at your institution can't find any revealing faculty meeting minutes, perhaps a mentor can answer the question, "Why me?"

Other Factors

Bill faced some negative attitudes in his new department. But he's a man, white, and American. Some faculty come into situations where they must contend with more than the usual political difficulties. If you're a woman, a member of a minority group, or a foreigner, the ladder to tenure may be somewhat more slippery.

Why were you hired? (There's probably more than one right answer.) Because you have special talents and experience? Then work to develop those talents and build on those experiences. Because you represent an underrepresented population? If you

were hired for that reason, why? To bring different perspectives
to your new department? Then you're likely free to be yourself.
To meet some quota or other pressures to "diversify"? Then you
may need to exercise a little extra judgment.

That doesn't mean to sell out, to deny your differences — not
at all. But you should be particularly sensitive to your situation,
to your environment. Some of your new colleagues may initially
resent you or even be apprehensive. Be sensitive to potential
conflicts. Don't try to avoid them; just weigh the consequences
carefully.

Remember: much of the progress made through affirmative
action has been at the lower levels. "Glass ceilings" and other
such barriers exist in academia as they do anywhere in society
where people have difficulty adjusting to differences. Don't be
suspicious of every colleague and every word and action, yet
don't be naive and idealistic.

Sometimes you may feel it's a no-win situation: you're
damned if you do and damned if you don't. If you volunteer for
committees, for example, some of your colleagues may consider
you overly aggressive or too eager to please, but if you don't,
then you're lazy or aloof or lukewarm in your commitment. Also,
as a former colleague pointed out, the dilemma is "especially
bad for female assistant professors who collaborate with male
'heavy hitters' " because it's easy to undervalue the contributions of the junior collaborator. And if a woman or a minority associates with other women or minorities, this can be viewed as
"ghettoization." As Kermit the frog laments, "It's not easy being
green."

Make the most of who you are and what you have to offer, so
your new colleagues accept you as an individual. In other words,
make it harder for anyone to simply label you in terms of your
differences. Network with people who can better understand
any particular obstacles you might face in your situation. But
don't assume anything about "friends" or "foes" — as you
wouldn't want your new colleagues to make assumptions about
you.

Could I Face Any Unavoidable Environmental Hazards?

Unfortunately the answer is "Yes." At least three come to
mind.

We've already discussed one: A major institutional budgetary shortfall that would force the board of governors to put a
cap on the number of slots open to new associate professors in
any given year. While they could all be promoted without any
salary raises, that would put faculty pay scales out of whack for
40 years.

Of course, looking on the bright side, the opposite could

happen: a generous benefactor comes out of the alumni wood-
work to endow accelerated promotions for outstanding young
faculty.

Another type of crunch is a pile-up of eligible tenure candidates at the departmental level. It happened frequently in the
1950-1960 decade, producing professional scrambles and personal vendettas. It could happen again as colleges and universities face massive faculty retirements in the 1990-2010 era.

At the college level of review these days, you might run up
against —let's face it — some sort of unofficial quota system, for
good or ill. A dean can be under heavy pressure to reflect in his
or her recommendations for tenure a university drive for affirmative action, multicultural diversity, pluralism, political correctness, or some such — or a faculty backlash against claimed
"diminution in faculty quality." You personally may or may not
benefit from the tension. That's just the way it can be, sorry to
say. (13)

There isn't much you can do about such hazards except
build the most impressive CV you can — and keep your fingers
crossed.

What About Fringe Benefits?

A fringe, according to Webster's, is "an ornamental bordering," but if so-called "fringe benefits" constitute 25% or more of
your total compensation package, as they may well do, you can
hardly call then "ornamental."

Benefits you should check into can include:

- Insurance — standard medical, dental, catastrophic
  health, life, disability (income continuation), family
  group, accidental death and dismemberment (including
  spouse and eligible dependents).

- Pension fund contributions.

- Social Security contributions.

- Travel allotments.

- Employee reimbursement accounts (tax-free).

- Tax-free annuities and deferred compensation.

- Paid sick, vacation, and parental-care leaves.

- Worker's and unemployment compensation payments.

- All sorts of "hidden perks."

You would have checked out the broad outlines of your
benefits before ever signing your letter of acceptance, but now
you should look into some important details on the big-ticket
items, such as:

<u>Health Care</u>. Does the institution pick up the whole tab, or

am I under a "contributory" plan? If so, is my monthly contribution a "fixed" amount or is it a percentage of costs? Can I choose a health insurance plan that allows me to consult any physician of my choice, or am I limited to a local HMO? If the latter, how do I get coverage when I'm on travel status? Does the plan cover dental care? extended mental or controlled-substance illness? out-patient counseling? How many days of paid sick leave am I entitled to a year? Do they carry over or lapse? If I'm down and out for a couple of days or weeks and my colleagues cover my classes for me, is that counted against my sick leave? What about parental leave? When I retire, what happens to any sick leave benefits I've accrued? my health care insurance rates?

Life Insurance. Does the institution carry any on me? my family? Is it term, straight life, or annuity? Do I contribute or not? What exemptions apply, such as the crash of a private plane or wartime? Does the coverage lapse after retirement?

Retirement Pay Program. Is my institution pledged to a stable plan, or is it looking at "reforms"? Is the program a state or denominational defined-benefit plan employing conservative investment strategies, or is it a national defined-contribution plan subject to the vagaries of the market? Can I choose between the two approaches? On what formula will my pension be based? Will summer teaching and outreach compensation be included in the computation? What's the size of the institution's contribution compared with mine? Is the fund sequestered or is it subject to political invasion? What's the track record of the investment board presiding over the fund — missing, matching, or exceeding inflation? How soon am I vested? Can I take my contributions with me if I switch institutions — with or without penalties? Is there a window of opportunity for early retirement? What entities will tax my retirement pay? Is there a deferred income-tax shelter option if I ever make enough salary to participate? Can I roll over my escrow funds into another investment — before or after retirement? Am I or am I not also covered by Social Security? Are recent department retirees happy about or disappointed in their experience with the program?

If your institution's personnel office is on the ball, it will have a handy-dandy fringe benefits explanation packet for you. Look into it right away because some voluntary benefits probably require that you sign up within 30 days of your appointment.

That packet can probably cover adequately the "official" benefits to which you are entitled, but don't neglect in your reconnaissance to check into any and all hidden perks as well:

Hidden Perks. Are there free or cut-rate tickets to athletic and/or cultural events? Are there free or cut-rate bus and/or parking fees? Access to campus recreational facilities? Economical cafeteria fares? Discounts on books and other logistical supplies? Child care services? Do faculty offspring get any breaks on tuition and/or fees? on admission requirements?dormitory space? scholarship funds? part-time campus jobs? Does the institution subsidize a faculty club building?

Along with hidden perks, you'd better check into hidden costs as well.

Hidden Dues. Are there any campus or community organizations I or my spouse are expected to join? at what cost? What is my expected "community chest" contribution level? Does my department maintain a "slush fund," "coffee kitty," or "social budget" to which I'm supposed to donate? How much a month? Is there an expected periodic campus foundation tariff? a campus research fund to which I'm required to turn over all or a percentage of any royalties I might earn on writings or patents? If I run up mileage while representing the institution around its constituency, will I be reimbursed or not? for off-campus meals and motels?

As time goes on, you'll undoubtedly think of other questions about benefits and tariffs. Don't hesitate to ask. Start with your department office factotum. He or she will know the answers or whom to consult. Don't rely on "locker-room experts"; go to the campus specialists.

The Fraying Fringes. As we've said earlier, we've always called them "fringe benefits," but the time has long since passed when you could think of them as a passing frill, what with benefits representing up to a quarter or more of your compensation package.

Here are some developments for you to keep an eye on.

Owing especially to burgeoning health care costs, you may start contributing more and more, directly or indirectly, to medical insurance as your institution feels the strain throughout the whole benefits system. stringent cost-containment strategies on the part of insurance companies are simultaneously leading to curtailments in actual coverage.

In the good old days of prosperity, many institutions developed expansive early-retirement opportunities to encourage the disappearance of high-salaried senior staff so new hires could be lured with visions of sugar-plums. Now that those plans turn out to be expensive, some college and university boards are looking at revisions.

Federal and state income tax policies have induced staff and faculty to avoid taxes by taking more of their pay in non-taxed, institution-provided benefits. When a college uses a dollar to buy fringes instead of paying that dollar in salaries, 100 cents can be used for benefits because fringe benefits haven't usually been taxed. But times may be changing. Not only are governments casting longing eyes on fringe benefits, institutions are casting equally covetous eyes on hitherto sacred perks.

"What's to be done?" asks Paul Strohm, editor of *Academe*. "A great deal can be done through organized, informed faculty intervention." (20)

So if you get "invited" to represent new hires on a campus fringe-benefits committee, you'll know what constitutes the agenda.

What About Logistical Support?

Again, you undoubtedly checked into the broad outlines of the topic before coming on board. Indeed, some of its aspects may have tilted your decision. Now's the time to pin down the details on such key matters as library resources, book and journal purchase funds, laboratory space and equipment, office space and equipment, long-distance phoning, fax access, instrumentation, computers, secretarial service, TAs/RAs, travel funds, leaves, instructional aids, in-house research funds, workshops and seminars for faculty on how better to meet your triad of responsibilities — the gamut of material that can make all the difference between smooth sailing and stormy weather in your navigation toward tenure.

But don't expect to get everything on a platter. As we suggested in Chapter 1, you've got to make your own fiscal investment in your career. If that means your spouse finds at least a part-time job and your children don't keep up with the Jones kids, so be it. The sacrifices are for six years, not a lifetime.

What Are Common Rough Spots and Sand Traps?

To stay in the fairway to tenure, it may help you to know why some professors don't shoot par. University scholars have identified these hazards:

- Personal problems, departmental quarrels, alcohol.

- Being unprepared to follow when the discipline or specialty takes a new twist.

- Complexities of grantsmanship or academic politics that can be a prerequisite to success for even the most creative scholar.

- Inability to understand the institution's definition of a "good" or productive faculty member, particularly if that definition is "fuzzy" or subject to change with the times.

- Gross methods used by reviewers to measure excellence in teaching, research, and service — relying on unsubstantiated gossip rather than taking time to read and evaluate solid data.

Some of these hazards you can avoid with skill; others are endemic to the game. Talk to your caddie.

What About Personal-Support Mechanisms?

- A professor is concerned because he knows the chair can smell liquor on his breath during daytime chats in the hall, but he can't shake the addiction.

- Another is at her wit's end because she's just received what she considers to be a grossly unfair reprimand from a superior.

- Still another is having such serious marital difficulties that it's affecting his ability to stay on track.

Farfetched? Not on your life. It could happen to you. So it's natural that you'd inquire into personal-support mechanisms on your campus should the need ever arise. At some institutions, faculty and staff with personal problems would have to muddle through a maze of counseling, employee relations, or other kinds of agencies before finding help. At others, a single one-stop resource is at hand.

At Midland, for instance, there's a central Employee Assistance Office that provides direction for any faculty, academic staff, or classified personnel who are struggling with personal, professional, behavioral, or medical problems.

Says its director: "We provide an opportunity for university people to sort out the things that are going on in their particular situations and to identify a broad range of options available for dealing with then. We tend not to do actual counseling, although we can get involved if we feel we can help within three or four meetings. What we emphasize is problem assessment and referral to the right resources at the university or in the city."

In turn, Midland has published a comprehensive employee assistance policy stating, among other things, that employees may use Center services during working hours and that all conversations, with a few exceptions covered by law, are strictly confidential.

You may find you're so fortunate as to have access to a like service. If not, you're obviously pretty much on your own — a significant negative institutional factor.

What Do I Do in Summer?

Assuming you're on a standard nine-month appointment (typically, only ag college professors are paid year-round, on the theory that their research opportunities peak during the growing season), you'll have the summer off.

What do I do? The temptation will be great to augment your income by teaching in the summer session, but that might bite seriously into your research pace. With luck your dean will have access to some discretionary funds he or she can use to offer summer salary research support to worthy young assistant professors.

A compromise would be to teach in a three-week summer session if your institution has such a calendar, and then use the remaining eight or nine weeks in laboratory or library. That, and taking a vacation — without which you and your family could go stir crazy. There's always the possibility, too, of combining vacation travel with research, attendance at a professional association convention, or enrollment in a teaching workshop.

Did we mention yard work?

What About Funding?

What keys open the department or college cash box? Research proposals? Requisitions for instructional aids? Requests for travel funds? All of the above?

Can I live forever on intramural "bootlegged" time and money, or will I be expected to generate extramural funding on my own? To what extent? How soon in my career? What support mechanisms are available to facilitate my search for grants? What's the going average of outside funding in my department per faculty member?

Such are key questions for you to plumb for answers early on.

To the question whether you're expected to attract some of your own funding, if the answer is yes, make no little plans. Sure, in terms of the size of an initial grant, you'll probably have to think small, but start contemplating already something much larger in scope — say, an institute, a center, a consortium, even a semi-independent named chair. Such devices seem to multiply on campuses these days like wire coat hangers in closets. Some are complexes of offices, some even buildings, others nothing but letterheads. Whatever, they appear to have a certain appeal to funding agencies. Scan, for instance, any academic newsletter and see how many academics cited are chairs, directors, or affiliates of those institutes and centers. It's almost as if in some circles the conventional department were becoming passé.

For example, the senior author (**ACS**) had a lot better luck attracting outside funding once he fabricated an inter-college Center for Environmental Communication and Education Studies than he did operating under a school rubric.

While such entrepreneurial efforts may usually wait upon your making tenure, there's nothing wrong with your reach exceeding your grasp — at least in your mind's eye.

One reviewer of this manual (a social science department chair in a state university) has this slant on the funding picture today:

One reason grant-getting is important these days is that
state support is getting more iffy than in the past. A grant-
getter is an important asset to a department, particularly
when at least some indirect costs from grants are funneled
to the department. Departments now seem to be considering new areas of specialization depending, at least in part,
on funding opportunities. A question: What's the sense in
continuing to specialize in X that can no longer be supported when Y has funding? Another question: Does the
tenure candidate work in X or Y? Wherein lies the future?

*(For more on attracting research funding, see Chapters IV
and VI.)*

What About Stress?

If you've been reading academic newspapers and magazines
lately, you know that campuses are highly stressful workplaces,
at least according to psychologists.

Young assistant professors, under the gun to publish or
perish, are particularly prone to suffer the effects of tension,
some of it self-induced, the researchers say.

If it's any consolation to you, Professor Walter H. Gmelch,
chair of the department of educational administration and supervision at Washington State University, reports that all members
of an academic community share the stress syndrome, although
the claimed causes can vary. (10)

Residence faculty are almost unanimous in identifying as
their top stressors "imposing excessively high self-expectations,"
"time constraints," and "lack of resources."

But so do almost all administrative and faculty groups.

Department chairs see themselves trapped between the pressures of performing as both faculty members and administrators. Upper-echelon administrator stressors stem from
institutional service requirements and leadership loads.
Librarians reflect both administrator and faculty issues; so do
cooperative extension personnel.

Apparently stress is simply built into academia, so you're
not alone. Fortunately, too, college and university administra-
tions are recognizing they can do something about the situation:
give faculty more control over their environment, offer supportive work and family policies, improve communication down and
up, provide health insurance for mental illness and chemical dependency, and allow flexible scheduling of work hours.

Probably your best antidote is simply to recognize that
hundreds of thousands have been this way before — and sur-
vived and flourished.

What About Work/Family Issues?

Is the climate of your campus sympathetic to dual-career couples? Are there collaborative arrangements with local employers to locate suitable employment for spouses? What about family responsiveness policies — maternity and family leave, reduced teaching loads, and adjusted tenure-track demands for parents of young children? Are there mentors and networks to support scholarly development for assistant professors with dual responsibilities? (11)

Is My Institution Censured?

You probably checked out long ago whether or not your institution is on the list of colleges and universities under censure by the American Association of University Professors. If you didn't, do so now.

The AAUP censures institutions when it finds they've violated the association's standards of academic freedom and tenure, which have become widely accepted in academia.

For example, in 1991 the AAUP's Committee A concluded that Albany Medical College dismissed a non-tenured microbiology professor without following due process when he declined a promotion to tenure in exchange for assigning title to the college for all his inventions and patents.

An institution can get off the AAUP list, but not without considerable remedial action. For instance, the South Dakota Board of Regents, which governs the state's six public four-year colleges and universities, has been under AAUP censure since 1962 — longer than any other institution. But now the Board seems to be on the brink of clearing its name.

Joining and staying on the faculty of an institution on the AAUP's blacklist can be hazardous to your academic health.

How Do I Keep From Getting Fired?

A brochure by approximately that title was issued in 1991 by *Changing Times Magazine*. Although aiming primarily at the business world and hence bordering on the patently "political," the editors nonetheless make some points not irrelevant to any campus scene:

- Develop your contacts, your networking, with peers, superiors, staff, and off-campus influentials.
- Know your institution's mission and adapt.
- Think — and act — positively; be cooperative, don't be a crank.
- Don't assume your competency is a given.
- Keep your résumé up-to-date and handy so you can argue your own case.

- Practice communicating orally and in writing more cogently.
- Go back to school in workshops or on your own.
- And the clincher: make yourself too valuable to lose.

What Is the "Culture" of My Institution?

In the words of Peter Seldin, prolific professor of management, academic culture is the unspoken language that tells you what's important, what's unimportant, and how you're expected to do things at your institution — the amalgam of beliefs, mythology, values, and tones that sets your institution apart, a term that describes rather than evaluates, concerned with perceptions rather than opinions. (18)

Why is it important to have a good understanding of your academic culture? Because you must be comfortable in a culture to succede in it.

Can a member of a college or university get an accurate picture of its culture? The answer is yes, but as an insider trying to learn about your culture you must do three things: (1) ignore your institution's promotional literature — it's probably written by a fugitive from a Madison Avenue PR agency; (2) disregard your own prior assumptions, biases, and beliefs; and (3) mentally record only what you see and hear. And first impressions can be valid.

Seldin lists the following 10 characteristics as some of the definable elements of an academic culture:

1. **Individual Autonomy.** What degree of responsibility, independence, and opportunity do you actually have?

2. **Structure.** To what degree are rules and regulations used to control faculty, students, administrators, and staff?

3. **Support.** How much warmth and helpfulness does the administration exhibit to subordinates? Faculty to students?

4. **Identity.** To what degree do faculty and students identify with the entire institution? With your department?

5. **Quality of Personnel.** How much confidence do administrators, faculty, and students display in each other's integrity and competence?

6. **Cooperation.** How effectively do people throughout the campus work together toward shared goals? What about people in your department?

7. **Decision-Making Process.** How much genuine consultation and collaboration exist in formulating functions and policies? At the top level? In your department?

8. **Risk Tolerance.** How much are you encouraged to be professionally adventuresome and innovative?

9. Communication Pattern. How well does complete, accurate, and meaningful information flow upward, downward, and across the institution? Within your department?

10. Sense of Community. To what degree do members of the college or university feel a sense of oneness, a tone of genuine caring and sharing for each other? In your department?

If you keep your mouth shut and your eyes and ears open, you should be able to get a pretty good reading on this continuum of institutional characteristics in a fairly short order. Members of site-visit teams and accreditation panels do it all the time in a week or so.

Don't expect to be utterly content with everything you sense. There is *no* perfect campus culture. On the other hand, if most of what you perceive is alien to your personal criteria, start sending out résumés right away.

SOUND SOURCES OF INFORMATION
Your Letter of Appointment

Although it was her first one, the letter Prof. Amanda L. Perkins wrote to your *alter ego* Bill at Midland University was explicit and helpful, perhaps because in her newness as botany chair she consulted an excellent <u>Chairperson's Manual</u> compiled by Kay U. Kerr of Colorado State University's Office of Instructional Services. (14)

If your own letter of appointment is more cryptic than clear, you might want to consider referring to that guide for clues to matters to be discussed.

With an award-winning track record in faculty recruitment and retention, CSU Professor Stephen D. Roper, chair of anatomy and neurobiology, has these useful talking points:

> <u>A newly hired faculty member deserves a clear explanation of what is expected over the next few years</u>. Detail the department's career criteria. The letter should include at a minimum the expectations regarding (1) teaching obligations (such as courses, number of students, when taught, and performance standards), (2) research activities (whether extramural grants are expected, whether the faculty member is to obtain salary support from grants, what level of productivity is anticipated), and (3) service activities (major committee assignments and so on). The letters I send to newly hired faculty members encompass our expectations for the first one to three years. These documents are quite comprehensive and typically run two to three pages in length.

> <u>The transition from Ph.D. graduate to new faculty member is a major change</u>. Whereas to this point the individual may have been protected and nurtured, that has now ceased.

That is why in our departmental letters of appointment we name a specific mentor or advocate for each new faculty member.

Protect the new hire from an overburdensome teaching/ service load in the first year. The first year is a critical germination time to set roots at our University. All my faculty concur in understanding the need to assume slightly greater teaching loads in order to ease the new faculty member's load, and this policy is explained in the appointment letter.

Provide appropriate resources as start-up funds. Resources such as equipment, discretionary funds, and space should be communicated in writing and honored in full. Ideally a new faculty member should be provided with sustained research support — a safety net for one to three years as the new colleague pursues funding. The letter will so state. It will also suggest that the new hire initially team up with a more experienced faculty member and submit a joint funding proposal, and point out likely journals, funding agencies, and campus aids in writing grants and preparing papers.

Point out how a faculty member can obtain national visibility. My letters of appointment speak to interdisciplinary collaboration and joint projects across the state and nation, offer travel support and encouragement to attend and present papers at national meetings, and suggest how to attract invitations for talks at other institutions.

The career of the spouse may be a consideration. In these days of "dinks" (double income, no kids) and "diks" (double income, kids), the career of the spouse or significant other may become a factor in retaining the new faculty member. My letters of appointment offer such assistance as the department might render.

As we say, if your own letter of appointment falls short of CSU's standard, try to figure out ways to bridge the gap in information and support. Don't just let uncertainties ride. Matters you don't clear up in the first month or so can fester indefinitely.

Departmental Meetings and Minutes

Your Midland *alter ego* was dreading his first department faculty meeting even before he reported in: "I won't know anybody and nobody will know me." The meeting turned out not to be scheduled until mid-September, to allow everybody to get their feet on the ground.

He had arrived early, in mid-August, at the "request" of the department chair so he could attend "orientation" sessions for new hires, sponsored by the Midland Center for Faculty Development. (They turned out to be worthwhile: no "This is the blackboard and this is a pointer" stuff.)

As the rest of the department began to filter in, Chair Perkins stepped to the fore, having read that Colorado State University handbook, and followed its prescription to the letter:

> <u>Monitoring the new faculty member's interaction with other faculty</u>. This is a delicate situation, requiring interpersonal communication skills. The department head can help by taking extra pains to introduce the new faculty member to other faculty, describing backgrounds and areas of possible mutual interest. Interactions outside the department with departmental faculty and persons from other areas of the university can be encouraged, even arranged. Setting up coffee sessions or lunches among small groups of faculty, including the new member, is a prime example. Every new faculty member needs to feel wanted and needed.

With luck, your own arrival will be as hospitable, so that by the time of the first faculty meeting you won't face it with utter fear and trembling. Even so, it will probably be best to follow that well-known adage that new assistant professors are to be seen and not heard; unless of course, you're asked to respond to a direct question, in which case take strategic evasive action without appearing to be totally dumb. Whatever you do, don't say, "Well, at Excelsior they did thus and so"; your new colleagues couldn't care less.

Keeping in the background has the advantage that it gives your undivided attention to the flow of the meeting. The agenda items themselves as well as the perfunctory or profound discussions they prompt will be the beginnings of your primer for learning your territory.

At Midland, departmental faculty meetings are habitually held on Friday afternoons after all classes are out. (Spouses just have to get used to late Friday dinners at least once a month.) Regardless of the state of the meeting, promptly at 5:30 Chair Perkins calls a pause in the day's occupation for what is euphemistically known as "the children's hour." Professor R. Hammond Louvre, the connoisseur, breaks out sacramental wine and everybody relaxes. (It's technically illegal to consume intoxicating beverages on Midland property, but nobody has ever questioned the department tradition.) Needless to say, the department meeting breaks up a bit later on a more convivial note than when it began. The ceremony may be the one device that keeps the two botany "camps" from shedding each other's blood on occasion. (One conundrum: if a new Midland botany hire is a teetotaler, what does he or she do?)

Don't draw the conclusion that all the Midland protocols we cite universally apply. For example, as one commentator writes,

"At small colleges, committee work is done at the campus level, not departmental. Faculty committees are composed of faculty across the disciplines who are voted in by the entire faculty. Yet much of what you say about departmental committees and meetings is equally applicable to such all-college committees.

"Incidentally, your advice to a new hire to be seen and not heard in such meetings is excellent. It takes a while to know the whole faculty, and you really need to recognize the different camps before you stick your neck out."

Regardless of what sort of department faculty meeting climate you find at your institution, look forward to those meetings and the clues they're bound to offer about institutional expectations.

One strategic decision may confront you at that first meeting: the chair may call for volunteers to serve on a new department faculty committee. Do you raise your hand? Some colleagues will frown on such an unseemly display of "pushiness"; others will applaud your willingness to assume the burdens of department citizenship. It's a judgment call. On balance, we'd say, "Go for it," particularly if the committee assignment has some relevance to your background and professional interests. The meek don't usually inherit the academic earth.

Besides paying rapt attention to the pronouncements and nuances at faculty meetings, you may want to go into department files and read the minutes of faculty meetings in years past — again, to get a feeling for your new territory. You may find some minutes so sparse they merely record who made what motion and whether it carried or failed, while others will have recorded every blow-by-blow of discussion to the extent the ultimate decision is practically buried in verbiage.

Nonetheless, past faculty meeting minutes can be well worth scanning.

College/Division Guidelines

Your college or division will likely have some sort of a criteria-for-promotion-to-tenure document. Because it has to apply to a wide range of departments, it will speak in broad generalities, but they can be helpful to an extent in giving you a sense of college priorities.

But you have to be conscious of the fine print. The Midland School of Forestry and Environmental Studies guidelines, for example, state explicitly that "school procedures and criteria are specific for faculty in the School, but they do not supersede University criteria" — and then later go on to say that a candidate for tenure in the School need demonstrate excellence in only one of the three of the triad, while University policy clearly states that all Midland faculty are expected to "perform over the full range of University responsibilities." To an assistant professor of forestry, it would represent "a puzzlement."

You may find the same sort of discrepancies in the literature of your institution.

Campus Policy Statements

The Midland *Faculty Handbook* (II) devotes much of its space on promotion-to-tenure to specifying the policies and procedures to be followed by all principal divisions. These rules you can use to anticipate the major steps in the process — or to appeal a mishandled review of your record.

Statements issued by such administrators as the Dean of the Graduate School/Research tend to be more explicit and thus enlightening, as we've seen in the delineation of Midland's research expectations.

One caution: make sure any administrative statement you consult at your institution is current. Outdated policy documents tend to have an extended half-life in departmental files.

Annual Faculty Activities Report Form

You can tell a lot about institutional expectations from the form of that form. For example, we're looking at a community college form; it has space for "Instructional Activities," for "College Service," and for "Discipline-Related Public Service and Outreach," but none for "Research." A land-grant college of agriculture form in hand starts out with space for "Extension Activities." A liberal arts and science college form in a research university starts out with space for "Research or Artistic Activities," while a four-year academy form starts out with space for "Teaching." All those variations tell you something.

Because it calls for all the data you ought to be keeping track of in detail, we reproduce the Midland University annual faculty activities report form here (as adapted by the department of botany and applied ecology):

Current Personal Data

Full name

University address and phone number

Midland address and phone number

Marital status

Name of spouse, if any

Names and birth dates of any children

All degrees earned, dates, and institution awarding

Area of research specialization

Rank at Midland, with date of appointment of present rank

Length and dates of faculty and/or professional service

Instructional Activities

Regular course offerings, by number, title, credit hours, number of students, number of labs

    Spring term

    Summer

    Fall term

    Winter term

Non-regular scheduled course offerings, by number, title, credit hours, number of students

    Spring term

    Summer

    Fall term

    Winter term

Continuing education and extension teaching (short courses, workshops, etc.)

Guest lecture activities (lectures given in colleagues' courses)

Student Advising and Counseling

Number of undergraduates for whom you are the assigned advisor

Graduate students (name, degree sought, schedule; if degree was completed, give date and full citation for thesis or dissertation.)

Major professor

Co-Major professor

Member, Steering Committee (other than those listed above)

Chair or Reader on thesis, exams, etc.

Research Completed or Underway

Grant-supported research (source, subject, amount, duration; list any graduate research assistants supported by each grant.)

Research proposals pending

School research (unsupported, bootlegged; state title, time spent)

Publications (provide full bibliographical citation; DO NOT use "with Jones" or "Jones et al."; detail any publications that were reported "in press" last year.)

Papers presented (give date, title, occupation, and location.)

(NOTE: Textbooks, reports, newsletters, circulars, and similar publications are normally considered evidence of teaching ability or public service and will be considered creative work only when they present new ideas or incorporate original scholarly research or performance.)

Public Service

Funded service (include consulting activities)

> Government agencies (federal, state, local)

> > Industrial and commercial groups, etc.

Unfunded service to government agencies, public interest groups, etc.

Professional Development

Activities in professional organizations (offices held; service as chair, participant, or consultant)

Professional society memberships

Other professional activities

> Editorial activity (journal, responsibility)

> Other (books, symposia, etc.)

> Reviewer (journal, number of manuscripts; agency, number of proposals; other)

> Participation in workshops, symposia, etc. (name, date, place)

Further education/retraining undertaken (leaves, workshops, etc.)

Foreign travel (when, where, purpose)

Noteworthy achievements (awards, licenses, inventions, citations, etc.)

Administrative and Service Responsibilities (including committee work)

Departmental-level

College-level

University-wide (include Research Foundation)

Statement for Annual Departmental Report Summarizing Significant Accomplishments During Reporting Period (limit to one or two brief paragraphs)

Future Plans, Ambitions, and Potential Contributions for Your Own Professional Development and Enhancement of the Department's Programs (not more than one page)

Any Pertinent Information You Feel Is Not Elicited by the Form (again, be brief).

Your own institution's faculty activities report form may vary in degree but not in kind. If by some odd chance your institution does not require an annual report, use the Midland form as a guide against the day when you'll have to document your promotion-to-tenure qualifications.

Goals and Objectives Report

You may or may not have to file an annual goals and

objectives report, as do Midland faculty members. Even if none is required, drafting one for your own azimuth is a constructive practice.

Unlike its annual Faculty Activities Report, Midland has no prescribed form for the goals and objectives document. Here's what the chair of the department of botany and applied ecology has written in a memo to her faculty:

> Each faculty member shall submit to the chair an annual statement of long-term goals and objectives for the coming year. These should cover research, teaching, and service activities. Outline professional development plans, being as specific as possible. Indicate how the chair and the department can facilitate the achievement of your objective. The report becomes the basis for your annual counseling session with the chair.

By formulating your own goals and objectives document, you can in effect subtly prescribe for review a set of expectations.

Counseling Sessions

Remember, if you were at Midland you would meet with your department chair in August or September to discuss those goals and objectives. Department tradition holds this to be a formative session in which you and the chair arrive at an agreement on your activities for the coming year. Since you're not tenured, the chair will also counsel you on how your goals and objectives are likely to affect progress toward tenure.

In April or May you would meet with the chair again to review accomplishments and productivity during the past year. This meeting occurs after the chair has made preliminary performance evaluations and salary adjustment determinations, but prior to actually submitting salary recommendations to the dean of the college. The chair will identify strengths and weaknesses in your record and suggest ways to effect improvement, particularly in terns of progressing toward tenure. The chair prepares a written summary of the review and gives you a copy to which you may respond. All documents then go in your personnel file.

As you can see, such semi-annual counseling and review sessions are extremely valuable to you, not only in terms of grasping departmental expectations but also in actually getting a sense of how you're coming along, at least in the eyes of your chair.

Not all counseling sessions need be scheduled, and the trick is to recognize an opportunity when it walks up and shakes your hand.

If a senior member of your search-and-screen committee spots you one noon hour brown-bagging in the faculty lounge, sits down at your table, and asks, "Well, how's the course going?" he may be simply making conversation and you can reply, "Fine, how's yours?" On the other hand, if there's a certain intensity in the air, you might think, "I wonder what he's heard?" and say, "I'm glad you asked. I'd like your advice about what I think I'm discovering about my teaching goals, the way students learn, and how the two mesh with the content of that course I'm assigned this term." (9)

And then see what happens.

If your institution doesn't formally schedule counseling sessions, you might try manufacturing the process with grace.

As good an excuse as any would be to seek the counsel of your department chair when you get back your first set of student evaluations after they've been through the department numbers-cruncher. You won't know whether to dance a jig or cry like a baby, because the summary will likely include a combination of a single numerical rating and a set of narrative student comments. Reconciling the two components can be the neatest trick of the week, a task of interpretation for which a seasoned professor is well-suited.

Midland uses a local modification of IDEA (Instructional Development and Effectiveness Assessment), a 38-item diagnostic form available from Kansas State University's Center for Faculty Evaluation and Development under the direction of Professor William E. Cashin, who has a 1989-90 data base of student ratings from 17,939 classes in 105 varied North American institutions. (7)

Your Midland *alter ego*, not without some trepidation, brought Chair Perkins a set of evaluations to look at from his second-term second-level course, Botany 335 — "Morphology of Flowering Plants." The chair had already observed that Bill was enthusiastic, full of energy, and always seemed to have students hanging around his office. So obviously he was popular, but his ratings didn't particularly reflect that. From her experience, Perkins spotted the problem: Bill was rigorous. Despite his accessibility and ability to impart excitement to a not-too-thrilling subject matter, the students complained about his toughness. That didn't bother the chair one bit, and she promptly advised Bill to maintain his standards, that students would come to respect him for it, that an "A" from Bill would take on a prized cachet around the department, and that his student ratings would go up accordingly. Perkins was also quick to point out that Bill's numerical rating was not out of line with that of other botany instructors in the IDEA data base.

That's how Peter Frederick of Wabash College (IN) recommends handling student evaluations. (9)

Periodic Program Review Report

Sometime during your probationary period your department will in all likelihood be subject to a periodic program review. You'll be well served if you view the process as an opportunity for you and your department to "take stock," and the resulting report can be helpful in discerning institutional expectations, individually and collectively.

There are two types of program reviews — internal self-study and external evaluation. Midland University uses the former every four years, the latter every seven.

To initiate the internal evaluation, the department chair appoints a committee of faculty members prior to the beginning of the fall term. The chair is not a member of the committee but serves as a resource. The committee must finish its report and submit it to the Vice President for Academic Affairs Office by March 1. The chair responds to the report, indicating those points with which he or she agrees or disagrees and emphasizing the aspects of the report that the University should particularly note. The dean of the college and the graduate dean also respond to the report. The report goes to a University internal review committee composed of faculty and administrators from other major units. That committee reviews the report to determine whether any proposed plans are supported by data.

The VPAA Office summarizes the report and proposes plans for the department for the next four years. A meeting to review the summary and plans then takes place among the VPAA, the graduate dean, the college dean, the department chair, and the chair of the department's self-evaluation committee, out of which will come (hopefully) a consensus report that will serve as a collective and individual guide.

Every seven years each Midland department is subjected to an academic program review by an external site-visit team of invited colleagues from representative institutions. The department gets to nominate some team members; the VPAA picks the rest and names the chair.

John B. Bennett, provost and vice president for academic affairs at Quinnipiac College (CT) and executive editor of the quarterly newsletter *The Department Advisor*, devoted the Spring 1991 issue to a thoughtful outline of what a site-visit team should look for and at, and hence how an assistant professor should tailor his or her career:

- Mission. How does the department stand historically/currently and directly/indirectly to what the institution as a whole is widely known or knowable for being and doing?

- <u>Demand for Services</u>. What is the current level of demand for the services of the department in teaching, research, and service, to include trendlines, patterns, and projections?

- <u>Societal Need</u>. What are the societal needs — geographic, demographic, political — to which the department should be responding as the ultimate rationale for claiming societal resources, and how well is the department addressing those needs?

- <u>Program Cost</u>. Is the department cost-effective in terms of such factors as faculty-student ratios, cost of instruction per student credit hour, indirect costs, contributions to other programs, revenue generated by externally funded research projects or by outreach activities, size of faculty in relation to its teaching/research/service track record, and proportion in each faculty rank — in comparison with in-house departments and with peer programs elsewhere?

- <u>Program Quality</u>. What is the department's "Nielsen rating" with respect to conventional measures of faculty caliber, relationships among departmental members, trends regarding faculty turnover, assessments of student potential and achievement, evidence of learning actually achieved in the department on the part of both students and professors, coherence of the curriculum as the nexus wherein faculty strengths and expertise are hooked to student needs, adequacy of such material requirements as instructional and research technology, and physical plant, library resources, and outreach logistics, and faculty involvement in program planning and execution?

Talk of evaluation or review will probably elicit from some faculty colleagues certain recitations of its manifold threats to traditional ways of doing things, or of malevolent administrative designs, as well as complaints about yet more burdens upon limited time and energy, Bennett points out. But he encourages assistant professors to participate with good will and reap the rewards of learning from what's working well and also from what's not. As he concludes, "Periodic self-study is the price of the self-regulated profession." (3)

Accountability and Outcomes Assessment

Responding to a rising drumbeat of dissatisfaction with the

quality of undergraduate teaching at Midland University, the Midland Board of Trustees mandated that the University have an accountability program in place by Jan. 1, 1990.

The resulting "Midland Accountability and Outcomes Assessment Plans and Procedures" calls for an annual evaluation of both University-wide and department-based educational outcomes, involving these elements:

- Undergraduate goals and objectives developed with external constituencies such as professional organizations, parents, employers of graduates, and alumni, indicating what students are expected to gain from their education.

- Assessment methods that evaluated how well the undergraduates have learned what the goals and objectives state they will learn — through standardized tests, observational data, reports of employers, alumni self-reports, capstone seminar evaluations, and other methods.

- Dissemination procedures to inform constituencies of how well Midland students meet the established goals and objectives. Departmental assessment procedures results become a part of the four- and seven-year reviews.

- Use of the results to review curricula and revise them if necessary, and to counsel individual faculty members. A newly appointed Faculty Council Committee on Instructional Development serves as the official institutional monitoring instrumentality.

Your institution may not have so formal a curriculum-and-instruction development program as does Midland, but read the writing on the wall: it says that on too many campuses undergraduate teaching has been weighed in the public balance and found wanting — and that assistant professors might well review their career priorities accordingly if they're to fit into what's being called "a new day — the '90s as the decade of undergraduate education."

Tenure Review Reports

Unless they're couched in the opaque language characteristic of all too many faculty-composed documents, your tenure review assessments could be just what they're intended to be — your very best guide to departmental expectations.

If the assessments cast aspersions on your student evaluation ratings, head for the campus instructional services center right away and sit in on lectures and seminars conducted by colleagues known for their teaching effectiveness. If the assessments make astringent comments on a worrisome lack of productive-scholarship pace, get on the stick. If they note a lack of service activity, look around for assignments with visibility. If you score low on interpersonal relations with colleagues, you might read Dale Carnegie's venerable *How to Win Friends and Influence People.*

On the other hand, if your tenure review reports rate at least a B+ in such regards, keep on keeping on with renewed vigor and confidence.

Your Monitoring Committee

You may be in a department where the crucial help/hurdle is an assistant professor monitoring committee, charged with at once mentoring and evaluating your progress.

A dean reviewing a draft of this manual asked us to include this comment:

> Such committees, if they're in place, deserve a scope of treatment. There are some serious ongoing debates as too whether such committee meetings should be open or closed, and what the committee's responsibilities are to the assistant professor they're tracking. For example, on my campus a recent failure to promote an assistant professor to tenure rested on his inappropriate use of statistical methods in his research. That error should have been noted by his monitoring committee the very first year of his appointment. Who is at fault? The aspiring assistant professor or the monitoring committee?
>
> My admonition to an assistant professor would be: "Use such a departmental committee if one is in place, but don't depend on it!"

What a sad commentary, but that's the way it can be.

Your Mentor

When Odysseus took off for the wars, he consigned his young son to the care of the fatherly Mentor, and so the term has come down to us implying advice, protection, caring, as the dictionary says.

Recently "mentoring" has become a "buzz word" in higher education as a variety of programs have come into use, particularly to help promote the advancement of minority group members and women.

But not much is really known about mentoring between faculty members. To bridge that knowledge gap, three ed psych professors recently looked systematically at how faculty at a public, research-oriented university in the Midwest actually envision and practice mentoring among themselves.

A result: faculty mentoring faculty is not common. When it occurs, it's mutually negotiated, primarily between persons of the same sex and between assistant and full professors.

Another result: demonstrating that mentoring is a complex, multi-dimensional activity, there appear to be four distinct types of mentors — friend, career guide, information source, intellectual guide (although multiple attributes can sometimes be combined in a single individual).

A conclusion: if you go looking for a mentor, know the type you're seeking; and faculty members willing to serve as mentors should acknowledge the kind of help they're willing and able to offer. (17)

You'll recall that at Midland your *alter ego* Bill was assigned a mentor in his letter of appointment from his department chair. You may or may not be in that situation.

There's no question that a willing mentor can be of signal assistance in leading you through institutional and interpersonal minefields. If you're faced with identifying one, here's a tip:

Why not try to recruit the chair of the department search-and-screen committee that recruited you? After all, he or she already has a big stake in your success, as do all committee members. If you don't perform with distinction, it's a reflection on their judgment. So the chances are that chair will be happy to offer valuable "advice, protection, caring." Lean on him or her as a coxswain counting cadence so you can row more effectively.

Collegial Track Records

The information can be hard to come by unless a friendly department secretary can help. But if you can get your hands on the records of what happened over the past five years or so to previous untenured faculty members in the department, you're in possession of a gold mine of clues to institutional expectations.

The personnel files of those fairly new associate professors now in the department certainly exist; whether they're open to your inspection, you'll have to determine. If you can review them, they'll tell you exactly how such and such an associate professor made it. (It won't do much good to look up the records of senior staff, because criteria for promotion and evaluation procedures are under relatively constant change these days.)

The records of assistant professors who tried and failed may or may not exist or be available, but if you can come by them, they can be an even more valuable guide to both generic institutional expectations and practical departmental politics.

If such a tactic strikes you as too much like snooping, forget it — or suggest it to a less scrupulous probationary peer. Let your conscience be your guide on this one. It's well to remember, however, Santayana's warning that those who are ignorant of history are condemned to repeat it.

Union Manuals

If you're at an institution with a faculty union or a facsimile of one, you may find its manuals a font of information about the P&T process, and particularly about grievance procedures should a candidate falter along the line. (1)

It's practically certain that your institution has a formal grievance procedure, since recent court decisions make such mandatory. It will likely provide that a faculty member denied tenure can file a grievance if he or she believes that the negative decision was based on an "improper evaluation."

As defined by Midland University rules (University Faculty 2224-6-07), there are two categories of "improper evaluations": (1) decisions made without adequate consideration of the pertinent facts by the individual(s) making the decision, or (2) decisions based on reasons that infringe on a constitutional right of the faculty member.

At Midland, the process for filing complaints alleging improper evaluation is codified:

Appeal for Reconsideration. Where the negative decision was initiated at the department level, the faculty member may appeal in writing to the chair within 14 days of the decision, identifying how the evaluation was improperly handled. If the chair concurs, he or she asks the dean of the college that the denial be reversed. If the reconsideration is negative, the faculty member may file a grievance with the college.

College Grievance Review. The appeal to the college must be presented in writing within 14 days of the negative department decision. The complaint is referred to the college Faculty Grievance Committee for investigation. Results of that investigation will be reported to the dean, who will inform the complainant.

University Grievance Review. Complaints alleging improper evaluation must be submitted in writing to the Vice President for Academic Affairs and thence to the faculty members of the Committee on Academic Freedom and Responsibility within 30 days of notification of an unfavorable college review. The burden of going forward and the burden of establishing proof is on the complainant (who may retain appropriate legal counsel).

Theoretically a complainant disappointed with an ultimate faculty/administration decision could carry his or her appeal on to the board of governors and then to the courts, but the hazards of becoming known in academic circles as a "litigator" are measurable, like wearing a scarlet letter, and many courts have been chary about entering into debates on academic merit.

As Midland faculty rules go on to prescribe:

Investigations of complaints alleging improper evaluation shall consider only whether the individual(s) making the decision(s) followed the appropriate procedures, considered the important evidence to a fair determination, and acted in a responsible manner. Neither College nor University grievance committees may substitute their judgment on the merits of the individual's performance for that of the academic unit concerned.

That last is a "sticky wicket," as they say. A faculty union grievance board may have quite a different opinion of "fair determination" or "responsible manner" than will the University's attorney.

In at least one state, the Legislature is contemplating a law that would permit independent panels of experts from other institutions to handle tenure-denial grievances based on sex or race discrimination. Passage of such a statute would create quite a precedent which neither faculty unions nor institution administrators might be happy about.

Hopefully you'll never be involved on either side of a grievance dispute, but it does no harm in briefing yourself on institutional and union points of view and procedures. It's all a part of knowing the territory.

Your Probationary Peers

You've had enough experience with grad student peers to know it's questionable whether to list peers under "sound" sources of information.

Some of your new faculty peers are going to be rocks of counsel and support, others frail reeds, still others all strengths in between. If there's any territory you've got to discern with precision, it's this one.

At Midland, Bill was in the company of seven untenured botany department members, at least one at each stage of the six-year marathon run. He discovered that several loved to tell exaggerated "war stories" about the grueling nature of tenure review sessions, that a couple of others were so close-mouthed as to be of no practical help at all, and the balance were gentlepersons and scholars who could be relied on to pass on practical tips and rumors.

If you could know from the gun with whom you'd be spending a career together in warm companionship and fruitful professional association, and which peers would fold their tents and silently slip away, it would be priceless prescience, but of course you can't know any such thing.

It's little comfort that your probationary peers initially have the same reservations about you!

The Grapevine

We're even less sure about listing the office grapevine as a "sound" information source. Some of the gossip you pick up can be right on the money, and some can be off by a country mile. The trouble is, you don't know which is which when you hear it.

The senior author's spouse knew he was getting promoted to tenure before he did (she picked up the word at a faculty wives' tea), but her guesstimate at the size of the concomitant salary raise turned out to be very wide of the mark. As ACS recalls:

> My very best grapevine was the janitor, or 'maintenance engineer.' Because I was a lark, I got to the office just as he was leaving his night shift, and we would fire up the coffeemaker — and gossip. Because we had a mutual love of duck hunting, we also shared a marsh shore blind on an occasional weekend. Whether he was just reading wastebasket detritus or actually perusing files, I never knew nor asked, but his sense of what was happening or about to happen in the department was encyclopedic. His most valuable advice to me was advance warning that the department capital budget was about to undergo an emergency freeze, which gave me time to process a requisition for a new mag-card typewriter (an early version of a word processor) before the blow fell.

That sort of grapevine is rare. Most of the over-the-transom stuff you hear you might as well forget and certainly not pass on.

But if you take that advice, you'll miss out on a lot of department camaraderie!

A department chair who reviewed this manuscript confides:

> I wish I could do a better job of getting junior faculty to (1) hear as much gossip as possible, and (2) contribute to that gossip as little as possible. For some assistant professors with a strong sense of powerlessness, gossip seems to be a means of protecting themselves from surprises — a new course preparation next year, an office change to a different floor, a shift in secretarial assignments, and so on. Yet participation in a grapevine network can be debilitating and lead to mild paranoia.

Campus Media

There are three types of "news" media you'll want to pay attention to — with varying degrees of interest and confidence.

First, there'll be a steady stream of memos from higher-ups. Department memos are "must" reading because they may announce a change in policy or at least a departure in procedures.

(A typical departmental memo: "I want to remind each of you to lock your doors whenever you leave your offices. I realize this can be inconvenient, but many times a quick trip to the mailbox can turn into a long wait for an elevator, or a hall conversation with a colleague can become extended. We try to ensure a secure building for you, and you can help by eliminating the open invitation an unlocked door can pose. Thank you." This may seem like "Mickey Mouse" stuff, but complying can protect your computer or purse from a roving thief.)

College memos are of indifferent caliber, assuming they're even grammatical; some will be relevant to you, others not; even so, you dismiss them at your own risk. Front-office communiqués will typically start out with "It has come to the attention of the Vice President for Administration that ..." Again, while most will be of only tangential importance, it's hazardous to toss them without at least a scan.

Second, there'll be a periodic all-campus house organ, giving you insight into the way the President (HEP position #01) views his or her — and your — world. It's not easy to write and edit such a publication. The chief PR officer has to phrase each sentence in such a way that it pleases or at least satisfies a varied audience — administrators, faculty, students, boards of governors, legislators, alumni, donors, and so on. For example, if a story downplays the significance of a racial disturbance on Greek Row, it can calm old sorority members while dismaying the dean of students and the faculty chaperones who were on the spot. You'll just have to learn to separate the wheat from the chaff.

Third, the campus student newspaper. Some are very good at investigating, reporting, and interpreting institutional issues, particularly those with an undergraduate angle; others are average; still others are flack sheets for either renegade student cabals or the President's Office itself. Again, you'll have to sift and winnow.

Whatever you do, don't ignore these campus media; no matter how dull or how slanted, they're a window on what somebody is thinking and doing. Sooner or later an item in one or another will be of vital import to you and your career, perhaps in the form of a practical "political" tip.

APPRECIATING THE PRACTICAL POLITICS OF GETTING PROMOTED

Let's get one thing straight from the start: we aren't using the term "politics" here in any invidious sense of back-room influence-peddling or crafty back-slapping and unseemly publicity-grabbing. We're using the term in the best Websterian sense of "the total complex of relations between persons in society."

Oh, we suppose if we wanted to sound academic, we could title this section "The Interpersonal Relationships,

Acclimatization Processes, and Acculturation Procedures Attendant to Achieving Promotion to Tenure in Colleges and Universities Today." But that would be both coy and inaccurate. Because we aren't talking here about any arcane theories; we're talking gut pragmatic.

While grasping fundamental institutional expectations is the rock-bottom basic strategy for making it in academia, it would be naive not to acknowledge there's a very human side to the success equation as well. And that's what we're going to outline now.

We say "outline" because if institutional expectations differ widely from campus to campus, you ain't seen nothin' yet compared with the kaleidoscopic variations in cultures, mores, ethos, and just plain accepted codes of conduct among institutions of higher education, irrespective of size, mission, location, and wherewithal.

So all we can do here is tick off the questions to which we believe you should seek answers specific to your situation in your particular institution. When we can with any assurance, we'll suggest likely approaches and even solutions, but you must take them with a grain of salt, given the lack of uniformity — institution to institution and department to department. In short, we're giving you the rules of a fun game of wild-card poker, not a sure-fire guide to winning. But win you can if you play your cards right and husband your blue chips.

The situation is analogous to your asking a question of a horticulturist, "What's the best variety of tomato to plant?" The answer can only be a bundle of questions: "In what type, fertility, and permeability of soil? In what growing zone with what amount of garden-plot sunlight? For what purpose — table use, salads, canning, ketchup, or sauce? For what preferred texture, size, and taste? Early fruitage, medium, or late? (Yes, a tomato is a fruit, not a vegetable, he or she will remind you.) Resistant to what diseases? With chemical or natural fertilizer and pest controls?"

And so it is with coming to appreciate the practical politics of getting promoted in your department at your institution.

In general, there are two broad types of political subjects, situations, or problems: those for which your principal challenge is to understand the going standards or requirements and adapt, and those for which you have to make a decision how best to weigh your personal code of ethics against the seeming demands of institutional constraints. The line between the two categories may be more apparent than real, so in the dichotomy you're about to see, feel free to switch a topic from one to the other as your sensibilities dictate. After all, it's **your** institutional environment to be mastered, and **your** promotion that's at stake.

LEARNING AND ADAPTING
Department Dynamics

You report into the office of your new department, walk up to the first desk and say, "Good morning. I'm So-and-So." A sassy receptionist in what looks like leotards grudgingly looks up from her screen to reply, "So?"

Or a professional but obviously bemused receptionist says, "Good morning, sir! And what can we do for you?"

Or a serge-jacketed receptionist breaks into smile, stands with hand extended, and says, "Good morning, Dr. So-and-So! We've all been anxious to meet you! Before I take you in to see Ms. Miles, may I get you a cup of coffee?"

In any case, you've just had your first brush with the character, the culture, the style of your department. Later in the day you get another silent briefing.

A "get-acquainted" faculty meeting has been called for 3:45. At 4:10 various professors are still straggling in. "Let's get the show on the road!" booms a voice from the head of the table. From off at a flank the chair says, "Oh, now, Frank, let's give everybody another 10 minutes. I really don't have much anyway." Desultory conversation continues.

Or: At 3:42 everybody is seated and ready. Promptly at 3:44 the chair enters the room with a flourish, stills the animated chatter with a rap on a glass, and says, "Welcome once again, people! Glad to see you're all on time as usual. As you can see from your copy of the agenda, we've got a good deal to go over, so let's get down to business. Ms. Jones, my secretary, will continue the practice of taking copious notes which will be in your boxes by noon tomorrow. First off ...."

Our fictitious scenarios may be a trifle exaggerated for effect, but they make the point that each university department has a unique way of parting its hair, so to speak. So from Day One, deliberately reconnoiter the dynamics of your new department, the better to be at home there.

Key objectives. All your initial efforts to understand the dynamics of your department should be directed at determining:

- What is expected of the department by the divisional CEO.
- What is expected of you by the department.
- The strengths and weaknesses of your compatriots.
- Other key people whose willing support is necessary to you and your department.

Key Questions. By whatever means are available and

acceptable, try to obtain a clear understanding of the answers to such questions as these:

- I've read my letter of appointment, but can I assume that my responsibilities outlined in it are consonant with the understanding of the faculty members who will ultimately evaluate me?

- How do my assigned responsibilities fit in with the responsibilities of the department? the college?

- What specific functions am I personally responsible for on my own?

- What standards must I meet in my first year? the second? beyond?

- What policies and standard operating procedures exist to assist me?

- What's the real power structure of the department?

- What are the formal norms I'm expected to comply with? Are these formal norms apt to be productive on my terms?

- What informal norms am I expected to follow? Which are likely to be productive? counterproductive?

- Who are the informal leaders in the department? What is the source of their power as informal leaders? Are the informal leaders positive or negative forces in terms of my meeting my responsibilities? In other words, who are strategic sources of support? of sabotage?

- What are the strengths and weaknesses of department support staff personnel? of my graduate students, particularly any TAs or RAs? of my undergraduates, particularly my advisees?

- Who are the key people who support department mission accomplishment? What are their positive and negative attributes?

- What are the strengths and weaknesses of the department in terms of each required function — teaching, research, service?

Such are essential questions driving your analysis of your new department. Getting a fix on the dynamics, the culture, the style, the character of your new surroundings and its denizens can be as intriguing as it is fundamental to the development of a personal azimuth, a career path.

On a small campus, identifying key people goes much beyond the department, to the whole campus, which, as one commentator notes, "will be quite obvious at your first college faculty meeting."

These pithy comments on "the human dimension" come from a senior professor who's been in six departments at four institutions:

> Tolstoy begins *Anna Karenina* with the observation that all happy families are happy in the same way, but all unhappy families are unhappy in different ways. So with academic departments. There is something in the chemistry of departments that makes them miserable or nurturing. I don't think it's possible to get a good sense of this as an outsider, but one can surely feel it as an insider.
>
> How does the tenure candidate fit in? You can't read it in a book. It goes beyond personal politics, I think, although sometimes that's the dimension blamed. It relates more to the mix that a person finds him- or herself in. Is there a good "fit" there?

Whatever your discipline, it's essential to sense the ethos of your calling — its content, traditions, culture. For example, here's the way Carla Howery of the American Sociological Association staff characterizes her discipline: (12)

> One thing we have going for us as sociologists: We're very comfortable measuring squishy things like marital happiness or alienation or urban decay, so we don't just stamp our foot and say, "It can't be done ...."
>
> Sociologists are also comfortable flipping from one method to another, good at understanding the limits of national norms across institution-specific data. We understand the problems of generalization; we're more savvy here than, say, faculty in the humanities.
>
> But sociologists are terrible about reaching consensus. They never want to reach consensus. People in sociology feed on differentness.
>
> Sociology has a "young" or "horizontal" curriculum. That is, one department's offerings bear little similarity to others'; there's a strong sense of "to each his own." Sociologists have a very strong commitment to that idea; even within departments it's very hard for a faculty to reach consensus about common goals.
>
> It's an interesting challenge for sociology. It helps that at least we know who we are.

If you're a budding sociologist, see how helpful that frank assessment is? If you're in another discipline, try to piece together a like analysis, the better to have a sense of "home."

Personal Development Plan

When it comes to the pragmatic politics of getting promoted, few practices can be so effective as to put in writing your own professional development plan, to include a five- or six-year timetable — with the advice and counsel of your seniors, peers, and other trusted people (who will be impressed by your self-reliance and diligence).

In other words, don't wait for somebody to order your career path. Then, about every six months, update the program based on your learning and development.

<u>Suggested steps</u>. Here are some thoughts as a guide to how you might go about developing a personal program:

- **Think in a quiet place.** Reflect about how you have performed in the past. Then visualize how you want to be able to perform in the future, given what you now know about the dynamics of your new department.

- **Identify your strengths and weaknesses** in such areas as these:

   Beliefs, values, ethics.

   Character traits.

   Knowledge of yourself, your subject matter, human nature, your position, your department.

   Directional skills — problem-solving, planning, decision-making, goal-setting.

   Implementing skills — communicating, coordinating, supervising, evaluating.

   Motivating skills — teaching, counseling, applying principles of motivation.

   Investigative skills — research, productive scholarship.

   Service skills — chairing, cooperating, seeking challenging assignments, sensing lay needs.

   Environmental factors — institutional, professional, community, personal.

- As you review your list of strengths and weaknesses, **think of at least one way under each topic you could improve, and a way you can reinforce or better your strengths.** Write them down. Seek feedback from valued counselors, regardless of rank. They will see things that you simply can't or don't see. If the feedback makes sense and feels right, accept and incorporate it.

- After you've identified weaknesses and ways to improve, for each weakness or desired improvement, **set a goal.** For example, let's say that one desire is to improve your counseling skills. Establish the following objectives:

   learn about human needs,

   improve ability to apply principles of motivation,

   improve communication skills,

   improve listening skills,

learn the ins and outs of under-graduate curriculum requirements.

- Once you've stated your goals, you're ready to continue: **develop plans to achieve goals.** Identify tasks that must be accomplished, put them in priority, and establish all the conditions necessary for each task. Write a simple plan to reach each goal. For example, if one of your goals is to improve your understanding of human nature, one of your plans might well be to sit in on lectures in an appropriate psychology course.

- **Evaluate.** For each goal, write out two or three ways of evaluating progress toward the goal. You are your own best evaluator if you're honest with yourself. Seek feedback, too, from informal raters — seniors, peers, students. For example, you might volunteer to take the "pop" quizzes in that course you're auditing.

It's *Your* Job

Your professional development program is the basis of a career path. While your reviewers have responsibilities to assist in your development, the real responsibility for your professional growth rests squarely on your own shoulders. If you have the necessary character traits — initiative, will, and self-discipline — such a program for yourself will reap great dividends in terms of both political substance and style.

The DAO

Increasingly, colleges and universities are designating the head, chair, director, or dean of a unit as its chief executive officer (CEO), and her or his adjutant as chief administrative officer (CAO). Next to your department chair (DEO), hardly anybody can so help facilitate — or founder — your academic career as can your DAO — the keeper of the keys, the power around the power.

Who is he or she? An assistant or associate professor in training as department assistant chair, or a tired full professor put out to pasture? Maybe an administrative specialist with a limited-term or indefinite appointment in that relatively new campus ranking midway between faculty and employee? Or perhaps a senior "classified," "civil service," or some such designation of long-time servant? Whatever — a crucial component of your department's culture.

Understand a DAO's natural tendency to be defensive and sometimes rigid: faced with largely routine tasks, everybody's "gopher," punching a 9-to-5 clock in a Grand Central Station surrounded by doctorates working on and off in relative freedom in private offices on various interesting assignments.

Yet beneath that austere exterior can beat a heart of gold if you can but sense its beat.

Discover what the DAO does and doesn't do or causes to get done or not done: typing projects not related to teaching? research proposals? travel arrangements? meeting scheduling? How much lead time does the DAO need or demand (depending in all likelihood on your position in the department pecking order)? What directions does the DOA want, resent, or appreciate?

How does the DAO react to your use of office equipment? copy machines, faxes, files, and so on? territorial or tolerant of interlopers? Does the DAO encourage and appreciate those who help themselves or does he or she want to exercise dominion? Does the DAO ride herd like an IRS agent on supplies and long-distance phone calls, or is there free access?

Be nice, be friendly, and respect the DAO's time constraints, the need to concentrate, to supervise underlings, and to answer first to the call of the chair. Remember the DAO on appropriate occasions — birthday, anniversary, Christmas, and so on.

A simple but essential requirement: complete every form the DAO gives you, properly and punctually.

Above all, acquire a sure feeling for the DAO's fundamental *gestalt*.

It may surprise you.

When the senior author (**ACS**) once joined a brand new interdisciplinary configuration, the acting chair pled with his faculty not to rile the old warhorse of a secretary he'd had to accept as a transfer from a determined dean's office. For six miserable months ACS walked on eggs, handling the DAO with kid gloves. Yet the more obsequious he tried to be, the more galling became the DAO.

Come August, however, ACS drew a reprieve to go on summer Army active-duty-for-training as a reserve colonel, taking out his hostilities at camp on innocent young lieutenants for two weeks. No sooner had he returned to campus than he got a brisk phone call from the DAO: "Where have you been? Report to my office right away." Before he could take off his uniform, so to speak, ACS barked back: "I'm **not** available at present. **You** come to **my** office at 1400." As he slammed down the receiver, he panicked: "My God, what have I done?" He need not have feared. Promptly at 2 p.m. the DAO appeared at his door, completely subservient. From then on, ACS never let the DAO forget who ranked whom — and the DAO responded willingly.

(Of course quite the opposite could have transpired. ACS once called the chancellor of his university "Sir" and he said, "Cut out that military stuff around me!")

In a small department at a university, or in a small college, cultivating a DAO may not be necessary. There won't be one.

Professorial Technology

Not only does it behoove you to become a master of the modern technology that can support your teaching and your research, adapting to the electronic age can smooth your career path by lubricating interpersonal relations.

For example, if you're facile with a word processor/computer, you can relieve the department office by typing an occasional manuscript from notes, then revising at the keyboard on the fly or from notes on hard copy. Or you can compose a form cover letter, then customize on your own for each occasion in a matter of minutes.

Another simple but invaluable high-tech tool is a personal answering machine. Without one, if you have your own office phone and can't be in your office from 7 a.m. to midnight, then you're likely to frustrate colleagues and students alike and play a lot of phone tag An answering machine may bother some callers to the point where they'll hang up on hearing your recorded voice, but most others will willingly leave messages — and greatly appreciate it if you get back to them promptly. (If opportunity knocks but once, how often can you expect it to ring in the absence of an answering machine?)

The real value in your becoming at home with gadgets is the subtle message it sends that you're a 20th-century person. Faint heart ne'er won fair promotion; when it comes to technological experimentation, fortune favors the bold.

Your "Personality"

What's to be the proper demeanor? Do you come on strong, eager, sell yourself? Or should you be the humble greenhorn? Should you be known for the campus and extra-campus contacts you cultivate, or should you be largely a department gardentender?

To what extent do you vary your "personality" depending on the working relationships you want to develop with key constituencies — the chair, college and campus administrators, senior colleagues, junior peers, staff, employees, collateral faculty, undergrad students, grad students, the community?

Obviously you can't be exactly one being to all people, but will a too chameleon-like pose open you to charges of "always putting on an act"?

The personality you present to your chair may be the most crucial of all.

Some assistant professors lean toward demanding a good deal of administrative maintenance. They display a continual need to talk with the chair about their teaching load, office location and size, exceptions to travel-funds policy in the department, the relative importance of committee assignments, and so on.

That sort of person can either summon up the chair's Samaritan instincts or exhaust him or her. We don't know whether it's better to be that kind of person or not.

Nor can we say with confidence a chair will respond favorably to the assistant professor who is constrained to keep the chair apprised of absolutely everything going on in his or her career. Every paper accepted for presentation at a conference, how a chapter revision is going, a recent phone call from a potential granting agency, advising work with a student organization, and so on — each topic can extend into a half-hour conversation with the chair in the lunchroom, in the hall, at a chance meeting in front of the building. While the chair may act pleased to hear of such accomplishments and will try to reinforce the faculty member's sense of self-worth, the chair may actually find such encounters needlessly time-consuming, not to mention confusing, since he or she has to try to keep every faculty member's agenda straight and current.

Probably the best tactic in the long run is simply to be yourself. That, and to hearken to these words from a department chair who reviewed this manual:

"In my book, among the best predictors of tenure potential is clear evidence — direct or indirect — of hard work."

Role Models

The professional activities and "political" stance of colleagues within the department — particularly not-too-senior colleagues — are something to divine quickly and surely. Your overt or covert choice of role model(s) will be something that your colleagues will be watching for as a measure of your own promise and compatibility.

It'll be advantageous for you if at least one of your role models is open to conversations about your problems and progress. Some idols have ears but they hear not.

Collegiality — "Getting Along"

A college is not called a college for nothing. Its root is *collegium* and its mark *collegiality*. While collegiality may be thought to encompass the cordiality or the camaraderie of a platoon, it is much more — the ground rules for "getting along" unique to academe.

With luck and/or foresight you'll pick a role model who personifies collegiality — the glue that binds a faculty.

Quinnipiac College provost and distinguished author

John B. Bennett has recently composed an important and power-ful definition of collegiality you can use as your lodestar:

> Collegiality in the sense of getting along with colleagues is more than just foreswearing hostility and belligerence. First, collegiality involves the disposition to credit col-leagues with a share of the power and authority residing in the *collegium*, a share roughly equal to the share one claims for oneself. And second, since higher education attracts people who might value their independence to the point of isolation, collegiality involves no less the willingness of each person to seek the judgment of colleagues on work in progress. ...

> Accordingly, a minimal level of cooperation with colleagues, an appropriate respect for their contributions, and a willing-ness to explore with them one's own ideas and work as well as one's teaching triumphs and frustrations seem essential for the conduct and continuation of the profession. Without some minimum intellectual reciprocity, the *collegium* no longer exists. ...

> Properly understood, collegiality does not stifle dissent or eclipse individuality. Indeed, it is only in the truly collegial department and college that diverse individuality can flourish. And ultimately it is this ability of colleagues to "get along" that is the prerequisite for expressions of col-legiality in governance and shared decision-making. (4)

Susan A. Cole, vice president for university administration and personnel at Rutgers, expresses much the same sentiments:

> The academy functions at its best when its members act in a commonsense fashion on the basis of their understanding of the traditions, expectations, and standards of the profes-sion. Further, in a litigious society, the academy must act af-firmatively to preserve its collegiality and traditions of academic decision-making. At their truest and best, such traditions abjure personal harrassment, exploitation of stu-dents and junior colleagues, and discrimination based on im-permissible grounds, and encourage the free expression of views and respect for one another as colleagues. (8)

Work Hours

When E.B. Fred was president of the University of Wiscon-sin, after leaving his own office very late he would invariably take a stroll around campus "to see what professors are burning the midnight oil." (It seemingly never occurred to him that what he was witnessing could be a janitor at work.)

You may have moved into a department of workaholics. Early in your career, show up some weeknight and some Satur-day to determine whether department custom expects you to labor all hours.

On the other hand, you may have joined a department where it's *de rigueur* to appear to have your nose to the grindstone as few hours of the day as convenient (which will simply mean that you either breast the tide or do your necessary work at home).

Whichever the case, it's a simple matter to conform, given an understanding significant other.

Calendar Times

In like manner, it may be the custom in your new department never to take a vacation, certainly not over the Christmas break. Again, check it out with a personal reconnaissance. You may discover that nobody's there except a couple of grad students. Or you may find a hive of worker bees.

When he was yet a bacteriology professor, the legendary E.B. Fred walked into his laboratory one night, looked around, and asked one of the grad students present, "Where are all my colleagues and where are all your fellow grad students?" "Well, you see, Mr. Fred," one student replied, "it's Christmas Eve!"

As we've said in another context, if you don't take at least a couple of weeks off in summer you can become a very dull academic. You don't have to go long or far, and you can keep in touch readily via electronic mail if you've got the requisite gear.

Indeed, you may have been attracted to your campus by the outdoor recreation opportunities its environs afford. The senior author (**ACS**) once got a phone call form a collegial friend in education: "We're trying our darnedest to recruit a promising young fellow from Harvard. He's a fishing nut. How about showing him some of your favorite trout and bass spots?" (Incidentally, for a fisherman to honor such a request calls for devotion above and beyond the call of duty.)

Again, whatever your calendar-time case, relax, enjoy — and accomplish.

Committee Work

In all likelihood your department will view committee work as a civic responsibility, one of the prices to be paid to keep the department micro-society functioning properly.

Some faculty members love to serve, some serve well but reluctantly, others have to be dragged kicking and screaming to the table.

So what do you do?

On the one hand, some departments will help protect your teaching/research time by understanding if you serve when called but don't volunteer, except perhaps for a project or ad hoc assignment down your alley, least of all for a standing committee that does anything but just stand, and for a long time.

Indeed, if you were to jump enthusiastically into committee work, some colleagues might view it as misplaced puppy energy or a lust for power.

On the other hand, some departments tend to load tiresome burdens onto the rookies, in which case it may be impolitic to shirk your responsibility.

In any case, grin and bear committee work as another of the rites of passage, being ever mindful, however, that in terms of brownie points it's normally outranked by teaching and research.

Expectations to Socialize

Your Midland University *alter ego* Bill and his spouse had scarcely moved into their modest town house in a faculty housing development than they found in their mailbox an invitation to attend a "start of the quarter" brunch at the home of Chair Amanda Perkins.

"I wonder how much they expect us to socialize here?" was the spouse's natural thought.

The answer to such a question is very much institution- and department-specific. Some departments at some institutions expect their faculty members to mingle often and long in a variety of social settings. Other departments at other institutions expect a bare minimum of togetherness.

Even within a department/college, an individual professor may be able to risk his or her own lifestyle. For example, in his long climb from instructor to professor to dean to president at the University of Wisconsin. E.B. Fred studiously eschewed hosting or even attending any social event other than a monthly poker-and-bourbon session with a half-dozen male cronies. A modern-day successor and his spouse, on the other hand, maintained a staggering social schedule.

You'll just have to feel your way. Chances are you'll discover a round of potlucks among probationary peers, plus an occasional sit-down dinner with senior staff or new-found department colleagues. When in doubt, don't hesitate to seek guidance from the person you identify as a social arbiter — faculty member or spouse.

Whom you invite and to what may be as diagnostic of your social grace as how often you entertain. Social events can be a useful and effective form of campus networking, but if you become known from your guest lists as a "social climber," the approach can backfire on many campuses. Better to be "omnivorous" — if that's the term — in your choice of house guests.

Without question, even a modest social life can put a dent in your family budget. Most colleagues will understand if you're sparing in issuing invitations. If you or your spouse are so fortunate as to be independently wealthy, don't flaunt it.

Whatever you do, don't sweat the socializing code you find. On most campuses, any days of measuring tenure credentials on the basis of drawing-room flair are long gone.

Dress Code

We have in hand a paragraph from the faculty guidebook at a Princeton-like academy, reading: "The school tie (presumably with elbow-patch jacket) is appropriate wear at all but the most informal (department picnic?) or formal (black-tie concert?) occasions."

On the other hand, in his novel *No Highway*, author Nevil Shute has a research director say:

> An unusual man is apt to look unusual. Mr. Honey sometimes presented an untidy appearance in his manner and clothes. I don't favor that, but I should be sorry to see the laboratory staffed entirely by correct young men in neat, conventional, civil service minds. We seek original thinkers with the untiring brain that pursues its object by day and by night. If the untiring brain refuses to attend to such matters as the neat arrangement of collar and tie, I do not greatly complain.

Those polar positions on dress codes may well suggest to you that, if socializing expectations are site-specific, dress codes are even more so.

Writing on "The F (for Fashion) Word" in the April 1991 issue of *Lingua Franca* after interviewing campus colleagues around the country, Valerie Steele has some delightful comments on the subject:

> Obviously, a university is not like a law firm, where the rules governing appropriate attire are both narrow and explicit. ... Peter Baldwin, an assistant professor of history at UCLA, remarks that academics are "under no pressure to dress well." And Deborah Kaple, a lecturer in sociology at Princeton, observes that some academics regard it as "one of the perks" of the job that they "don't have to pay attention" to how they dress. But if everyone in academia is happily doing his or her own thing, why is it so often the same thing? ...

> "Theoretically, anything goes," says Susan Kaiser, author of *The Social-Psychology of Clothing: Symbolic Appearances in Context* and associate professor at UC Davis, "but in practice, within a small-group context, such as a department, a subtle kind of negotiation goes on. We influence each other." ...

> In academic circles, many professors say, clothing is perceived as "material" (not intellectual) and, therefore, "beneath contempt." There is a sharp division between "the life of the mind and that of the body." ...

> Among leftists, fashion is also regarded as "bourgeois," and

so they often "go out of their way to distance themselves" from it, observes Michael Solomon, editor of *The Psychology of Fashion* and chairman of the Department of Marketing in the business school of Rutgers University. Aging " '68 types" are often "aggressively informal," agrees Baldwin, and "deliberately dress down for class." But even conservative professors often look barely respectable. ...

In the modern American context, to wear jackets rather than suits is to adopt a lesser degree of informality compared, for example, with businessmen or, closer to home, college administrators. But to wear a sports jacket and tie imparts an impression of formality and authority.

As a result, there is something of a split between professors who wear ties and those who don't. Baldwin distinguishes between "the Harvard compulsion to cravats versus the California obligatory tieless look." ...

Blue jeans are the operative garment. ... How better to assert solidarity with the young than to dress like them? ... A professor might be the oldest, most powerful, and least hip person in the classroom, but his antiestablishment clothing signified that he was a free spirit opposed to pernicious hierarchical distinctions between the teacher and the taught. ...

The sweater, either alone or under a jacket, is another garment frequently worn by male academics. ... The majority of professors seem to wear baggy, stretched-out sweaters in boring colors and cheap materials.

Women academics are "a disaster," insists one female professor in California, citing frumpy suits, sensible shoes, and outmoded haircuts. With their "asexual clothes and handbags [that] are satchels," with "no makeup or jewelry," laments one woman professor at an Ivy League university, the "subconscious message" of her collegial sisters is: "If I could, I'd be male."

Certainly, femininity is out. So is anything too conspicuous or body-revealing. Like most female professionals, the majority of women in academia tend to minimize any sartorial eroticism while maximizing status signifiers. "Most female faculty look like bankers and lawyers, even when the men are in polo shirts," is the succinct assessment of a UC San Diego scholar.

Yet upon closer inspection, women academics do not really look like bankers, lawyers, or business executives. Sad to say, they lack marketplace flair. Skirts, for example, tend to be significantly longer than those of most professional women: to mid-calf, when the fashionable length is slightly above the knee. The jacket (the female executive's badge of authority) is seen less often in academia, where professors tend to wear separates. ...

Can a style of dress hurt one's professional career? True to

form, most academics deny that it makes any difference
whatsoever. But a few stories may indicate otherwise. ... (19)

Well, there you have it. At least you can say this for dress
codes: they're easy to discern. Just look around your department. Whether you opt to conform is, in most situations, up to
you, but your response will say something.

As Polonius said in *Hamlet*, "The apparel oft proclaims the
man." (Presumably, if Shakespeare were writing today, he would
say "person.")

Environmental Impingements

Housing, health care, schools, spousal employment, recreational and cultural opportunities, libraries, stores, family
budget, competent tradespeople, commuting time — a gamut of
concerns can impinge on your institutional duties, at times
markedly — particularly if you're a stranger in a strange land.

The character of one department may be such that colleagues couldn't care less about such personal concerns and will
expect you not to bring them with you in your briefcase to the office. Callous? You bet. But it's a fact of life in some certain situations.

On the other hand, the caring culture of some departments
can be positively cloying.

An early tip-off as to what style you've inherited can be the
conduct of the department CEO. If he or she asks nary a word
about how you're personally settling in, you can assume the
department expects you to be strictly professional in your
habits. If he or she wants to know all the details of your adjustment, you may almost be tempted to invent a problem so that
the department chair can fulfill his or her need to be "helpful."

Depending on your own personality, you may be more comfortable in one situation or the other, but they're not much
amenable to change. It's another case of going along to get along.

Salutatory Titles

As a matter of fact, you can get a feeling for one important
aspect of institutional style — how you address people — by consulting a *HEP Directory* before ever coming to a campus.

Take a look at the description of Midland University. Although Midland is an institution of some pretensions, there's
not a "Dr." in the house — except, of course, in the School of Allied Health Professions. On the other hand, at Cobalt College
across the state, practically everybody's a "Dr."

It's all a matter of style. If you're at a "Dr.-less" institution,
no matter how proud you are of your new Ph.D., don't call yourself or anybody else "Dr."; you're a plain "Mr." or "Ms." If, however, you're at an institution that advertises its roster of Ph.D.'s

at every opportunity, emblazon yours on your office door.

All this may seem like the height of the inconsequential, but nothing is so diagnostic of campus status as its employment of salutatory titles. In fact, you can almost say that the more prestigious an American university today, the more it will frown on the use of the title "Dr." for any faculty member except a bona fide M.D. or D.D.S., while the more "wannabe" a campus the more it will encourage you to display the title — at home and abroad.

The Town-and-Gown Minuet

In some campus communities the line between town and gown is quite distinct, with senior academics looking down their noses at their plebeian counterparts, and assistant professors viewed askance if they cross the border.

In other campus communities, faculty and citizens share a general camaraderie. Local professionals are invited to give guest lectures, and deans take turns as chairs of city service clubs.

Whatever dance card you inherit, don't let it get in the way of forming friendships with your immediate neighbors, with the parents of your children's pals, with church acquaintances, or with the like.

Twenty years from now you may discover that your warmest relationships are not intra- but extra-institutional, or you may be content with a closed campus circle.

Job Offer Etiquette

Some departments assume their assistant professors are constantly on the market, and may even take pride in their being so. Other departments will view any sign of wanderlust as evidence of disloyalty.

As a professor on probation, you owe it to your career to make yourself available, provided your job-hunting doesn't get in the way of your current responsibilities or rattle the chair's cage. (Given the academic grapevine, there's no way you can keep any perambulations secret, at least not for long.)

Without question, an attractive job offer from a competing institution can be compelling leverage, **but** — never threaten to leave without being prepared actually to go if you're bluffing and your bluff is called.

The senior author (**ACS**) has an indelible memory of a probationary peer who took an offer letter to the dean's office in hopes of accelerating his pace toward promotion or at least of generating a healthy salary raise. When next seen, he blurted, in surprise and dismay, "I ... I ... I ... I'm going to Excelsior!"

DECISION TIME
Relations With Students

From the perspective of professors as leaders in relation to their students, there are roughly three leadership styles they can adopt — depending on their personal backgrounds and proclivities, the level of the student, and the mores of the department.

A professor is using the **authoritarian leadership style** when he or she tells students what's to be done and how, without incorporating their interests or ideas. When using the **participative leadership style**, a professor involves students in determining what to do and how to do it, yet retains final decision-making authority. In the **delegative leadership style**, a professor delegates decision-making to a student or group of students, yet retains responsibility for the results of his or her students' decisions.

The style you would use for a particular situation would depend on your analysis of the situation and your judgment of who has the necessary information to solve the problem or to accomplish the task. Your creative thinking is a key to the correct choice of role. Your beliefs, values, character, and experience will influence how you think. The way you think will determine how you apply what you know and what you do.

A professor can use a quick, flexible mind if he or she is to stay with or ahead of the rapidly changing forces in faculty-student relations on campuses today. He or she must continually identify and foresee shifts in important actors and forces. As the situation changes, he or she can change the mix of actions and style. One mix of actions and one style may work one time and be ineffective the next. Only by exercising good judgment can you successfully meet the demands of complex, stressful, changing interpersonal and institutional environments.

We've been talking here, or course, about your professional stance *vis-à-vis* students. When it comes to personal relations, increasingly the advice: **don't.** Instances of sexual harassment are repeatedly being brought to light these days, and faculty are always at risk, whether the accusations are true or groundless. (15)

The Midland botany department had to set up a special human relations committee last year just to deal with allegations of sexual harassment and discrimination.

Personal relations with undergrads have always been questionable, while it has been accepted that professors and their graduate students sometimes got together romantically, but that could be changing, particularly in a situation where the professor has evaluative or supervisory authority over the student, as

in a course or with an RA. Even in consensual arrangements the
risk is great the relationship will end on a sour note with the
student charging harassment.

Faculty almost never are able to defend themselves completely in such situations, even when the charges are absurd.
On the other hand, in instances where faculty are totally to
blame they deserve severe discipline.

While there are seldom written institutional guidelines
covering personal relations with students, the soundest oral advice probably is, **don't.** As one reviewer of this manuscript commented, "One is less likely to get into trouble playing around
with a dean's spouse than with a student."

Moonlighting

Some departments encourage their faculty members to earn
outside income by accepting consulting fees or similar emolu-
ments, assuming the work is related to your academic expertise
and doesn't interfere with your salaried duties. Indeed, an active
consulting life can be a badge of distinction. Sometimes your
public service activities can lead to such arrangements.

Other departments frown on outside work, particularly if it's
unrelated to your professional competence, on the theory that
the institution has bought all your time or that tainted money
can be involved. Some institutions require that you report mi-
nutely all outside income, from whom, and for what. Others
want to know about it in very general terms. Others ask nothing. In rare cases you may be expected to contribute all or part
of your profits to institutional coffers.

Honoraria in lieu of expenses or just plain reimbursed expenses seldom qualify in departmental eyes as outside income. Nor does
substituting extensively on your youngster's paper route. Subbing as
a seasonal store clerk probably would qualify, along with a certain
amount of opprobrium. Military reserve pay seldom is considered as
reportable income, nor are you usually docked for the necessary ar-
mory or summer-camp time. A call to active duty would be a different matter, necessitating a leave without campus pay.

For some strange reason, patent and book royalties usually
occupy a niche all by themselves, being considered a natural ac-
companiment of scholarship, even though the institution may
have underwritten a good share of the production costs. When
royalties bulk really large, some grateful professors donate a
percentage to a campus fund. For example, from 1928-29 to
1989-90, donor-directed gifts netted the University of Wisconsin-
Madison $7,858,620 through the Wisconsin Alumni Research
Foundation, a considerable share of that amount coming from
Harry Steenbock and his vitamin D irradiation patent personal
royalties.

In short, the ground rules respecting moonlighting are so many and varied that it behooves you to double-check before you start operating *ex cathedra.*

A gratuitous word: don't build any outside income into your family budget; it's too ephemeral. Use it for extras.

Conformity Codes

As Emerson said, "A foolish consistency is the hobgoblin of little minds." Wherever they may be, most faculty members agree; it's a badge of the profession.

And yet each campus has distinct limits on the degree of inconsistency it tolerates, particularly in its untenured staff. Put another way, campuses vary in the size and scope of *lebensraum* they give their faculty members before imposing quiet ostracism.

A crucial aspect of appreciating the practical politics of getting promoted in your department/institution is determining the conformity codes under which you find yourself — and complying or not as a situation dictates. So diverse are those situations that it's impossible to generalize about them and about your reaction. The one ground rule we can suggest is this:

Respect the bounds of peculiarity on your campus, yet maintain a personal code of conscience. When the two are in utter conflict, recognize it as decision time.

Political Action

Your Midland *alter ego* Bill had scarcely gotten his first quarter squared away when he found in his campus mailbox an invitation to join a campus "Save the Lagoon League." On inquiry, he finds the situation to be thus:

Where a small watershed empties into Lake Midland at the northern edge of the campus, a 20-acre "lagoon" — or "marsh," depending on your perspective — has existed since the glaciers. In spring its willow-lined margins are the haunts of both waterfowl and campus lovers. Now in its wisdom the campus planning commission has opted to convert the lagoon into a subterranean culvert and use the captured land for a faculty parking lot. Most campus administrators are delighted; some faculty and many students and alumni are distraught, as well as are the county lake management technicians.

Your *alter ego* recognizes immediately that in the conflict he has an ideal case study for the new department program in biological conservation/sustainable development, but should he personally get involved in the league? He can't plead that the matter is irrelevant to his scholarly interests; quite the contrary, it's tailor-made. But can he risk the public exposure his participation would inevitably bring to focus? A tenured faculty member can let his conscience be his guide, but an assistant professor may have to be circumspect.

Given the "political correctness" imbroglio that has made colleges and universities the topic of a multi-media news blitz, you may well find yourself in a situation different in kind but not in degree from that of your Midland *alter ego.* Do I or don't I? We won't presume to prescribe an answer other than to suggest that the one person you ultimately have to live with is yourself.

Networking

Some departments will openly encourage you to work formally and informally with colleagues both within and beyond your department, and there are real advantages to so doing.

For example, by discussing your projects with department colleagues, not only will they be alerted to your enterprise, you will benefit from their input, enthusiasm, and even nagging. By linking up with colleagues across campus, you gain outside perspectives and interdisciplinary approaches — both of them intelligent and unembedded in disciplinary constraints.

Extra-campus conferences can be an intellectual banquet, exposing you to an even wider range of thought and manner, and to a broader world of scholarship. To get away, offer to trade missed classes with a colleague. Such an exchange can carry bonus benefits: the colleague will know of your off-campus status, you and he or she will establish a working relationship, the substitute may be impressed by your class and your preparation, and the liaison can lead to team-teaching or research collaboration.

But not all departments are eager to share your talents outside, as your Midland University *alter ego* Bill was surprised to discover. His former Georgia professor, now dean of the Midland forestry and environmental studies school, invited him to chair a planning-and-evaluation committee for a student in their non-thesis master's degree program. Chair Amanda Perkins ruled, "Absolutely not!"

Her reasons were both profound and picayune. As Perkins explained, Midland had no mechanism for transferring such graduate advising work from forestry to botany and, given current tight budget constraints, it was mandatory that botany not squander any of its scarce economic resources beyond Pendarvis Hall. Secondly, some of their colleagues would think it beneath the dignity of the botany department to be associated with "that forestry trade school."

So, before you engage in too many beyond-department forays, check out the situation, weather, and terrain.

Pressure Points

Anybody who has ever consulted an osteopath for a back

ailment knows the doctor can usually find a pressure point or two that will relieve the distress after proper massaging. Just so with department dynamics.

Early on it was obvious to your Midland University *alter ego* that, for the good of both the new applied ecology program and his own career, he had somehow to make peace with his recalcitrant theoretical botany colleagues.

A little detective work revealed that there were both profound academic reasons and personality peculiarities for their opposition:

Although a botany master's program had traditionally been a 24-credit regimen, six credits of which were required thesis credits, the department/college committee structuring the new biological conservation/sustainable development program had opted for a pattern of 30 course credits with no mandatory thesis. That was like waving a red flag in front of a bull. How could botany's high standards be so defiled? (And wouldn't grad students flock away from lab programs into the new configuration?)

Bill set out to do some diplomatic fence-mending. At an early meeting of the program planning committee, he proposed a compromise: why not retain the 30-credit regimen so that students would be exposed to a necessary range of materials, but let's include in the 30 a four-credit research-paper-in-lieu-of-thesis requirement, said paper to be done up in such a fashion as to meet learned journal or research proposal standards? That turned out to be a happy solution to the matter-of-principle conflict.

The personality problem was tougher to handle. The acting chair of the new program was simply not a very likable person, and he had compounded that debility by being of uncertain caliber: not only had he come into the department with 18 years as a dendrologist with the USDI National Park Service in lieu of a Ph.D., he also held a joint appointment with "that" forestry school across the way.

As a first step, Bill proposed that the acting chair of the program take over the grad student program planning and evaluating assignment (on forestry time) that Bill had been asked to assume by the Midland forestry school, thereupon relinquishing his acting chairship. While it would have been logical for Bill to become the applied botany program chair, such a move would have been premature. Rather, he proposed that the program be administered at least temporarily by a three-person committee — one card-carrying cytologist, one geneticist (who was actually a "closet ecologist"), and himself, with the geneticist serving as chair pro tem. It was hard to argue against that strategy, and indeed nobody did so with any conviction. Even the dendrologist was content. (The only dismayed person was the forestry dean.)

Whether the makeshift strategy could hold together indefinitely, Bill wasn't sure, but it was a better shot than continued cold war. At least at the first meeting of the triumvirate, everything went smoothly. So Bill had taken a significant step at finding a key pressure point and mending fences. Chair Perkins was understandably impressed with his adroit handling of what had been a messy situation.

You can be on the lookout for a similar role of osteopathic diplomacy wherever you are.

Conferencing

Without question, as sound a political move as any is to attend at least one conference a year in your field, particularly if you're invited to present a paper; and many departments will "pop" for the cost. The attendant prestige-pro-promotion is measurable — unless you acquire a reputation as a mindless traveler.

An even sounder political decision is to host a conference on your own turf, provided you do it with savvy: figure about an 18-month lead time in which to line up funding and program participants; get yourself an administrative assistant of some kind; assemble a broadly based planning committee, to include extra-campus as well as all-campus representatives of appropriate agencies and organizations; pick a general topic or theme with some local relevance; select keynote speakers and panel members having reputations for pithy remarks with news media "bite." The credibility you gain from chairing a hometown conference multiplies manyfold a trip or two.

(This demur from one reviewer: "I would **never** recommend that an assistant professor take on such a charge!")

Your Midland University *alter ego* Bill figured out that the best way to capitalize on that lagoon vs. parking lot business was to use it as a peg for a regional academic conference along the lines of his department's new biological conservation/sustainable development theme. For the conference kickoff he got a promised appearance by Gaylord Nelson, former U.S. Senator from nearby Wisconsin, "father" of Earth-Day, now general counsel for the Wilderness Society, who had recently made headlines with the ethic, "When somebody destroys something made by man, he's called a vandal; when someone destroys something irreplaceable, something made by God, he's called a developer." For the principal presenters Bill picked emeritus professors John Cobb, Jr., and Herman Daly, authors of the current book *For the Common Good: Redirecting the Economy Toward Community, Environment, and a Sustainable*

Future. But to keep the agenda balanced, Bill invited as presenters as well two forceful Midland urban planners to promote the parking-lot option — and to save the seminar from the charge that it was "staged by environmentalists." The resulting conference should stimulate student, faculty, administration, and public thinking — and lend visibility to the department and its new M.A. program.

Keep your eyes open for a similar opportunity where you are.

Leadership and Character

If all that's transpired so far in this section on practical politics seems to you like gamesmanship beneath your dignity, depending on your personal likes and professional standards, you could be right.

But there's one crucial aspect of qualifying for promotion to tenure you can't duck, and that's the responsibility you bear for yourself and your chosen profession to demonstrate incontrovertible hallmarks of leadership and character.

<u>Hallmarks of leadership</u>.

- Know yourself and seek self-improvement.
- Be professionally proficient.
- Seek and take responsibility.
- Make sound and timely decisions.
- Set the example.
- Know your colleagues and students and look out for their well-being; keep them informed.
- Develop a sense of responsibility in your students: ensure that any task is understood and accomplished.
- Practice teamwork.

<u>Hallmarks of character</u>.

- Integrity: searching for and doing the morally right thing.
- Maturity.
- Will.
- Self-discipline.
- Flexibility.
- Confidence.
- Endurance.
- Decisiveness.
- Coolness under stress.
- Initiative.
- Justice.

- Empathy or compassion.
- Sense of humor.
- Creativity.
- Humility.
- Tact.

Now if all that sounds like a bunch of platitudes, so be it.

A Balancing Act

Because our forthcoming chapter on teaching is longer than our chapters on research and on service, one reviewer of the manuscript accused us of "overemphasizing teaching and trivializing research" and, by implication, service as well.

We don't mean it to be taken that way. "Balance" among the three is the desideratum, at least at many institutions. Again, it pays to know your territory.

The same reviewer has a constructive approach to the issue:

> A proper view of the "balance" issue is to place it in a career-span context. The probation period is a time for a new professor to prove to him/herself and the world that she/he can make significant contributions to a scholarly guild. This is the time to take advantage of every bit of "nurturing" and released time that your department is willing to provide.

> Professors' desires to be stellar teachers and do awesome research are wonderful, but can't they be given less emphasis for the short five-year (from arrival on campus to submitting your papers) probationary period? What makes for "balance" within a department is that different folks are in different phases of focus on teaching, research, and service.

> The crucial thing that needs to happen during the pre-tenure period is to make a transition from being somebody's graduate student to being a scholar in one's own right. This challenge requires carving out one's own scholarship turf or, as one of my professors once described it to me many years ago, "finding your own dead horse to flay."

> Also, on my campus people are sometimes denied tenure for lack of "programmatic" research, meaning that they flit from one related research question to the next. (Of course, this is at times a "code" for "We don't like your dialect.") Many assistant professors don't have the luxury of waiting around to analyze the feedback from one study before planning the next. (Which is why lots of biologists choose for subjects animals that have a short gestation period and life cycle.)

> Emphasis on a five-year research plan/program is essential.

A FINAL P&T CHECKLIST

As a capstone to your learning the territory, we suggest you locate a copy of the official form on which, five or six years from now — the fates willing — your recommendation for promotion to tenure will be initiated by your department and reviewed by higher echelons before being placed — again, the fates willing — before the board of governors.

If your institution has no such form, you may find it useful to check the following Midland University form, covered by a memo of transmittal from the college dean to the department chair.

Chances are this Midland form is very similar to the docu-mentation you and your chair will be asked to produce and package. At any rate, it certainly contains sure clues to the type of information you should start collecting and cataloging from Day 1.

Consult it conscientiously — and confidently.

However, in doing so, recall what brought you in the first place to seek a career in academia. It certainly wasn't money alone. Wasn't it the stimulus that comes from being around bright people — colleagues and students? The opportunity to contribute, discover and share knowledge? The ideal of service? So don't try to reduce your assistant professorship to merely a quantitative quest for tenure, important as that may be. Your probationary term can be qualitatively richer than that. Live it professionally to the full.

<u>MIDLAND UNIVERSITY</u>

COLLEGE OF LETTERS AND SCIENCE

<u>Interoffice Communication</u>
DATE: November 15, 1991
TO: Professor Amanda L. Perkins, Chair
      Department of Botany and Applied Ecology
FROM: E. Howard Harrier, Dean
RE: Faculty Promotions to Tenure

    1. Attached you will find the University's new standard form to be used in recommending all faculty for promotion to tenure.

    2. It is important that this form be followed as exactly as possible, both to ensure uniformity in review and to forestall procedural grievances.

    3. Please bring this form to the attention of all members of departmental tenure review committees, and particularly to the attention of all probationary members of the department.

    4. Eighteen (18) copies of the recommendation and your rating are to be submitted for each candidate going forward. This Office will need the materials by January 4, 1992.

    5. Evidence must be provided for each major point on the form. Use full names, including initials, to help us in the

preparation of our request to the VPAA.

6. In the case of faculty who hold appointments in more than one department, you are reminded that recommendations from all departments (and colleges, if applicable) are required. Contributions to interdisciplinary programs should be included and should also be evaluated by the appropriate peers.

7. You are reminded that in the case of faculty who are in the sixth year of their probationary period, a decision must be made as to whether they will be promoted to tenure or whether they will be given notice that their employment will be terminated at the end of their final year (or after a grace period). Notify us of those such faculty whom you are not recommending for tenure, along with material relevant to your decision.

EHH:cpr
Enclosure
cc: College P&T Committee

FORM FOR RECOMMENDING PROMOTION OF FACULTY MEMBERS TO TENURE AT MIDLAND UNIVERSITY

I. <u>Name of Faculty Member, Current Rank, and Department</u>.

Append a current curriculum vitae.

II. <u>Action Requested</u>.

Promotion to which rank, or tenure, or both.

III. <u>Number of Years of Professional Experience</u>.

This figure should be a total of the number of years of experience in teaching, research, professional practice, and extension work. It should reflect the total number of years of professional service and should not be limited to the years of service at Midland.

IV. <u>Midland Personnel Record</u>.

Ranks held and date of appointment to each rank.

V. <u>Present Responsibilities</u>.

Teaching. Describe responsibilities for teaching. Give the title, catalog number, and number of credit hours of courses taught during the last five years (by quarter). State approximate number of students in each class. If courses were team-taught, indicate percent of course taught by candidate.

Research and Artistic Creativity. Describe responsibilities for research and artistic creativity.

Extension and/or Professional Practice. Describe responsibilities for extension and/or professional practice.

Student Advising. Does the candidate serve as academic

advisor to undergraduate students or graduate students?
How many of each?

International Assignments. List international assignments on Midland projects during the last five years. Include project title, number of months served, and major
accomplishments.

Others. If contributions are made outside of the assigned
categories shown above, describe the nature of these contributions.

VI. Reasons for Promotion and/or Tenure (to be completed
by chair)

Identification of Area(s) of Excellence. The University's
standards for promotion and tenure indicate that a faculty
member must perform in: (1) teaching and advising; (2) research, scholarship, or artistic activities; or (3) extension
and/or professional practice. Identify the area(s) in which
the candidate excels.

Teaching Performance. Give a thorough analysis of the
faculty member's teaching capability and performance since
the date of the most recent appointment. Indicate special
qualifications by evaluating such items as: interest in students, advising skills, instructional methods, ability to
stimulate student interest in subject, competence in subject
matter. Submit evidence to support the analysis, including
evaluations by students and peers.

Performance in Research or Artistic Activities. List
major publications since the date of the most recent appointment. Use documentation format appropriate to your discipline. Evaluate the publications in terms of the level of
research ability reflected and their contribution to knowledge. Comment on the quality of journals in which the publications have appeared and the nature of their review process. List significant outside funding obtained. Appraise
ability to attract, stimulate, and develop the research talents of graduate students. For multi-author publications,
describe the shared contributions. Submit single copies of
key publications separately so that they can be returned to
the candidate following completion of the review.

**Performance in Extension and/or Professional Prac-
tice (if applicable).** Give a thorough analysis of the faculty
member's extension and/or professional practice capability
and performance since the date of the most recent appointment. List major accomplishments in professional practice.
Evaluate the importance and quality of the individual's extension and/or professional practice in terms such as
demonstrated expertise in the discipline; ability to instruct,
inform, and assist the clientele; and the extent to which the
individual displays leadership, initiative, and creativity in
the application of the discipline.

Service Activities. The University's standards for promotion and tenure require that all candidates must have demonstrated excellence in at least one of the following: institutional service, professional service, or public service. Cite the ways in which the candidate has met this requirement. List departmental, college, and university committee memberships and evaluate contributions to each. Appraise relationship with colleagues in terms of cooperativeness, helpfulness, and willingness to assume share of responsibilities in the academic community.

National Professional Standing. Appraise national professional standing, such as memberships and offices held in professional associations, and professional awards and honors received.

Evaluation by Departmental Colleagues. If this recommendation is the outgrowth of consultation or action by special evaluation techniques, such as a committee on faculty promotions, please indicate.

Evaluation by Peers from Outside the University (to be solicited by the Chair or department review committee). The Chair or the committee shall solicit letters from qualified, impartial reviewers, with the understanding that, insofar as possible, access to them will be limited to persons involved in the promotion/tenure decision. Between three and six letters should be sought, with at least one of the reviewers being suggested by the candidate. A copy of the candidate's CV and other relevant materials should accompany the letter of request. The reviewers should be asked to be specific and to comment on particular aspects of the candidate's scholarly contributions and their impact on the field, as well as, where possible, to compare the candidate with others in the field at the same stage of their career. The Chair should assess the letters and should prepare a summary to be transmitted with the package, including an explanation of why those persons were selected in terms of their general qualifications in the field as well as their specific contributions to this review. To preserve confidentiality, the letters themselves should be transmitted with the package to the Dean and subsequently to the VPAA and will be retained in the Office of the VPAA. The essence of the letters should be shared with the candidate in a way that protects the anonymity of the evaluator.

References

1. Anderson, Charles, "Academic Bargaining Successfully: Some ABCs" (Washington DC: American Council on Education, 1991, pamphlet).
2. Astin, Alexander, *The American College Teacher: National Norms from the 1989-90 HERI Faculty Survey* (Los Angeles: UCLA Graduate School of Education Higher Education Research Institute, 1991).

3. Bennett, John B., "Academic Program Evaluation," *The Department Advisor*, Spring 1991, pp. 5-8.

4. Bennett, John B., "Collegiality as 'Getting Along,'" *AAHE Bulletin*, October 1991, pp. 7-10.

5. Boice, Robert, "New Faculty as Teachers," *The Journal of Higher Education*, March/April 1991, pp. 150-193.

6. Carnegie Foundation for the Advancement of Teaching, *Identifying Comparable Institutions* (Washington DC: John Minter Associates, 1990).

7. Cashin, William E., and Ronald G. Downey, "Instructional Development and Effectiveness Assessment" (Manhattan KS: Kansas State University Center for Faculty Evaluation and Development, 1991, pamphlet).

8. Cole, Susan A., "Professional Ethics and the Role of the Academic Officer," *CUBA Journal*, Fall 1991, pp. 37-41.

9. Frederick, Peter, "Changing Collegial Conversation," *The Department Advisor*, Spring 1991, pp. 1-5.

10. Gmelch, Walter H., and P. Kay Wilke, "Stress in Higher Education," *The Journal for Higher Education Management*, Winter/Spring 1991, pp. 23-33.

11. Hensel, Nancy, *Realizing Gender Equality in Higher Education* (Washington DC: George Washington University Educational Resource Information Center Clearing House on Higher Education, 1991).

12. Howery, Carla, Interview with Barbara D. Wright, "Discipline-Based Assessment: The Case for Sociology," *AAHE Bulletin*, November 1991, pp. 14-16.

13. Jimenez, Carla, "Legal Issues: Unlawful Discrimination," *The Department Chair*, Fall 1990, pp. 10-11.

14. Kerr, Kay U., *Chairperson's Manual* (Fort Collins: Colorado State University Office of Instructional Services, 1989).

15. Paludi, Michele, and Richard B. Barickman, "Ivory Power: Academic Sexual Harassment," *The Department Chair*, Spring 1991, pp. 5-6.

16. Powell, Gen. Colin, quoted in "What's Next, General Powell?" *U.S. News & World Report*, March 18, 1991, p. 5.

17. Sands, Robert G., L. Alayne Parson, and Josann Duane, "Faculty Mentoring Faculty in a Public University," *The Journal of Higher Education*, March/April 1991, pp. 174-193.

18. Seldin, Peter, "Personal and Professional," *The Chronicle of Higher Education*, May 8, 1991, pp. A15-17.

19. Steele, Valerie, "The F Word," *Lingua Franca*, April 1991, pp. 17-20.

20. Strohm, Paul, *et al.*, "Fringe Benefits: Under Attack," *Academe*, May/June 1991, pp. 9-21.

21. Sykes, Charles, and Brad Miner, Eds. *National Review College Guide: America's 50 Top Liberal Arts Schools* (New York: Wolhgemuth and Hyatt, 1991).

22. Wesson, Marianne, and Sandra Johnson, "Post-Tenure Review and Faculty Revitalization," *Academe*, May/June 1991, pp. 53-57.

III
THE TEACHING CHALLENGE

In a sense this chapter may not seem necessary. For most faculty teaching is not a major concern along the path to tenure and promotion, for two reasons.

First, it's generally right there in your contract, inevitable. With research or service work there are choices: you choose whether or not to do it, how much, what kind, when. With teaching you usually receive your assignments: the experience is thrust upon you.

The second reason why teaching isn't usually an obstacle is that, at many institutions, only horrible instructors have traditionally been denied tenure or promotion on the basis of teaching alone. Student evaluations may not matter much. Evaluations by colleagues may not be any more important; a recent study by John A. Centra indicated that 94% of faculty raters judged their colleagues' teaching as "very good" or "excellent."(6)

Fortunately for our students, that situation is changing as voices rise to demand better instruction. But that trend may make your upward path more difficult. If the decision-makers want to promote teaching without relaxing expectations for scholarship and service, you'll need to be more efficient in your efforts to teach better.

Teaching provides intrinsic rewards and motivations. It can be a real joy to work with students, to help them develop, to challenge them to realize their potential, and sometimes to learn together with them. But beware: as a colleague at Midland University warned Bill Campion, "Teaching can be like a black hole, drawing away your time and energy. And suddenly — you're up for tenure with your CV out of balance."

In this chapter, we have two goals: to hit the essentials of good teaching and to suggest ways to maximize recognition of your efforts at tenure time. If you feel tempted to skip the first part of this chapter and read only the second, we encourage you to at least skim the pages on the essentials of teaching.

REPRESENTATIVE STANDARDS

In this, as in the succeeding two chapters, we're setting your sights high by quoting what a major university tells a candidate about its "standards to be applied in judging qualifications for tenure."

Initially, the institution states that "evidence of a candidate's teaching in a discipline, scholarly excellence, and productivity" includes "teaching and the development of teaching materials" right along with research and service.

The "criteria" document goes on to say that "evaluation of teaching ability and performance takes into account the wide range of approaches to teaching." These include "lectures, discussion sections, seminars, institutes, workshops, media presentations, laboratory instruction, in-service training, media courses, correspondence courses, individual tutorials, advising and consulting, and consultative exchanges with client groups."

While no candidate is expected to be equally proficient in all teaching situations, "proficiency *must* be demonstrated in those teaching situations most appropriate to the candidate's teaching responsibilities."

Evidence used to evaluate teaching ability and performance will include:

- Surveys of student opinion.
- Assessment by colleagues, based on direct observation.
- Course outlines, bibliographies, scripts, program development, and other teaching materials.
- Assessment by teaching assistants, workshop participants, trainees.
- Record of student advising, consultations, and research supervision.
- Development of new courses and teaching materials.
- Client and peer evaluations of program presentations.
- Success of students: in your course, in later courses for which yours is a prerequisite, in careers based on majors in your field, and in high-profile areas — when they receive important fellowships, gain admission to prestigious graduate programs, present papers at conferences, and publish scholarly articles and books.

The guidelines conclude: "A balanced judgment of teaching ability *must* rely on more than one kind of evidence."

So, at this and comparable institutions at least, excellence in teaching is clearly essential for aspirants to an associate professorship.

At many research institutions new faculty may learn through experience that excellent teaching is considerably less important in practice than in principle. Even at liberal arts colleges, urban colleges, and two-year colleges — institutions where teaching has generally been held in higher esteem — there may be subtle shifts to stress productive scholarship. Once again, it's a question of knowing your territory — and realizing that not all expectations are in writing.

YOUR PERSPECTIVES ON TEACHING

AFTER 20 YEARS IN THE CLASSROOM ...

New faculty may feel that they shouldn't have any problems teaching, since they've only recently emerged from the classroom experience as students — they may also have served as graduate teaching assistants. This assumption is risky, for several reasons.

Faculty tend to teach as they themselves were taught; it's what they know and it has worked for them. But there are other approaches and techniques. And students aren't all the same. Most faculty are more intelligent than the average student. More important, they have a greater interest in the subject matter. And they're probably more comfortable in academic surroundings; after all, they've chosen to settle down there.

Approaches and techniques handed down from one generation of faculty to the next need to be examined and revised. Otherwise we could all just meet to talk in the marketplace, as they did in ancient Greece, or conduct all academic activities in Latin, as they did in medieval Europe, or just lecture from the podium as ....

SAME OLD SYSTEM

Many faculty stick with what they know. Some want to go beyond the tried and true, but they feel that educational research and pedagogy are a separate discipline, a terra incognita populated by such strangers as Dewey, Piaget, and Vygotsky. Not to worry: you don't need to be an expert in research on teaching and learning to try something a little different.

At a recent American Association for Higher Education conference one presenter was overheard telling another, "I don't know if this session will work, but we'll just try it." The candor, the honesty, and the enthusiasm were more inspiring than "canned" presentations that have proven "successful" over and over and over and ....

The lesson: don't always play it safe. Your students expose themselves to mistakes and failure constantly. You may be an expert in your field, but you can't know it all. You may be the one in charge in that classroom, but you can't make everything work out right.

Think of "teaching" as "facilitating." Your job is to make your students' environment conducive to learning and to provide activities that promote their development.

WHAT'S YOUR STORY?

What's your particular situation? Some beginning instructors are assigned established courses, complete with design and materials, while others may enjoy total autonomy, with the freedom and responsibility of creating their own courses. For most, the scenario is somewhere between those two extremes. So just move through the following sections and find what works for your particular situation.

CONCEPTUALIZING YOUR COURSE AND YOUR GOALS

Whether you're creating a new course from scratch (a challenge we'll cover later in this chapter) or, as is more likely, adapting an existing course to meet your particular objectives and perceived student needs, the process of course development is the same — and it can be scary. But you shouldn't feel overwhelmed, not if you examine each aspect carefully.

In preparing a course, the question "**Why** are you teaching?" is more fundamental than "**What** are you teaching?" The question "**How** do you want your students to **change?**" is more central to your purpose than "**What** do you want them to **learn?**"

Then you should ask yourself the following questions:

- Where are we beginning? Who are my students?
- How can I facilitate their learning?
- What are our circumstances? That is, class hours, time outside of class, classroom size and layout, resources.

For further guidance, you might try the more comprehensive, two-page worksheet for planning courses developed by Kathleen T. Brinko of Appalachian State University.(4)

GOALS: WHY ARE YOU TEACHING? HOW DO YOU WANT YOUR STUDENTS TO CHANGE?

It's easy to think just about primary goals, the essentials of your field of study: students will learn this material, students will be able to solve these problems, and so forth. But there are other goals that may be secondary to your subject area but which are also very important, in a larger context. Many of these goals will likely be cognitive (knowledge and intellectual skills), while a few may be affective (attitudes, values, interests). Your particular goals might include critical thinking, better reading comprehension, verbal and writing skills, appreciation of the values and opinions of others, teamwork, research skills, understanding personal differences ....

Some teachers think of those goals as icing on the cake: if you make progress toward those goals, it's a bonus. A colleague likes to call those secondary goals "the mortar that holds all those bricks together." It's a question of attitude. Some instructors view secondary goals as a bonus or, worse, as a frill that detracts from the time and energy available to achieve the primary goals. For others the secondary goals suggest ways —

often quite creative — of pursuing the primary goals.

Start with the basic question: What are you teaching? Then ask: Why? What is the value of what you intend to teach? How do you want your students to be different because of your course?

As some have put it, "Defend your course." Be specific. Make a list of general objectives: students will understand the causes of World War I, students will know the distinctive character-istics of species of mammals, students will be able to explain philosophical differences between Descartes and Pascal, stu-dents will write a program to sort records by any one of seven fields. These will be your primary goals.

Then consider what other goals would be worthwhile in your course. In a course for majors or minors, these goals could be closely related to the discipline. Just ask yourself, "What helped me succeed in my field? What do I wish I'd learned when I was studying that area of my discipline? What knowledge or skills are most useful to practitioners in this field?" In a general course for students with diverse interests, the secondary goals might be larger. With first-year students, for example, you might want to encourage intellectual curiosity, to help develop study skills, to promote cooperation.

YOUR STUDENTS: WHERE ARE YOUR STARTING POINTS?

The next aspect of planning is often more difficult. Who are your students? An introductory class of beginners and visitors? A more advanced class? A class of senior majors? Grads and post-grads? Non-traditional and special students?

What knowledge, experience, and skills will your students bring to your course? Why are they taking your course? Don't make any unwarranted assumptions. Colleagues who've taught similar courses recently can be a source of valuable suggestions.

When Bill arrived to teach his first class, he found that a few of his students were older than he, two by several years. He was concerned, since a colleague had warned him about older students:

> Because they're more experienced in the 'real world' they tend to have higher standards, more definite expectations. Sometimes it's frustrating because they're more likely to focus on the bottom line, on acquiring information and skills, and less on learning how to think.

But Bill had thought hard about his course goals; they were solid and realistic, and he felt ready for any challenges.

Amanda Perkins, chair of the botany department, had also helped prepare Bill for his students by providing him with some demographics. So Bill knew that about 18% of students taking courses in the department were part-time students and that about 20% of the full-time students were working part-time as well. He also knew that Midland attracted some 22% of its undergraduates from out-of-state and that MU recruiters were particularly successful in metropolitan areas around the Midwest and the East Coast. Plus, Perkins had noted proudly, the campus had students from a dozen foreign countries. Bill, a country boy from Georgia, hoped he'd be able to reach all of his students, despite their different backgrounds and situations.

Today's colleges and universities are not well prepared to meet future demands [because] student populations are steadily graying. The baby boom is over and the pool of 18- to 24-year-olds is declining. By 1992 some 49% of higher education students will be 25 or over. Of these, 19% will be over 35. ... Teaching strategies have to change to accommodate the older student. The three words are time, place, and pace.

Time means when they study, like Saturdays or in the evening. These are busy people. They have families, they have job commitments. They want to call the shots; they don't want faculty to do it.

By place is meant where they study. They want some flexibility. Going to classrooms on a campus is not for many adult students. They won't do it.

Pace is just that, the pace at which they learn. They want to learn at their pace, not the instructor's.

Those three ideas are the most radical ideas in higher education you could ever talk about. They require looking at the student and asking when do you want to learn, how fast do you want to learn, and where do you want to learn. You make the choices and we'll provide the flexibility. That's pretty much unheard of except in certain new institutions that are popping up in the private sector.

— Jerold Apps, *Higher Education in a Learning Society* (San Francisco: Jossey-Bass, 1988), pp. 1-2.

The composition of your classes may well be similar. Statistics from the U.S. Department of Education for fall 1987 (the most recent federal report) show that while 65.7% of full-time first-year students were under 21 years old, 6.8% were 30 or older — and 38% of part-time students were 30+. Some 37% of students beginning their college studies in fall 1991 were planning on working to pay their expenses, 4.8% with full-time jobs.

There were slightly more women than men enrolled as undergrads in fall 1987 — 3,299,312 to 3,163,754. In fall 1990, 84.3% of first-year students were Euro-American, 9.6% were African-American, 2.9% were Asian-American, 1.5% were Mexican-American, and 1.3% were American Indian. Two-year institutions had the highest minority enrollment percentages, with 23.7% at private schools and 23% at public, while four-year institutions showed minority percentages of 16.9% (public) and 15.3% (private). In 1988 there were 361,000 foreign students, about 205,000 of them in undergraduate programs. The top countries represented were China, Taiwan, Japan, India, and the Republic of Korea.

Students with disabilities constitute important minorities: according to one source, 7.1% of first-year students have disabilities — vision (2.2%), hearing (0.9%), speech (0.5%), learning disabilities (2.2%), and health-related disabilities (1.3%). Another source sets the figure at 10.5%. Some students have economic disabilities: 17.2% of first-year students in fall 1991 estimated their parental income as less than $20,000. Finally, many students are first-generation collegians: 40% reported that their fathers hadn't attended college and 42.8% said the same of their mothers, while the percentages of students whose parents had no high school diploma were 11.8% (fathers) and 9.1% (mothers).(7)

These are just statistics, interesting numbers that provide merely a suggestion of the many differences among the more than 13 million students at our more than 3500 colleges and universities. Whatever the demographics may be for your classes, it's clear that the more you know about the backgrounds and abilities of your students, the more effective you'll be as their teacher.

If possible, survey students at the start of the semester. Ask for a show of hands to a series of questions: Who's studied phantasmagoric parapsychology? Who knows the principles of pataphysical science? Who can explain the differences between widgets and doohickeys? Or pass out index cards and ask students to give their name, phone number, major, previous courses in the field, and additional relevant background.

Another approach is to give a diagnostic test, with questions that touch upon the various areas you intend to cover in your course. A simple diagnostic: ask for definitions of key terms to be used in your course and examples illustrating those terms. Of course, you should make clear to your students the purpose of the diagnostic test. Students can be easily overwhelmed by such tests as they begin the course.

Just as you want to have a good idea of who your students

are, you should also be familiar with learning styles. This area of research has attracted a lot of attention in recent years. You can get a good introduction in *Learning Styles: Implications for Improving Educational Practices*, by Charles S. Claxton and Patricia H. Murrell (Washington DC: Association for the Study of Higher Education, 1987).

Once you've developed an idea of who your students are and established where you want to take them through your course, you should consider what methods and materials will best suit that journey.

Some of Bill's colleagues at Midland University administer the Learning and Study Strategies Inventory, developed by researchers with the Cognitive Strategies Project at the University of Texas-Austin,(29) or the Motivated Strategies for Learning Questionnaire, designed by researchers associated with the National Center for Research to Improve Postsecondary Teaching and Learning.(22, 23)

Once they've gotten an idea of how their students fit into the 21 MSLQ categories, they can choose more appropriate approaches to their material, as suggested in another NCRIPTAL publication, *Teaching Tips for Users of the Motivated Strategies for Learning Questionnaire (MSLQ)* (Ann Arbor: University of Michigan, 1989).

Since he was short on time, Bill decided to skim *Learning Strategies and Learning Styles*, ed. Ronald R. Schmeck (New York: Plenum, 1988), for a general introduction, then read *The Learning-Style Inventory* by David A. Kolb (Boston: McBer, 1985) and used "The Kolb Model Modified for Classroom Activities," by Marilla D. Svinicki and N.M. Dixon (*College Teaching,* 1987, 35:4, pp. 141-146) for ideas on better shaping his teaching methods and assignments to his students.

For another perspective, you might try reading about the Kolb model. (17, 27)

HOW CAN I FACILITATE LEARNING? METHODS AND TECHNIQUES

Lecture

> Our teachers never stop bawling into our ears, as though they were pouring water into a funnel, and our task is only to repeat what has been told to us. I should like the teacher to correct this practice, and right from the start, according to the capacity of the mind he has in hand, to begin putting it through its paces, making it taste things, choose them, and discern them by itself, sometimes clearing the way for it, sometimes letting it clear its own way.

These words come to us from 400 years ago, in the advice of Montaigne, who advocated a head that was "well-made" rather than "well-filled." To help make his point, Montaigne quoted Cicero: "The authority of those who teach is often an obstacle to those who want to learn."

Traditionally, instruction has often been in the form of a lecture, sometimes defined as "a process by which the notes of the lecturer are transferred to the notes of the students without passing through the mind of either." But a lecture doesn't need to be simply a mindless reading of material. And there are times when a lecture may be the most effective means of instruction — if done well. Jim W. Corder, an English professor at Texas Christian University, recently argued eloquently in the affirmative:(9)

> Arguments that lectures are pedagogically unsound are invalid because they are based only on bad lectures. ... We often don't examine what makes a lecture good or differentiate the good from the bad, so we wind up opposing *all* lectures.

Corder pointed out two advantages to lectures:

> First, at their best, they dramatize the creation of knowledge. ... Second, lectures can show the consequences of knowledge — show what comes of knowledge, how it can be used in ways not previously seen or guessed. Good lectures exemplify possibility. ...
>
> To suppose that all or most classes should be arenas for active or experiential learning is as simplistic as to suppose that all or most classes should be lecture classes. No method is right for everyone in all circumstances.

If you decide that lecturing would be the most effective means of teaching a certain segment of your course, you should be attentive to the following aspects:

- **Structure.** If you decide to read your material (Is that really the most effective method?), pay attention to syntax and punctuation. Often a sentence that works great on the printed page can be too long, complex, or stilted. Listeners, unlike readers, can't stop and run through a sentence a second or third time. Be aware particularly of long sentences, dependent clauses, and comments within parentheses or dashes. Compensate orally for visual clues: pause after each paragraph, and bridge between sections with transition phrases, such as "Next we consider ..." or "This brings us to ..." Better yet, prepare an outline on a transparency to display with an overhead projector.

- **Volume.** Too low and your students may have to strain to hear you. Too high and they may develop headaches or tune you out. Increase volume to emphasize something important or to make your students more attentive. For larger classes, you may be able to get a cordless microphone from your instructional media center. Also, you may find it useful to warm up your voice before class, like an actor or singer.

- **Articulation.** Pronounce your words carefully, but without exaggeration or affectation. Your articulation should help convey your meaning, not distract from it.

- **Pace.** Moderation is the key: neither so rapidly that you and your students tire out, nor so slowly that you bore them. Although listeners tend to find lecturers who speak more rapidly to be more competent and persuasive, you should bear in mind that your goal is to teach, not to impress. Slow down when presenting or explaining difficult material. Speed up to underline changes in content or mood or to make your students more attentive.

- **Pauses.** Use short pauses to emphasize something, to mark a shift in direction, to gather your thoughts, or to allow students a moment to reflect or react, or to finish noting what you've just said. Avoid the tendency to fill pauses with meaningless sounds ("ah," "um," "OK") — and the mechanical "Any questions?" or "Do you understand?"

- **Pitch.** Vary your pitch naturally. Listeners may interpret a monotone as a sign that you lack interest or confidence. But avoid a repetitive pattern of pitch which doesn't fit the meaning of your words; leave that delivery to broadcast journalists reading unfamiliar, prepared scripts. Concentrate on the meaning of your words, not the sound of your voice.

- **Body.** Make sure that your students can easily see you, not just disembodied head and hands above a podium. Use movement: gestures and motion visually supplement the aural, but nervous fidgeting, repetitive and meaningless gestures, and constant activity are distracting, while any motion may undermine your efforts to explain complex material.

- **Face.** Relax and let your face naturally express how you feel about your material and teaching in general. Many instructors feel that they should be reserved, serious, formal, impersonal; students may interpret their facial expressions as signals of boredom, disinterest, or even hostility.

- **Focus.** Look at your students whenever possible; make eye contact with each. Look at your notes only when necessary. If you look at the ceiling, out the window, or at the clock, your students will do likewise.

- **Appearance.** Remember that your clothing, hair, and makeup convey an image. Many students (and your colleagues?) believe that grooming reflects attitude. Should you dress up? Should you go casual? It's your decision, of course — but it's wise to remember that you're likely not totally free to choose.

Most instructors are aware that students don't always follow every single word; in fact, they may get lost for considerable lengths of time. Students may experience four kinds of mental lapses during a lecture, according to Mary Budd Rowe, a chemistry professor:(24)

- **Short-Term Memory Overloads.** If new ideas come too fast, short-term memory — the mental buffer zone for temporary information storage — may overflow. Researchers estimate it takes between five and 10 seconds to transfer information from short-term to long-term memory.

- **Momentary Misunderstandings.** If a student doesn't immediately grasp an idea, confusion results. The student must make sense of the new idea, fit it into what he or she already knows and understands, or it can't move into long-term memory.

- **Translation Troubles.** When instructors use terms other than those used in the text or previous lectures, students may have difficulty making the necessary translation. They may struggle to integrate familiar and unfamiliar terms, to determine what they mean.

- **Sidetracks.** Something is said that leads the student into another train of thought, distracting him or her from the lecture.

Rowe recommends a two-minute pause every eight to 12 minutes, to let students review their notes with each other, fill in missing material, clarify unclear concepts, and briefly discuss what they're learning. Short breaks not only lessen the damage of mental lapses, she says, but they also seem to help prevent them.

Three other strategies are helpful in minimizing mental lapses. Keep your terminology as consistent as possible. If you need to introduce new terms, put them on the board, an overhead, or a handout, and define them. When presenting a new idea, moving to another phase, or changing direction, try to make contextual connections: "Now, in the case of XYZ — which, as you recall, is a variant form of ABC used for ..."

Finally, a brief comment by Page Smith:(26)

> I must confess that my own attitude toward lecturing was deeply influenced by my experience in teaching Dante's *Divine Comedy* in a seminar. When I suggested to my students that they devise some modern hells for modern sins, two students in the seminar offered interesting hells for professors-who-neglected-their-students. They proposed that the professors be required to listen to lectures for all eternity. The only point of dispute between them was whether it would be worse torment for professors to have to listen to their own lectures or to those of an especially dull colleague. I have never been able to feel the same way about lecturing since.

Demonstration

Sometimes it may be most effective to provide a demonstration of a process, such as to solve a problem step-by-step. There are several essential points to keep in mind:

- Make sure that students can easily see the board, the overhead, or the lab table that you use for your demonstration. (An overhead is superior to the board, if only because you can face your students as you demonstrate.)

- Work through your demonstration at a pace that allows your students to follow, to take notes, to understand the process, and to formulate any questions.

- If you write on the board or an overhead, allow students time to copy your words of wisdom. Bear in mind that while you may have a 4' x 8' board or a series of transparencies with overlays, the students are limited to notebooks that are 8 1/2" x 11" or smaller. If you plan to fill large areas or multiple transparencies with your demonstration, you might want to mention this in advance, so they can plan better.

Questions

If you choose the route of show (demonstration) and tell (lecture), you should try to involve students through questions whenever possible. Sometimes instructors feel that they're allowing students plenty of opportunities to ask questions, while students feel quite differently.

It's not enough to end every few sentences with a quick "Any questions?" or "Do you understand?" before continuing. As a reviewer wrote in the margin of this manuscript,

'Do you understand?' is the *worst* question. Students are often embarrassed to say 'No.' They also know from experience (i.e., tests) that understanding isn't often a yes-no sort of process: they may understand enough to follow you, but not to use the information. If they say 'Yes,' can you be sure they understand as well as they should? If they say 'No,' you still don't know *what* they don't understand. If this question is a filler, silence is better. If you really want to know if students understand, ask questions that require them to demonstrate their knowledge or lack of it.

When you ask for questions:

- Give your students time to reflect on what you've said.
- Scan their faces for signs that things may not be completely clear.
- If you've made several points, you might ask for questions about each, to break the material into more manageable chunks.

It's often more effective to ask a few review questions from time to time. Keep in mind the following techniques:

- Start with easier questions, then work up to the more difficult ones.
- Ask questions that are relevant and productive.
- Vary your question types and structures.
- Keep your tone exploratory, not threatening. Questions should be a way of assessing the results of the learning process, results that depend on the instructor as well as the students.
- Phrase your questions in as few words as possible.
- Give your students sufficient time. Instructors often feel uncomfortable with moments of silence, and research has shown that they often allow students too little time to answer questions. Try to simulate the reaction process: mentally repeat the question (as students might in order to absorb it), think about the answer (at their speed), then imagine phrasing the answer.
- Move out toward the class, among your students if possible.
- Call on a student by name — and avoid establishing patterns. (The laws of random probability shouldn't favor students who sit in front or students who get good grades, for example.)
- Repeat the question, but not every time and certainly not immediately.
- Offer some sort of a clue.

- If you allow adequate time for answers and there are none, reshape the question, but avoid changing it more than necessary. It can be very frustrating for a student to be close to offering a response, only to have the instructor substantially change the question.

- Answer the question yourself — but only as a last resort. This is an admission of failure, which easily undermines student participation.

Then, when your students answer your questions, there are a few points to keep in mind:

- Make sure the other students hear and understand the answer.

- Acknowledge the answer. Not just mechanically ("Yes," "OK," "Good," "Uh-huh"), but with at least a brief comment.

- Correct wrong answers. Encourage your students, but not by accepting answers indiscriminately.

- Bring your students into the answers. When you get a response, try returning it to your students: "What do you think about that?" This works best with responses that express opinions or value judgments, but it can also work for right-wrong answers.

- Build on the answers. Follow up an answer with a question or two. Don't aim all your follow-up questions at the student who gave the answer, or your questioning may be perceived as a punishment. Probe the class.

Lectures and demonstrations can be efficient ways of conveying material, but there are other methods that are often more effective — particularly since you want instruction to be more than merely a transmission of information or a display of skills.

What's really exciting is when both instructor and students learn, from the sharing and interaction of ideas, in a symbiotic relationship. As a colleague explains it, "It's by learning with a teacher that students develop their potential; it's by learning with students that teachers remain questioning and alive — and often how they come upon their best ideas for innovative research."

Lectures (a.k.a. "show and tell") tend to be just a one-way street, as E. Glassman observes:(12)

> I realized that when I lectured I was the one who learned the most. I was the one whose thinking skills were enhanced and whose creativity was stimulated. I played the active learning role: the students' was passive, often consisting of listening and trying to decipher what I was saying during the lecture.

Instructors may feel compelled to use teacher-centered methods such as lectures or demonstrations so they can cover more material. But they should carefully consider the following remarks by Jean MacGregor, associate director of the Washington Center for Improving the Quality of Under-graduate Education at Evergreen State College:(18)

> Learners are diverse individuals whose understanding of reality is shaped by their gender, race, class, age, and cultural experience. Therefore, teaching is woefully inadequate if it is construed as an enterprise of "transmission" or "coverage." And learning is woefully limited if it is thought of as simply an exercise in "receiving" and "reflecting."

Toward More Active Student Involvement

There are many ways to involve your students more actively in their learning experiences. The choices depend on your particular circumstances, which include the subject, class dynamics, your personality, and logistics. Think of active learning experiences as expeditions into the wilderness. Choose an activity, prepare appropriately — then take a chance!

Class Discussion

This is perhaps the most basic form of class participation. In fact, it's easy to be casual about discussions. But if you don't put energy and interest into them, why should your students? You may be very familiar with class discussions, but you should take a few moments to read "Discussion Teaching Method," an article by William M. Welty, director of the Center for Faculty Development at Pace University (*Change: The Magazine of Higher Learning*, July/August 1989, pp. 41-49).

To keep a discussion going, John H. Clarke, director of the Learning Cooperative at the University of Vermont in Burlington, offers the following suggestions:(8)

- Keep a visual record of student contributions: jot them on the board or a transparency.
- Use your record — to link contributions, to compare, to provide closure.
- Convert student questions to statements, then solicit other opinions.
- Convert student opinions to questions to involve reticent classmates.
- Turn questions of interpretation back to the group.
- Use student assertions to draw examples from others.
- Ask questions that encourage inference, prediction, analogy, or synthesis.

- If the discussion lags, convert the last student contribution to a new question or assertion.

- When a student makes an important contribution, label it with his or her name — the Jane Theory or the Mike Question — and use it as a pivot or anchor for further discussion.

When Bill used the board to record student contributions, he quickly became aware of some important factors involved in the dynamics of his classes. Although he'd anticipated problems in getting his students to participate, one problem surprised him — a handful of students tended to dominate the discussions, discouraging the others.

So, Bill changed his style slightly. First, after asking a question, he paused a little longer before calling on any student. Then, he chose one of the last students to raise a hand, although he realized he was risking frustrating the more eager students. He also tried to ask questions that allowed for several answers, so he could involve more than one student per question and encourage divergent thinking.

At times, though, some students simply spoke out. Then, rather than be overly strict about protocol, Bill simply acknowledged their contributions, then called on other students to comment. Occasionally after class, he sought out one of the more dominant participants and quietly asked him (they were usually males) or her to stay for a moment. He then thanked the student for being so interested and enthusiastic, but pointed out that it was important to have everyone in the class feel free to participate in discussions. One of the more dominant students got upset, but the others more or less graciously agreed to be less aggressive. Bill didn't really feel comfortable with that way of handling the problem, but he was relieved that the aggressive students generally allowed the others a chance. He resolved to talk with his colleagues about the problem and ask for suggestions. After all, he realized, what works in one situation may flop in another.

Group Discussion or Problem-Solving

Although discussion involving your entire class can be effective, it's usually better to divide your students into smaller groups, with three to five in each. Depending on the subject and class composition and dynamics, you may decide to group students according to interests, abilities, or personalities. You might try the 12-item questionnaire that Thomas E. Muller, a business professor at McMaster University, has developed to form "balanced" groups.(21)

Make sure that you set a time limit, clearly define what you expect of the group activity, and indicate what sort of follow-up you want: you may want to have each group report to the class or have each student write out as homework a summary of the what happened in his or her group. Then move around among the groups to encourage participation of every student and to answer any procedural or factual questions that might arise. It may seem obvious, but if you expect group reports you should allow adequate time: nothing is more frustrating than to have a great discussion abruptly ended by the clock.

There's a growing effort nationally to involve students more actively in the learning process through collaborative and cooperative learning, which emphasize small work groups. Advocates maintain that not only do students learn more in groups than individually, but they also benefit emotionally. A good introduction is *A Guidebook for Cooperative Learning*, by Dee Dishon and Pat O'Leary (Holmes Beach FL: Learning Publications, 1984). Faculty interested in exploring the advantages of discussion and group work might read *Classroom Communication: Collected Readings for Effective Discussion and Questioning*, edited by Maryellen Weimer and Rose Ann Neff (Madison WI: Magna Publications, 1989).

Many instructors find small groups difficult. It's like a three-ring circus: you need to organize more flexibly, motivate the performers, set it all in motion, then step out of the spotlight and be everywhere at the same time. It may be useful to consult *Small Group Teaching: A Trouble-Shooting Guide* by Richard G. Tiberius (Toronto: Ontario Institute for Studies in Education, 1990).

But, as a colleague insists, many instructors find it easier to work with small groups than with whole classes — "less of a show, fewer machines to maneuver, less prep, at least after the first few times." But, she points out, "planning for small groups means preparing a smorgasbord of options, paths, and questions, which requires multi-analysis of materials." Whether you find it easier or more difficult, you owe it to your students — and to yourself — to explore the possibilities of small groups and cooperative learning.

Debate

This method may be most appropriate when there are two sides to an issue, but it can be valuable when there are several perspectives, since gray areas challenge critical thinking. This activity is generally best suited for smaller groups, where more students can get involved. You may want to keep track of the debate by listing on the board the points made by the parties. Once again, a follow-up can be valuable; you might ask students to take notes, then write up a summary or a position paper for homework.

Role Play

This sort of activity is often more difficult, since it requires a certain theatricality. It's also more difficult to involve a lot of students. But it can be a logical choice in foreign languages, for example, or an interesting change of pace in the social sciences, where students can act out attitudes, historical figures, literary characters, philosophers, and so on.

One instructor has a method of organizing role plays that allows her to maintain control but without intruding. She prepares slips of paper describing each role, assigns a few roles to begin, then hands out others one by one according to the flow of action. This "progressive playwriting" lets her shape the activity as it develops, by her choice of roles, and then stop it at any point, by not handing out any more roles.

Simulations and Cases

This sort of "real-life story problem" activity can stimulate and challenge a class. It may be most effective at the end of a unit, as a review that requires students to apply the knowledge they've acquired. Although this can be a class activity, it's generally more effective in smaller groups. With simulations and cases, follow-up is crucial: What conclusion did each group reach? How? Make sure that the students understand that *outcome* may be less important and less informative than *process*.

If cases sound like an interesting possibility, you might start by reading *Teaching and the Case Method* by C. Roland Christensen and Abby J. Hansen (Boston MA: Harvard Business School, 1987).

What Else?

There are other methods; your colleagues may have suggestions and there are shelves of journals and books that can provide more options. Cynthia Weston and P.A. Cranton provide a comprehensive and organized overview of the range of methods in their article, "Selecting Instructional Strategies" (*The Journal of Higher Education*, May/June 1986, pp. 259-288).

Just keep in mind your goals — both primary and secondary — and the abilities and dynamics of your class. And remember the words of that anonymous conference session participant: "I don't know if it'll work, but we'll just try it."

ASSESSING STUDENT CHANGE

When you consider your methods of facilitating learning, think also about your ways of assessing the results. Focus on the questions that serve as guidelines for your course: "How do you want your students to **change?**" "**What** do you want them to **learn?**" The next question is logical: "How can your students show you what they've learned and how they've changed?"

The primary traditional means of assessment is the exam. The best word of advice here, as in so many aspects of teaching: make sure it fits. Use exams only if they are carefully designed and appropriate to your goals. Supplement testing with other forms of assessment. Be sensitive to exam anxiety and its effects. To alleviate anxiety, Bill wrote out a series of sample final exam items and distributed copies to his students.

Finally, you may want to have your students grade you on your exam effort. You might simply attach a short evaluation form to the exam, asking such questions as:

- Did the content you expected to see appear on this exam?
- Were the questions clear? List the number(s) of any question(s) that seemed unclear.
- Are you satisfied with your responses to most of the questions?

The evaluation should contain space for a grade and additional comments.(19)

Since many students are naturally reluctant to criticize, for fear of possible "grade retaliation," it's wise to have them separate their evaluation from their exam when they turn them in, to form two piles (with evaluations face down). When Bill followed this procedure for the first time, he noticed that several students, when turning in their evaluations, shuffled the others in the pile. Although he believes that their precaution was unnecessary, it seemed to reassure them, so he now makes a practice of periodically shuffling the stack of evaluations as students turn them in.

A good alternative to exams, in many disciplines: projects. Of course, there's the term paper, in a variety of forms — a comprehensive "thought piece," a detailed analysis, a research article. You might ask students to find, read, and analyze journal articles on a certain topic. You could have them create their own exam, a switch that lets them show how well they understand not only the material but also its relevance. Don't hesitate to experiment: just focus on your course goals and go with the creative flow!

If you have first-year students, you may want to consider some advice on assignments offered by Bette LaSere Erickson and Diane Weltner Strommer.(11) They caution against assigning term papers and projects as "especially ill-suited" for inexperienced students:

> They ask students who know little about a subject to identify topics of special interest prematurely and require in-depth study before students know what resources could or

should be consulted. Attempts to provide the directions and guidance freshmen need turn into impossible tasks because we cannot supervise what are essentially independent study projects for twenty or thirty or more students. The most serious reservation about these assignments, however, is that they do nothing to encourage freshmen to study on a day-to-day basis.

Erickson and Strommer recommend various alternatives:

- Shorter papers, four or five pages, less ambitious than the typical term paper or project.

- Assignments with focus, not simply general advice, "Think about this for next time."

- Assignments that produce something tangible — a solution to a problem, a list,

- Outline, a paragraph, a newspaper clipping.

- Activities that promote understanding and thinking.

- A variety of assignments, to appeal to different learning styles.

- Frequent, short assignments to help your students keep up and study regularly. You don't need to grade all these assignments; focus on some in class discussions, skim through others to check for misunderstandings, and designate some as practice exams.

For many courses, particularly with smaller classes, you may want to assign homework. Although students may complain about frequent assignments, these can help motivate students to prepare regularly — an especially important consideration with first-year students or in required non-major courses. Assignments also lessen the weight of exams, reducing test anxiety. Major drawbacks: grading assignments can be time-consuming and exhausting, students also have a greater opportunity to avail themselves of resources that can distort your assessment of their learning (i.e., they may cheat).

Grades

Finally, as the last aspect of assessment (but definitely not the bottom line): grades.

> Grade: "An inadequate report of an inaccurate judgment by a biased and variable judge of the extent to which a student has attained an undefined level of mastery of an unknown proportion of an indefinite material."(10)

That's a depressing thought, especially since most faculty are obligated to give grades of some sort.

Most faculty use either straight percentages or a curve. But here again, conventional methods are not necessarily sound. In their study of grading, Gerald S. Hanna and William E. Cashin reached the following conclusion:(13)

> Each of the common bases for assigning college grades — *percentage* and *class-curve* grading — has only limited meaning and lacks a sound rationale. Neither satisfies the major criteria for student grading systems. *Anchor measures* enable the advantages of norm-referenced grading to be achieved without introducing the evils of class-curve grading. ... They, therefore, are recommended for use in assigning college grades.

An anchor measure may offer the most reliable basis for grading systems. An anchor measure is "a device with which one can judge or 'take bearings' of the status of a class." If several sections of the same course, all following the same syllabus and using the same text, take the same final exam, that exam can be used to reveal differences in achievement among the sections, allowing instructors to adjust grade distributions within each section accordingly.

But if there aren't any suitable data to allow you to anchor the grades for your students, what do you do?

Many instructors devise some sort of compromise between straight percentages and a curve. Some will anchor their system by comparing the scores of certain students whose grades in the course have been relatively stable. Of course, there's no such anchor for the first several grades or if there are few or no students whose grades offer reliable stability. The best alternative may be simply to give grades frequently, so the weight of the final grade is spread out, students have greater motivation throughout the term, and there are less likely to be surprises at the end.

Bill always returns tests and major graded assignments before class, as students arrive. He allows his students enough time to review their work, then puts up an overhead transparency with the following information —

- mean grade: 81.3%
- median grade: 83%
- range of numerical grades for each letter grade and number of students receiving each letter grade:

92-100	A	6
89-91	A-/B+	4
82-88	B	8
79-81	B-/C+	5
70-78	C	6
60-69	D	2
0-59	F	1

He then asks if anyone has questions about the *material*. Students with questions about their *grades* must talk with Bill before or after class. But since every student knows how he or she fits into the class profile for each test or assignment, Bill rarely needs to deal with the matter of grades. (And he then files the grade distribution information along with a copy of the test or assignment, just in case questions arise later.)

Essay items are particularly tough to grade. How can you make that chore easier?

First, when you construct the essay question or topic, imagine what points you'd like the students to make in their essay and calculate the breakdown. Sure, it's simpler to just decide on five essays at 20% each. But then, when you have to grade them, you pay for that simplicity. If you consider the material to be covered on the test as consisting of a certain number of elements, you can weight these elements according to their importance and then construct questions or topics. It may violate expectations of symmetry to use items worth 13, 22, 18, 23, 16, and 8 points, but it certainly makes grading easier.

It's also vital to explain to your students your grading criteria. Some students learned in high school to impress teachers with rhetoric, while others were successful in giving just the facts, however crudely organized an expressed. If you know what you want, you should be able to make your expectations clear to your students.

A few days before a big exam, Bill likes to put a sample item on a transparency. He then talks it through with his class, as if they were one collective student taking the exam. They all suggest points to be made, discuss the relative merits, then organize the elements of their answer. Bill then weaves the pieces together into a straightforward answer, choosing his words with care but not meticulously, occasionally "rewriting" himself. He then plays the role of the teacher, grading the elements as organized on the transparency. The students understand that what matters in their essays is substance, yet they gain a better appreciation for the way that the substance is expressed.

Finally, when you grade essays, you should consider establishing a curve. Some faculty avoid using curves, for various reasons — fear that they contribute to grade inflation (as if one instructor could have that great an impact on a problem that's been around for decades), that they suggest an "easy mark," that they seem too subjective.

But Bill finds that curving makes sense. After grading the essays and calculating a percentage, he looks at the paper with the highest grade, any F or low D papers, and a paper receiving the median grade. If those grades seem appropriate for the particular students and for their performance, then Bill follows straight percentages. But if he feels that the top paper was better than the grade, that the bottom papers don't really deserve such a low grade, or that the median really should have been higher, he adjusts the grade profile slightly, by perhaps 3%-5%. He never gives his students lower grades than they earned; he simply admits that his test was perhaps too easy and he chalks it up as a learning experience.

Finally, keep a record of your grading behavior for each test or assignment. What elements did you expect in each essay? How detailed did you want the essays to be? How flexible were you? What alternative elements did you accept? In which areas were your students particularly weak? Such a record allows you to more knowledgeably and confidently deal with any students who might later come to you with questions about a grade. Of course, you also have a head start on constructing tests and assignments for the next time you teach that course.

Many instructors worry too much about giving grades. They fear gaining a reputation as Old Softie or Heart of Stone — or that student evaluations will hurt their chances at receiving tenure. Yes, some students may be obsessed with grades, but don't get caught up in their anxiety. Sure, the GPA is important, but your single course grade shouldn't make the difference between the ideal employment and just another job, between grad school and the cold, cruel world. Some students may not understand or accept it, but you're far more important in how you help your students develop than in what grades you give them. As for any concern about whether you should bend your principles in order to get better student evaluations, that's a question of knowing your territory — and your conscience.

CHOOSING MATERIALS

TEXT(S)

When choosing materials for your course, there are two extremes: choose a textbook or create your own materials. With the former you generally sacrifice freedom to pursue your specific goals with your particular students as you would like; but the latter decision may entail a great deal of time and effort, sometimes unnecessarily. Furthermore, remember that authors, reviewers, editors, and marketers have spent untold hours and dollars to create accurate and interesting products. Students often don't react as well to home-made materials simply because they lack professional touches.

The best strategy is often to choose one or several textbooks, then mix and match sections, supplementing with other materials. One word of caution: expense. Instructors eager to expose their students to an intellectual smorgasbord may forget that textbooks can be very costly. Sometimes a good alternative is to place certain materials on reserve, so students can read them at the library. But remember that many students have jobs or careers, difficult schedules, family responsibilities, and/or disabilities that might make reserve readings inconvenient or even impossible.

How do you choose a textbook? Glenn Ross Johnson, former director of the Center for Teaching Excellence at Texas A & M University, suggests that instructors consider the following criteria:(15)

- Authors: knowledgeable in the field?
- Reviews: favorable?
- Topic emphasis and sequence: appropriate and adaptable to your course objectives?
- Content: accurate and current, sufficient details, level appropriate to the background of your average student?
- Bias: free of national, racial, sexual, and other bias?
- Concepts, principles, generalizations: appropriate and clearly developed?
- Explanations: clear and succinct?
- Reading level: appropriate for your average student?
- Table of contents, preface, index, appendices: adequate and useful?
- Titles, headings, subheadings: helpful for visualizing the organization of the content?
- Summaries, review questions: appropriate, leading students to generalize, apply, evaluate, and think critically?
- Sources, bibliography: adequately documented, appropriate, current?
- Illustrations, graphs, tables, maps, charts: accurate, clear, appropriately located and labeled?
- Format, layout, type: clear and interesting?
- Price: reasonable for the use you intend?
- Construction: convenient size and weight, durable?
- Instructor's manual: supplemental materials, teaching aids, review and test questions, strategy suggestions?
- Supplemental materials: suitable for the text and your situation?
- Assessment: test items or other devices for evaluating learning and assigning grades?

In selecting your textbook(s), don't go with only what you know. Sure, maybe it was the greatest book in the world when you were taking that intro course a few (!?) short years ago. Times change — and fast. Ask your colleagues. Keep up with new publications through your journals and announcements in *The Chronicle of Higher Education.* Request review copies of every relevant book that appears on the market. Take the time to skim every volume, making notes about coverage, quality, strengths, and weaknesses. Keep a file of reviews for each text.

A recent development has been the customized text. Instructors can compile readings from various sources, then have a photocopy service compile the readings and make them available to your students. Here again, though, you should pay attention to cost. The legal decision March 28, 1991, in *Basic Books v. Kinko's Graphics Corporation,* will make copy services very wary about reproducing any text, regardless of size, without paying royalties, which should make custom texts considerably more expensive. Also, unless there's a market for used copies of your custom text, it could actually cost your students even more than traditional textbooks. (Of course, your students will all want to keep their copies of your book forever, but some may be forced to be pragmatic.)

If you're accustomed to seeing photocopied anthologies substitute for texts, guess again. A March 1991 federal Circuit Court of Appeals ruled that, far from being protected by "fair use for educational purposes" doctrine, the practice violates publishers' copyrights unless you get permission in advance. Gaining that permission can be a time-consuming and expensive process, since you have to write to each copyright holder and be prepared to pay royalties. ...

For a modest fee plus any required royalties, two companies will do your work for you: the Anthologies Permission Service and the National Association of College Book Stores. Some professors may simply prefer to ignore the interpretation of the law and continue to pass out [photocopied] course materials — provided they can find somebody willing to risk reproducing the clippings.

Better seek the counsel of your institution's attorney for the latest developments in the course-packet business before you discard placing materials on reserve at campus libraries or requiring your students to purchase a text or texts.

— Debra E. Blum, "Securing Copyright Permission," *The Chronicle of Higher Education,* Sept. 11, 1991, pp. A 19-20.

OTHER RESOURCES

A custom text may be too ambitious for new faculty. So you
choose the best text available, then make "patches." These ancillary materials may consist of short readings, time lines, diagrams, specialized glossaries, guides for difficult readings,
sample test questions — whatever might make the text fit your
course better. Some you prepare before the term, some as you en-
counter needs throughout the term. And whatever you do, do it
with care: make sure your materials are helpful, accurate, and
clear. As Horace said of his poetry, "I have built a monument
more lasting than bronze." Remember: your materials are not
only for your students, but for the world — including those who
will review your tenure dossier.

Consider human resources as well. It may be very beneficial
to invite outsiders to your class.

- Invite guests who can make valuable contributions to
  your class, through their expertise or perspectives that
  differ from yours. You may want to present together: students can be stimulated and informed by a lively exchange between two experts — especially if they
  disagree.

- Prepare your guests with information about your course
  and your students.

- Prepare your students: tell them about your guest and
  encourage them to think of questions to ask.

- Use the contributions of the guest in subsequent classes:
  refer to them in discussions and relate them to new
  material.

Don't limit your consideration of instructional resources to
the classroom. What outside resources could contribute to the
learning experience? Would it be appropriate to take a field trip
to a museum, a business or government facility, a movie, a lecture or other presentation, another class? Would it be useful to
display student work outside the classroom in some way — publication, demonstration, exhibition?

Our students have been characterized as the "MTV Generation." Whatever the extent of truth in that statement, you
should consider the dimensions of your classroom environment.
When you present something, do you automatically put it on the
board, even though you've prepared it thoroughly in advance?
Do you tend to walk into class with five pounds of handouts?

If so, then you may want to add some pizzazz. Visit your
campus instructional development center for some tips on using
audiovisual materials. Sometimes it's really true that a picture
is worth a thousand words — and it's certainly easier to prepare

charts and diagrams in advance than to throw them up on the board in midsentence. If you use AV materials appropriately, you'll find that students understand better and pay closer attention.

But avoid overkill or misuse. Some instructors go wild with AV materials, building up a dangerous (and exhausting) dependency on colors and graphics. Don't depend on content to grab and hold their interest, but don't work so hard to interest them that you lose sight of your purpose. In short, aim at the ideal advocated by Horace— *utile et dulce*, mixing useful and enjoyable.

YOUR COURSE OUTLINE

ORGANIZATION/STRUCTURE/POLICIES

Once you've planned your course — what you want to do, why, and how — draw up an outline for your students. Pedagogically, this is a good idea, and in terms of your personnel dossier, it's essential.

Student evaluation forms virtually always contain questions about course organization, which can be helpful in preparing your outline.

- How effective was the instructor in making clear the goals and objectives of this course?

- How clear were the goals, aims, and requirements of this course?

- How well organized was the instructor?

Your course outline is your students' first impression of your organization. It should generally include the following items:

1. Course Number and Title, Credits, Semester, Class Time and Location

2. Your Name, Office Location, Office Hours, Office Phone

You might choose to provide your home phone number as well. If so, however, it would be wise to indicate hours during which students may call you. For some it's a sign that you really accept calls at home. To others it sends a message that you don't want to be bothered at 3 a.m. (Students tend to have unusual schedules, and the questions that bother them most sometimes come at the worst times.)

3. Course Description

Give students, in just a few sentences, reassurance that they belong in your course or warning that this isn't what they expected. Descriptions in your institution's catalog may serve as a model. Make sure that your description matches the official description: students have the right to expect what's promised in the official course description.

You may also want to indicate your expectations of student

level and background. Some faculty avoid specifics, for fear of scaring off students and risking cancellation of their course. Others believe that their courses should be open to all, regardless of level and background. Check with your department about policy and with your colleagues about practices.

4. Course Goals

Where are you going in the course? How will students be better because of a semester with you? They may already be enrolled in your course, but you still have to sell them, because they should share responsibility for their learning. Be as specific as you can for your subject matter, without burying your students with a comprehensive and detailed list.

5. Attendance Policy

Is attendance required? For every session or just for certain selected sessions? If you require attendance, how will you encourage students? Frequent written assignments to be collected? Pop quizzes? A grade for attendance? Will you excuse any absences?

6. Assignment Deadlines and Policy

How strictly will you enforce deadlines? Set policies that are practical and that you can adhere to fairly for all. And remember: it's easier to start out tough and loosen up than to start lenient and then have to clamp down.

7. Readings

Make sure that your students understand the difference between "required" and "recommended" — and make sure that you don't expect them to read materials that you only recommend. You should probably keep your recommendations brief, so as not to overwhelm your students, as some may feel obliged to read everything. If you want to suggest a large number of materials, it may be better to distribute a series of lists at intervals throughout the semester. This can be particularly effective if you find that some students are weak in certain areas; it's easy to modify your recommendations to include background (remedial) readings.

8. Guidelines for Succeeding in Course

Indicate that you intend to have lectures or discussions or group projects or written assignments or whatever. What preparation will you expect for each class? What will be your primary focus — general concepts? details? facts? analysis? How would you suggest that your students study? What should they do if they feel inadequately prepared for a particular unit of material?

9. Policy on Academic Integrity

Students are often fuzzy about what's allowed and what's not. You should cite the text of your institution's policy; if there isn't any, formulate your own. The policy should include plagiarism as well as in-class cheating.

Example: "Plagiarism: the deliberate use of any outside source without proper acknowledgment. 'Outside source' means any work, published or unpublished, by any person other than the student."

What's the institutional procedure when cheating or plagiarism is suspected? What are the penalties? Be prepared to enforce the policy and make sure that your students understand your position.

During the course, make it clear when you are allowing or encouraging cooperation and teamwork. If you let your students use their texts or notes for a test, make sure that they understand the rules of the game.

Try to anticipate ethical questions. For example, what if a student uses for your course an assignment submitted in a similar form for another course? Can students share notes or research? Remember: we don't all share the same assumptions about these matters.

Finally, understand that if you suspect dishonesty your reaction can lead to legal complications. For example, read the Opinion piece by Robert L. Wolke, emeritus professor of chemistry and founding director of the Office of Faculty Development at the University of Pittsburgh, in *The Chronicle of Higher Education*, May 15, 1991, and the series of follow-up letters June 12, June 26, and July 3.

In brief, when he suspected a student of cheating on an exam, Wolke suspended his grade, apprised him of the charges, got a written statement from the proctor, and notified the dean, following the prescribed university procedures. Wolke says that the student's father, a lawyer, phoned and wrote letters, requesting copies of all evidence and threatening to sue. The university attorney, concerned about legal complications and institutional liability, advised Wolke to drop the matter and give the student a suitable grade. Frustrated, Wolke sent the dean a retraction, together with the mathematical calculations to justify his suspicions. His report concluded that "there is still a perfectly good one in 29 trillion trillion chance" that the similarities in exam answers were a coincidence. Wolke then gave the student an A+. "The moral for students?" he asks rhetorically. "If you have a lawyer handy, go ahead and cheat like crazy. Universities are pushovers." The moral for faculty? Draw your own conclusions.

EVALUATION GUIDELINES

How will you know how well your students are learning? Class participation? Written assignments? Quizzes? Tests?

Projects? Journals? Which activities do you intend to grade? How? How much will each activity or category count toward the final grade? If you give numerous homework assignments or a series of quizzes, will you drop a few of the lowest grades?

Since this aspect of a course is generally of paramount importance to students, you should be clear about what you expect of them. Make sure, however, that they — and you — understand and remember that learning is not simply a question of grades.

A final question here: What about extra credit? Students may not ask this question at the start of the term, but you should be prepared for it as the weeks pass. There are various advantages and disadvantages.

advantages of exta credit

- It allows students the opportunity to explore specific areas in greater depth.

- It may promote more individual instructor-student relationships.

- It can increase motivation.

- It provides "grade insurance" for the weak and the worried, as well as for serious illness or other problems.

disadvantages of extra credit

- It encourages students to confuse *quality* and *quantity*, which undermines their efforts.

- It may result in inflated, misleading grades. There's a difference between an A for A-level work and an A for B-level work supplemented by extra credit.

- It tends to shift students' attention from course content and class participation to extra credit projects.

- It adds to your work and it can be an administrative nightmare.

What's your concept of grades? A reward? If so, then extra credit makes sense. An indication of ability? Then extra credit would undermine the accuracy of those grades. A simplified and powerful form of feedback? You need to determine how extra credit supports what you're doing in your course.

If you decide to allow extra credit, here are a few recommendations:

- Maintain your focus. This is essential. Extra credit should be aimed at your course goals. Students can do additional problems or readings, with a report on each.

- Return extra credit work promptly, with feedback.

- Set a deadline for extra credit. Students should know

their grade status and act to remedy any bad situation before the final week.

- Outline the ground rules. Some instructors refuse to allow extra credit to rescue a failing student or raise a D to a C.

- Establish standards. Is a mediocre effort better than none at all, especially as it probably reduces the time and energy spent on required work?

- Determine the weight of the task. Don't treat extra credit work subjectively, in terms of "brownie points" or a "halo effect." What will be the percentage impact on the final grade?

- Work with each student interested in extra credit, if possible, to set guidelines. The students will benefit more from their extra work, you'll build a better relationship with the individual students. ... and you're also less likely to receive work done for another course or even by another student.

A MAP: YOUR SYLLABUS

The syllabus should serve as a map for your journey through the semester. It should provide enough detail to direct your students, but not so much that they feel overly programmed. Think of your role as that of a tour guide: you want your schedule to indicate the major sights and activities, but allow freedom to explore side roads according to the interests and needs of your clients, serendipity, fate, and human elements.

Your syllabus should indicate exams and major deadlines. You should outline the principal units of the course: what you intend to cover week by week, maybe even session by session. For further suggestions, consult the guide by Malcolm A. Lowther, Joan S. Stark, and Gretchen G. Martens, *Preparing Course Syllabi for Improved Communication* (Ann Arbor: NCRIPTAL 1989).

Finally, consider the advice offered by Howard Altman, director of the Center for Faculty and Staff Development at the University of Louisville:(2)

> Since the course syllabus becomes a written legal covenant between the instructor and the students in the course, each syllabus should end with a caveat of the following sort: "The above schedule and procedures in this course are subject to change in the event of extenuating circumstances." This caveat protects the instructor and department if changes in the syllabus need to be made once the course is underway.

Welcome to the '90s!

As an example of a course guide, here's what Bill prepared for one of his courses:

Botany and Applied Ecology 311:
Introduction to Applied Ecology

Instructor:
> A. Wilmot (Bill) Campion
> 435 Greene Hall M W F 12:30-1:30 T R 9:00-10:00
> 637-8245 (office)
> 624-7713 (home: evenings between 7 and 10, please)

Term:
Spring 1992

Time and Place:
> Lecture M W 1:50-2:40 213 Mendel Hall
> Lab/Quiz F 1:50-2:40 Sites to be announced

Credits:
3 (an additional one-credit option is available to B&AE majors performing a course-related independent study project

Prerequisites:
> For B&AE majors — B&AE 101, 102
> For non-majors — any introductory biological science course

Teaching Assistants:
To be selected and introduced

Course Description:
> Botany 311 will introduce you to "the science of community" — "the study of the interrelationships of organisms and their environments" — and to the role of applied ecology in environmental management today. In a larger sense, this course will introduce you to a philosophical world view that says to us, "I am a part of my environment and my environment is a part of me."

Course Goals:
Botany 311 has two distinct yet compatible goals:

- to explain the technical tools and econo/social setting of the applied ecologist today;

- to elucidate the concept of "ecological awareness" — the realization that the community to which each of us belongs includes soil, water, air, plants, animals, and people — and the corollary concept, "ecological conscience" — a will and a way to protect the health, integrity, stability, and beauty of our humanity-land community.

Texts:
Odum, E. Laurence, *Introduction to Applied Ecology* (Garden City NY: Hill & Dale, 1991), $39.95, University Book Store.

Campion, A. Wilmot, "The Ecology of the Chesapeake Bay," Chesapeake Bay Commission Technical report #26 (Baltimore MD, 1990), $4, Speedo Copy Service.

Phloem, Ruth, "Identifying State Flora," Midland University B&AE Department Bulletin #16 (Midland ST, 1987), $4, Speedo Copy Service.

<u>Materials and Equipment</u>:
Standard field notebook, clipboard, hand magnifying glass, tweezers, field clothing (including waterproof footgear).
<u>Recommended Readings</u>:
Stamen, Charles, *Memoirs of a Field Ecologist* (Harper's Ferry WV: National Park Service Press, 1989).
Leopold, Aldo, *A Sand County Almanac* (New York: Ballantine, 1986).
Schoenfeld, Clay, *Everybody's Ecology*, 2nd edition (Cranbury NJ: A.S. Barnes & Co., 1989).
Hendee, John, *et al., Wilderness Management* (Washington DC: GPO, 1980).
<u>Suggested Readings</u>:
See attached bibliography.
<u>Term Paper</u>:
A lab report on your plant inventory of your assigned study plot on the Midland Lagoon littoral.
<u>Exams</u>:
Four pop quizzes during the quarter. (Typical question: "Briefly explain the substance and impact of Section 102(2)(C), 1969 National Environmental Policy Act.")
Two-hour essay/multiple-choice final. (Typical question: "The 1985 State Water Resources Management Act bans timber cutting within how many feet of the shoreline of all navigable waters? (a) 50, (b) 100, (c) 200, (d) 300, (e) none of the above.")
<u>Attendance Policy</u>:
I believe I'm reasonable, but I want to prepare you for the real world, so attendance is required, both for lectures and for lab/quiz sections. However, I understand absences can be inevitable. If you feel you have a valid excuse, come talk with me. You're allowed two unexcused absences; each additional absence will lower your course grade 1%.
If you miss a scheduled exam, you must arrange with me to make it up. If you have a legitimate excuse, there won't be any penalty. If you miss a pop quiz without an acceptable excuse, you'll receive a grade of 0 and the 1% penalty. If you turn in your term paper late without an acceptable excuse, you'll be penalized 1% for each day late.
<u>Policy on Academic Integrity</u>:
I'll enforce the policies laid down in Section IV, Subsection A, *The Midland University Student Handbook*.
<u>My Expectations</u>:
I don't grade on a curve. Everybody who earns an A will get an A; everybody who goofs off will get a D or an F. I want all of you to succeed, and I'll meet you at least halfway.
<u>Your Responsibilities</u>:
To get the most out of this course, treat it as a professional experience. Be here on time for every class. Study the texts.

Scan the recommended readings. Dip into your choice of suggested readings. Be a field team player. Take abundant notes. Understand not only *what* we're doing, but also *why*.
Postscript:
This is my first year teaching at Midland. Around week seven and at the end of the term you'll have two chances to evaluate me. We're all in this together, to learn: that partnership is the essence of higher education.
   Week 1 (1/14-1/18)
Reading: *Introduction to Applied Ecology*, chapters 1, 2, 3
M W: Introduction to B&AE 311, Applied Ecology: A Brief History
F: Discussion of history of applied ecology, assignment of study plots on Midland Lagoon and instructions for term paper
   Week 2 (1/21-1/25)
Reading: *Introduction to Applied Ecology*, chapters 4, 5
M W: Applied Ecology: Econo/Social Setting
F: Discussion of econo/social aspects of applied ecology
   Week 3 (1/28-2/1)
Reading: "Identifying State Flora"
M W: Methods of Field Research
F: Lab
...
   Week 15 (4/29-5/3)
M: Review, evaluation, term papers due
W: Review (practice exam)
F: Review (discussion of practice exam)
   Final Exam: T 5/7 3:00-5:00 (site to be announced)
N.B. The above schedule is for guidance only and may change in the event of extenuating circumstances.

GOING INTO ACTION

THOSE FIRST FEW MINUTES
   For many instructors — both rookies and veterans — the first meeting can be very difficult. It's normal to have butterflies in your stomach, but here are a few suggestions to help you get them to fly in formation:

   • **Use the entire hour productively.** First impressions are crucial, so make sure you set the right tone.

   • **Take care of business.** Provide the necessary administrative information, such as the procedures for adding or dropping courses and your school's policy on religious holidays. Take attendance.

- **Introduce yourself** and share your relevant experiences. You're there for a reason; let your students understand your background, and your interests (professional and other). Students naturally want to know who's going to lead them on this learning journey, so be yourself.

- **Find out who your students are.** You might pass around index cards and ask for names, phone numbers, major, background in the discipline, and reasons for taking the course. You may also ask each student to stand and give a short introductory spiel: name, major, hometown, campus residence, why they're taking the course, what they expect to learn, or whatever. (Students like to know who's taking the learning journey with them. This also encourages them to form networks from the start. It's also good for them to hear the various needs of their classmates, so they can better understand why you spend time on matters that they may consider to be of little value or interest to them personally.)

- **Plan at least one activity** to get your students involved. It should involve the physical: have them stand and introduce themselves, ask for a show of hands (Who has the textbook already? Who's taking this course as an elective? Who took Intro to Xerology last term?), conduct a milling exercise (maybe a scavenger hunt: have each person find a student from a neighboring state, a junior, a chem major, a left-hander ...). Make them feel their presence in your class.

- **Cover the appropriate resources.** Many instructors will talk briefly about the texts and other materials, giving advice on using them, explaining strengths and weaknesses. If your course involves work at the library, a lab, the museum, the planetarium, or other facility, make sure that your students know where the facilities are located, their hours, procedures for using them, and how to get their questions answered or take a tour.

- **Encourage questions** from the start. Be specific — "Any questions about these three points?" "Is it clear how I expect you to prepare for each class?" Treat every question with consideration. Remember: the only stupid question is the one they don't ask. Make your students comfortable about asking questions.

- **Assign some work.** Some instructors like to give "diagnostic" homework, to find out how well their students are prepared and/or how they think, organize, and write.

Some use the first assignment to get their students to go out and buy the texts, use the library or lab, or whatever.

According to your personality and teaching style, you may benefit from the following guidelines:

- **Use prompts as necessary.** We all have faults, both faculty and students. Remind yourself by placing one or more index cards on your desk or podium or as bookmarks: just a word or two — smile, be patient, eye contact, ask for questions, don't fidget, slow down, use gestures, move around — whatever might be useful.

- **Think about humor.** Some experts warn against using any humor, because it might offend some students or because it's not natural for certain instructors. Others advocate humor as a way to facilitate learning. Heed the Ancients: know yourself. And be sensitive to your students.

CLASSROOM PROTOCOL

Before you enter the classroom, at the beginning of the term and before every class, you should think about the social dynamics of your microcosm — and whether you should establish policies and guidelines beyond the strictly academic. In brief, there are three basic questions.

What can your students expect from you?

They should expect you to guide their learning, to set relevant goals and reasonable expectations, to respect them as people, to maintain an atmosphere of respect and support, to be fair and open, to challenge and motivate them to develop their potential, and to be honest with them.

This means assigning work that focuses on course goals and neither insults their intelligence nor surpasses their abilities. And it means that you promptly return their written assignments and tests, with coherent and helpful feedback.

Think of yourself as a "facilitator" for your students. You're not responsible for their learning, but rather for making the environment conducive to learning and providing activities to involve them as actively as possible in learning. One instructor suggests keeping in mind the old line, "Not a sage on the stage, but a guide on the side."

(Although it's not something that your students might expect from you, you should also take precautions for their safety. If you teach evening classes or in remote locations, during your first meeting you should remind your students of potential dangers. Encourage them to form groups when leaving for home or parking lots. Many students often feel secure around campus, especially students from smaller communities. Don't encourage paranoia, but it may be wise to issue a regular reminder to take care. After all, one of your responsibilities is to help prepare your students for the real world — and it's all around us, even on campus.)

What can you expect from your students?

That's a tough question! It's probably most important for you to expect them to take responsibility for learning and for them to respect each other and support the learning environment.

What can your students expect from each other?

You need to ensure a balance of enthusiasm and freedom with sensitivity and respect. This issue is of growing importance, as campus policies designed to protect the right of every student to an environment conducive to learning run up against the legal protection of the First Amendment. Your students probably don't expect you to have the wisdom of Solomon, but they have the right to assume that you'll be sensitive to their feelings and their expectations and that you'll supervise their environment.

This means, unfortunately, that you'll need to maintain discipline. A few guidelines for dealing with students who disrupt the environment:(28)

- Deal with them individually (not in groups), in person (not over the phone), outside of class (not during class).

- Keep it reasonable. If you or the student are emotional about the issue, suggest another meeting.

- Focus on behaviors that disrupt teaching and learning: anything else is basically a personality conflict, a "me vs. you" situation.

- Face challenging questions or statements honestly and openly. Fight the temptation to react defensively, to bluff, to rely on your authority. Don't pull rank.

Usually discipline isn't a big problem. If you experience difficulties, you might want to read "A Model for Resolving Classroom Conflicts and Enhancing Student Commitment" by Esther E. Hamilton (in *The Organizational Behavior Teaching Review*, 12:2 [1987-88], pp. 40-50).

INAPPROPRIATE SOCIAL DYNAMICS

A final word of advice, unnecessary for most faculty but vital for some: don't become socially involved with your students. There's a difference between being friendly and being unprofessional (or worse!). What would be inappropriate behavior? Your campus may have guidelines. A simple rule of thumb: don't go anywhere or do anything with one student that you wouldn't do with any or all of the others.

NAVIGATING THE COURSE

With solid planning and a good first class, you should be well on your way to providing your students with a healthy and interesting learning environment.

You should prepare for every class. Some instructors simply reread their notes — which should never become dusty or worn out. This is minimal preparation. For others, preparation may involve a complete set of plans, with visual aids and handouts, and a notation of approximate timing for every module. At minimum, you should reread the text or textbook section before you cover it in class. In addition, each term you should read at least one recent book or article for every unit of your course.

The main piece of advice here is to not fall into a routine, to remain attuned to the effects of your preparation. If you stumble through class after class, if your students seem lost, if you regularly run on past the bell or end abruptly five minutes early, consider changing your approach to preparing your class.

The next piece of advice, intended for the meticulously organized and/or extremely nervous: follow your plans as a map, not a religion. They should remind you of where you want to go during a specific class and help you get there, but they should never be more important than the learning activities. If you feel like you're running the class with your lesson plans in one hand and a stopwatch in the other, maybe you should read this paragraph again.

Finally, back up to look at the forest from time to time. Students may become lost in details and lose track of the big picture, the greater meaning of what they're learning. Some instructors keep a journal of each class, briefly recording their impressions while they're still fresh, a practice which compels them to reflect on the progress of the class and provides an outlet for their emotions. Other instructors immediately revise their lesson plans and notes, to have a head start for the next time they teach that course.

No matter how busy you are, you and your teaching are worth a few minutes of thought. What went well? Why? What didn't go so well? Why not? How would you do it better? As a former colleague would say, "If you can't learn, you can't teach."

MOTIVATION

The spirit may be willing, but sometimes only the flesh seems to be in attendance. How do you keep students' interest alive and healthy? How do you get your students to do the work when they're distracted and overwhelmed by other responibilities and pursuits?

From the start you should encourage appreciation of your subject. Students should understand the value of what they're doing: every lesson and assignment should have clear purposes, every "what" should be accompanied by "why." And as you explore details along your learning journey, make sure that your students don't lose track of the big picture.

You should also show your interest — not as a rah-rah cheerleader, but as an enthusiastic participant in the learning process. How do you feel about what you're teaching? Some faculty can teach intro courses for years and still feel the excitement of guiding their students through the early steps. They know that their subject has meaning and value, and that conviction and their love of the subject make them enthusiastic about bringing others into their "home" and making them feel welcome there. And that enthusiasm is often generally contagious.

OK, you point out, that may be fine for the classroom, where your presence inspires enthusiasm and motivates your students to ask questions, provide answers, and discuss. But what about outside the classroom? How can you motivate them to read and do other assignments?

The traditional, facile answer is to collect the written assignments and test them on the rest. This is known as motivation by the letter, not by the spirit. At times this may be the best way, but there are certainly others.

When students turn in written assignments, they should receive more than just a grade or a check. Give them coherent and helpful, balanced feedback, noting at least one strong point and suggesting one area for improvement. And write on each assignment a brief note — to congratulate, to console, to put the grade into perspective, to suggest a few ways to improve, to invite a student to come talk with you. Such comments can motivate your students as well as guide their learning.

Sometimes students don't bother to read assigned material because the instructor tells them that it doesn't matter. Not in so many words, of course, but if you simply repeat the material in class or never refer to it in any way, students soon realize there's not much purpose in preparing. If your students seem unfamiliar with material from the readings, even if you're certain that a significant number didn't even look at the readings, don't repeat the material in class. Sure, it's easier for you to "cover the material" that way. But students who didn't read quickly learn that it doesn't matter and students who did read are punished with boredom for their efforts.

Don't just tell students *what* and *when* to read; tell them *why* and *how*. Why did you choose this reading? How does it fit into class activities? What do you plan to do with it? Discussion? Test? Integration into a later activity? How do you want them to read? For a general sense? With a focus on certain points? For a subtext?

If you plan to use a reading in class, do so. One instructor noticed that many of his students weren't doing the readings. So, in one class, he asked how many students had done the reading. (This question works better than "Who didn't do the reading?" because there's a certain inertia to overcome to raise a hand.) When some students didn't answer in the affirmative, he gave them handouts with the case studies that he'd planned for class, then asked them to leave and write commentaries on the cases. With the students who remained, he conducted an excellent discussion. And the students who hadn't prepared learned their lesson.(25)

One of Bill's colleagues suggested another tactic. She gives her students a quiz over the material before she leads a discussion of it. The quizzes don't need to be difficult or take much time: she merely covers the basic points of the reading, for a grade. Her students usually learn quickly that she's serious about the readings she asigns.

It's not enough just to get your students to read, of course. Glance at their books. Are the pages covered with highlighting? That could indicate problems: too many students simply scan the readings and mark things for later reference, without really trying to understand them or to grasp their place within the larger picture. Then, when they need to discuss or review the material, it may be almost like reading it for the first time. (Recently a professor at Yale University was quoted as blaming highlighting pens for "retarding the education of university students by distorting and cheapening the way many read.")

You might want to encourage your students to proceed by paragraphs or sections of several paragraphs. They read a chunk of material, then jot in the margin a few words to summarize that material — not to repeat the "what" but to note the "why." Why did the author write that passage? How does it relate to the preceding material and further the direction of the chapter?

In essence, your students are creating subheads for each paragraph or section. This involves understanding, analysis, synthesis. When they need to discuss or review the readings, they have signposts that lead them through the material.

One of the best ways to encourage more thought when taking notes is to allow students to use those notes for tests. (Of course, you may have to use more thought in creating your tests!) To avoid simple regurgitation from pages upon pages of facts, you need to stress higher-level cognitive work, requiring application, analysis, synthesis, and evaluation.

Jules Janick, a professor at Purdue University, uses a novel approach. For the final exam he lets students prepare and use "crib sheets." The rules:

- Students may use both sides of a single 8 1/2" x 11" sheet of paper.
- Notes must be handwritten — not typed — and signed. (No mass production!)
- Students must turn in their crib sheet with the exam.

His students learn to analyze, synthesize, and evaluate the course material. Then, if exam results are disappointing, Janick reads the cribs for insights into the reasons.(14)

PARTICIPATION

The best way to encourage participation is to plan interesting (irresistible) activities and truly appreciate whatever your students might contribute.

But how?

One instructor prepares questions on index cards, structured like those outlines you learned to do in fifth grade. He first lists the main points to be covered in the discussion. Then he classifies his questions. At the "Roman numeral" level he puts his easiest questions — facts. At the "capital letter" level are questions that go beyond recall, to require slightly more thought. Finally, at the "Arabic numeral" level within each section are the "why" questions and items requiring analysis, synthesis, and evaluation. A quick glance at his cards and he can choose questions appropriate to the level of his students during any given class period.

Sometimes he leaves the classroom in smiles, describing the discussion as "level three all the way!" Occasionally he only mutters, "We couldn't get out of level one." If the discussion wanders away from his prepared questions, he lets it go as long as the results are worthwhile. (As he puts it, "Better *their* direction enthusiastically than *my* direction pulling teeth!") Then, he simply works a transition into the next group of questions.

If you decide to encourage participation by grading it, consider the system used by Kevin Melvin, a professor at the University of Alabama. He explains at the start of the term that he intends to evaluate both the quality and the quantity of class participation. No grade will be lower than C- except in cases of excessive absences. He keeps an informal record throughout the term.

Then, the day before the last day of class, Melvin asks his students to rate the contributions of their classmates as high, medium, or low. He asks them to put about the same number of students in each category. For each student Melvin considers his grade and the median peer rating: if the peer rating is higher than his own grade, he averages the two; if the peer rating is lower, he uses his grade alone for participation. In classes ranging in size between 15 and 27 students, Melvin reports high correlation between the peer rating and his grade. The system may not work quite as well, he suspects, with very small or large classes. (20)

What if you get assigned to a large class, a sea of 50 or 100 or 200 faces?

- **Plan activities.** Set aside a certain period of time for questions, to focus attention. Answer as many questions as you can within that time, then move on. Don't spend too much time on one question unless it interests a lot of your students. If a student seems very attached to a question or very lost, offer to continue the discussion with him or her after class or during your office hours.

- **Think "action."** When you prepare lesson plans, try to find various ways to involve your students more actively. Some instructors use the "directed ellipsis." For example, rather than begin, "When Abraham Lincoln freed the slaves with the Emancipation Proclamation in 1863," you might pause and let students fill in the blanks: "When Abraham Lincoln freed the slaves with the ... yes, the Emancipation Proclamation in ... yes, that's right, 1863." (One instructor plays up the theatrical with a fine performance as "the Absent-Minded Professor.") This method takes more time than a straight delivery of the material, you need to be attentive to cuing your students, and sometimes you may feel like an auctioneer, wearily waiting for the right bid, but it's a good way to involve your students.

- **Show that you appreciate input.** Thank your students for questions as well as for answers. As a colleague once pointed out, you should be in control like a lion-tamer: be confident but on your toes. Sure, it's easier if you just keep those animals locked in their cages or whip them into submission, but the goal is to keep it exciting for lions and tamer alike.

- **Work with what they give you.** ("George brought up a good point after class yesterday ...." "Colleen suggested an interesting possibility in her essay ....") This can be very effective with a "comment box." Keep a box outside your office and bring it to every class. Encourage your students to contribute. Then, use the input in your presentations. (One instructor admits to dropping in one of his own on occasion, especially at the start of the term or during "dry spells.")

A good guide to the special conditions of bigger groups is

Teaching Large Classes Well by Maryellen Weimer (San Francisco: Jossey-Bass, 1987).

OUTSIDE THE CLASSROOM

One area in which faculty show great diversity is in office procedures. Some set generous office hours and respect the right of students to have access to an attentive instructor. Others neglect this duty and treat students as an inconvenience. Set appropriate hours, announce them — and keep them. Nobody expects you to just sit there in your office waiting. If no students drop by, it's valuable time to prepare for your classes, read, write, maintain correspondence. But if a student comes by, drop everything and concentrate on that student's needs.

Since more and more students have responsibilities beyond their studies — jobs, family, campus and community extracurricular activities — faculty must remember that no schedule fits all. Maximize your availability: you might let students make appointments outside your regular hours, encourage them to call you at home (during certain hours), make sure they know where your campus mailbox is located, give them the department phone number so they can leave messages, set up an answering machine if you have an individual office phone.

Being available for your students isn't just the right thing to do. It also pays dividends when they do their term-end evaluations — which helps your tenure dossier. So if you feel like skipping out on your office hours, consider the odds: Is it likely that a student will come by? Is it likely that colleagues will notice the student waiting and perhaps grumbling? Is it likely that the student will complain or make a comment on your evaluation? Is it likely that the tenure jury of your peers will find you guilty of neglect?

When you meet with students, be attentive to what Iver Bogen, a professor at the University of Minnesota-Duluth, calls "shadow messages" — subliminal statements. Where is your desk in the office. Does it form a barrier? What do you have on your walls and on your desk? What is your reaction when students drop in — inviting or inconvenienced? Do you keep looking at your watch or out the window? As the song goes, "Every little movement has a meaning all its own."(3)

CHECKING ON YOUR PERFORMANCE

STUDENT FEEDBACK

You plan, you organize, you give your class blood, sweat, and tears. Then what?

If you wait for students to volunteer feedback, you may have a long wait — and the results are likely to be complaints, not compliments or constructive comments. Many instructors simply judge their teaching from student performance on assignments and tests, then expect the term-end evaluations to fill in the gaps and bring everything together.

It might be wise to try spot checks throughout the course. One example is the one-minute paper suggested by K. Patricia Cross and Thomas A. Angelo, in *Classroom Assessment Techniques: A Handbook for Faculty* (Ann Arbor: NCRIPTAL, 1988). At the end of a given class period, perhaps a month or so into the term, you simply ask your students to answer the following questions, anonymously:

- What's the most important thing you learned during this class today?
- What question(s) remain(s) uppermost in your mind?

A colleague prefers two open-ended statements:

- What I value most in this class is ....
- I wish this class would ....

In *Teaching College Freshmen* Erickson and Strommer reprinted a somewhat more detailed evaluation form, the Class Reaction Survey in use at the University of Rhode Island (p. 105). They begin with a general assessment of that class period in terms of improvement needed — none, little, some, or considerable. Then the same four grades are used to assess the instructor in 10 areas, covering preparation, clarity, variety, use of examples and exercises. Finally, students grade the class — excellent, good, satisfactory, fair, or poor — and indicate why they rated it that high, as well as why they didn't rate it higher. The survey takes less than five minutes and, best of all, it's in plain English.

Three points to remember if you create a questionnaire:

- Establish a clear rating system. Some favor a five-point system, for symmetry (almost always, often, sometimes, occasionally, hardly ever), while others argue that such rating scales let student take the path of least resistance, the middle rating. Any more than seven points: too complicated. Fewer than four: not worth the effort.

- Make sure that every item is simple and straightforward. For example, rather than "Instructor presents material in an interesting manner, explains carefully, and answers questions sympathetically," it's better to divide the item into three, one for each instructional function.

- Vary the direction of the items, for greater reliability of results. For example, you're likely to get more accurate results if you put "Instructor speaks with expression" and "Instructor answers questions rarely or poorly" (mixing good and bad), rather than "Instructor speaks with expression" and "Instructor always answers questions well."

Another means of inviting student feedback involves more effort. Researchers at the University of Washington recently studied student reactions to course evaluation procedures.(1) They found that students preferred a method of class interview which allowed them to meet in small groups with a facilitator but no instructor, to discuss the class, to "generate their own categories of response," and to "check perceptions of teaching effectiveness with others in the class." The study also showed that students were more satisfied with evaluations at midterm than at term end and when the instructor provided an "extended reaction" to their evaluations.

This study suggests the following approach to student evaluations. Around the middle of the term, set aside some time to discuss the class. Divide your students into small groups, at random. Ask them to share their opinions and to take note of all feedback and suggestions, without identifying the contributors by name. Then leave, to return at the designated time and collect the notes. Consider them, then formulate some sort of response, to present to your students the following class if possible. (If you hold the discussion the last day of the week, you allow yourself a weekend to reflect.)

This approach to evaluations would take a little more time and energy, of course. But consider the conclusion of the University of Washington research team: "It is disturbing to find that students evaluated as least satisfying the predominant, traditional means of collecting student opinion about teaching effectiveness: the use of individual, standardized rating forms administered at the end of courses with limited instructor reaction." (p. 205)

SELF-MEASURES

Some instructors, especially with a little experience, can assess their teaching themselves, fairly objectively and without too much anguish. You don't necessarily need an elaborate procedure.

Richard B. Chase, a professor in the University of California business school, offers his personal money-back guarantee: he promises reimbursement of book expenses plus $250 toward class fees to any student who isn't satisfied with his course (*Wall Street Journal*, March 19, 1991). It's an interesting idea. Ask yourself at the end of every class, "How many of my students would be asking for their money back for this class session?"

VISITS

"O wad some Power the giftie gie us To see oursels as others see us!" What Robert Burns longed for can be yours. Invite a colleague from your department to visit one of your classes. Have him or her unobtrusively sit out of the way and observe everything — your techniques and behavior, the reactions of your students, the dynamics of the class as an ecosystem. Then meet for a few moments as soon afterward as possible, to discuss observations and interpretations. Bear in mind, of course, that this is just one person's opinion, based on one class, but the experience might provide you with some valuable insights — and a valuable letter at tenure time.

Sometimes you may prefer to invite an instructor from another discipline, especially if no colleague in your own department seems an appropriate choice or if you would prefer an "outsider." In perspective, the "outsider" can experience your class as a student. For example, if you teach chemistry, you might find someone who teaches biology or zoology, maybe even someone in English or anthropology. An "outsider" is more sensitive to discipline-specific matters, such as concepts or vocabulary which might make it more difficult for your students to understand you.

You may be able to bring into your classroom a member from the instructional development staff. This may be the most effective way to get valuable analysis of your teaching and suggestions for improvement.

If an observer visits your class, what is he or she likely to expect? One of Bill's colleagues told him that she uses the following checklist when she evaluates an instructor:

- Careful planning.
- Start (on time? brisk?).
- Pace (fast enough to maintain interest, but not lose students).
- Variety, length, and sequencing of activities.
- Creativity.
- Humor.
- Contextualization of learning (how does this class fit into the larger context?).
- Participation (how many students? how substantial their output?).
- Learning checks (questions, exercises ...).
- Style of dealing with questions.
- Style of dealing with challenges to authority.

- Ending (on time? "not with a whimper but a bang"?).

Still another option may be to have one of your classes videotaped. You can then view the video alone or with a colleague or member of the instructional development center. This takes a certain amount of courage, but the benefits can be easily worth the effort.

What if you can't or don't want to get a visitor and your campus doesn't provide videotape services? You could use an audiotape recorder. Set it up where it won't be too conspicuous and where you can get good sound quality for the entire room. If you teach in a lecture hall, you'll probably need to set up at least one additional microphone to record student responses and questions.

What can you learn from an audiotape? Certainly not as much as from a video or a visit. But you can at least focus on your delivery — volume, tone, pace, pauses, annoying mannerisms. And an audiotape may be less obtrusive to students, less likely to affect class dynamics.

You can also learn a lot about the dynamics of your class environment. You might want to try the Cognitive Interaction Analysis System, developed by Glenn Ross Johnson, or the assessment instrument developed by Ned A. Flanders when he was at the University of Minnesota. Both systems help you track the verbal activities of your class, which may provide some valuable insights into the dynamics of your classroom interaction. (For details on the CIAS, consult Johnson, *First Steps to Excellence in College Teaching* [Madison WI: Magna Publications, 1990], chapter 6. Flanders describes his system in *Analyzing Teaching Behavior* [Reading MA: Addison-Wesley, 1970], pp.28-29.)

THEN WHAT?

Unless your assessments during the term reveal that your course is a disaster, it's probably wisest not to attempt any major changes, just a few tweaks here and there. A rider who thinks about changing horses in midstream should first consider adjusting the saddle and harness. After the term ends you can design plans for improvement.

Many inexperienced instructors take student input about their teaching far too personally, and often too seriously. If you're unsure about making changes in your organization, procedures, methods, or style, you might want to discuss the matter with an experienced colleague in the department or somebody at the center for faculty development.

Take note of all the comments, think about them, decide what fixes are feasible during the term, then set the others aside for the following term. A course is like a boat: instructor and students are working together, with the instructor providing guidance and the students pulling on the oars. The boat can feel shakier at the helm than on the benches.

THAT FINAL ASSESSMENT

STUDENT RATING FORMS

Your institution, division, or department will probably provide you with student evaluation forms. Whether they're required or not, use them. If there are no standard forms, create one. Make sure that your students understand how important the evaluations are, both for you and for future students. Evaluations should be anonymous. Assure your students that you'll read their evaluations only after turning in their course grades. Then leave the room while the students complete the forms.

You may also want to discuss the course in class. Students might be reluctant to criticize, particularly so close to grading time, but some may be eager to offer some valuable suggestions for improvement. Some may be more interested in venting their feelings — but that's also a worthwhile result, especially if you can handle the situation effectively and gracefully.

Read the evaluation forms after you've turned in your final grades and had a moment to relax. Set aside some quiet time, away from distractions: the evaluation forms should make you think and you should be ready to develop ideas. Take note of any comments or suggestions. Remember: your students aren't experts on teaching and they may have some biases, but their perceptions and opinions are very important.

Also keep in mind the words of consolation Chair Amanda Perkins offered Bill at the end of his first term at Midland: "Every prof gets a few comments that 'this was the worst course ever.' It's hard, but you just can't overreact to such criticisms. It's only natural for all of us, especially new faculty, to focus on the negative comments and forget the many positive reviews." She's right: you can't please all of the students all of the time. (But keep trying!)

When administering and reviewing student evaluations, be aware that research has identified certain factors that may undermine the validity of the results, including:(5)

- **Expressiveness.** Student ratings may be influenced more by style of presentation than by substance. But if you're attentive to making your classes interesting as well as informative, you shouldn't be concerned about this factor.

- **Student motivation.** Instructors tend to receive higher ratings in classes where students entered the course with an interest in the subject or were taking it as an elective.

- **Level of the course.** In general, the higher the level, the better the ratings.
- **Workload/difficulty.** Contrary to popular belief, students tend to give higher ratings in difficult courses where they have to work harder.
- **Purpose.** Ratings tend to be higher if the students know that they'll be used in personnel decisions.

Keep these factors in mind when you consider your ratings; you might also want to mention any appropriate factors when you write up your assessment of the course for your records and your tenure dossier.

Finally, if your department doesn't use an adequate student evaluation procedure, you might suggest checking into the Instructional Development Effectiveness Assessment (IDEA) forms (Kansas State University, Center for Faculty Evaluation and Development) and the Course/Instructor Evaluation Questionnaire (CIEQ), designed by Lawrence M. Aleamoni, a professor of educational psychology at the University of Arizona (Comprehensive Data Evaluation Services, Inc., Tucson).

SELF-EVALUATION

A relatively quick "checklist for developing instructional awareness" is proposed by Maryellen Weimer in *Improving College Teaching* (San Francisco: Jossey-Bass, 1990):

- *What do you do with your hands?* Gesture? Keep them in your pockets? Hold onto the podium? Play with the chalk? Hide them so students won't see them shake?
- *Where do you stand or sit?* Behind the podium? On the table?
- *When do you move to a different location?* Never? At regular 10-second intervals? When you change topics? When you need to write something on the board/overhead? When you answer a student's question? At what speed do you move? Do you talk and move at the same time?
- *Where do you move?* Back behind the podium? Out to the students? To the blackboard?
- *Where do your eyes most often focus?* On your notes? On the board/overhead? Out the window? On a spot on the wall in the back of the room? On the students? Could you tell who was in class today without having taken roll?
- *What do you do between content segments?* Say OK? Ask

if there are any student questions? Erase the board?
Move to a different location? Make a verbal transition?

- *When do you speak louder / softer?* When the point is
very important? When nobody seems to understand?
When nobody seems to be listening?
- *When do you speak faster / slower?* When you want to
emphasize an important idea? When you're behind
schedule? When you're having trouble understanding
students' questions?
- *Do you laugh or smile in class?* When? How often?
- *How do you use examples?* How often? When?
- *How do you emphasize main points?* Write them on the
board/overhead? Repeat them? Ask the students if they
understand them? Suggest ways to remember them?
- *What do you do when students are inattentive?* Ignore
them? Ask questions? Interject an anecdote? Point out
the consequences of not paying attention? Move out
toward them?
- *Do you encourage student participation?* How? Grade it?
Call on students by name? Wait for answers? Verbally
recognize quality contributions? Correct student
answers? How much class time is typically devoted to
student talk?
- *How do you begin / end class?* With a summary and conclusion? With a preview and a review? With a gasp and
a groan? With a bang and a whimper?

Being aware of your behavior in the classroom is only the first
step, but it's fundamental to improving your teaching.

EFFECTIVE GUIDES

Perhaps the best single guide to assessing your teaching is
How Am I Teaching?, edited by Maryellen Weimer, Joan L. Par-
rett, and Mary-Margaret Kerns (Madison WI: Magna Publications, 1988). It's a compilation of 12 forms for evaluating
everything instructional, including:

- your classroom environment,
- your course materials,
- your attitudes,
- your classroom procedures,
- your teaching style and behavior,
- your stimulation of cognitive and affective gains,
- your relations with your students, and

- specific problems.

There are forms for you, your students, and peers. Everyone can provide you with input about your course; changes, of course, are up to you.

A recent work, *Faculty at Work: Self-Assessment Guide*, by Robert T. Blackburn and Janet H. Lawrence (Ann Arbor: NCRIPTAL, 1991) should also help you evaluate your efforts and their effects.

Challenge yourself to make your teaching more effective. Consider again the example of the business professor who offers his students a money-back guarantee. Ask yourself at the end of the term, "How many of my students would be asking for a refund for this course? Why? What would have made the difference?" And then, because time is also a teacher, ask another question — "How will my students feel about this course in five years?" (That's a question often asked in tenure and promotion decisions.)

MOVING ON

INSTRUCTIONAL IMPROVEMENT PLAN

It's very likely that you'll find some negatives in your student evaluations and self-assessment. There may be sins of omission as well as commission, things you'd like to add, approaches you'd like to try. But it's only human to read the evaluations, do your self-assessment, sing and dance or rant and rave — and then take a break to charge up for the next term. Life goes on.

But you should take a little time to work up an instructional improvement plan. Simply list the content areas covered and the methods used, then make at least one suggestion for improving each area. This will serve as the basis when you plan for that course again. If you're moving on to other courses the following term, consider areas of similarity in material or methods. What did you learn that might apply to your new courses?

WHO'S OUT THERE TO HELP ME?

One important thought to bear in mind, especially when reviewing your teaching: you may be alone in the classroom, but you're not alone in your efforts.

First, you can turn to colleagues in your department or related disciplines. This can be awkward, but it also may well be worth the effort. Why should students be the only ones in the educational enterprise to form study groups and support networks?

There are also, on most campuses, trained personnel. It may be a Center for Instructional Development, a Department of Curriculum and Instruction, a Center for Teaching Excellence, a

Division of Instructional Support — but they're out there, ready
and willing to help you.

Don't hesitate; don't wait for problems to develop. Some instructors conceive of instructional support in terms of urgent
care. But those people aren't doctors and the facility isn't an
emergency ward. It's better to think of your center as a facility
for instructional wellness, a pedagogical health club where
knowledgeable, experienced, committed, and usually very enthusiastic people will help you make the most of your efforts.

You can learn a lot from workshops and seminars on teaching your specific subject matter. But if there aren't any such activities in your discipline or related areas, consider attending
workshops for graduate teachers in your discipline. Not only
will you have an opportunity to learn some tricks, but as someone between a novice GT and an expert faculty facilitator, you
may encourage by your presence a more open exchange of ideas.

Reach out beyond your campus. You may want to join an organization committed to teaching in your specific discipline. Or
become a member of the Professional and Organizational Development Network in Higher Education — a.k.a. "The POD
People." (For information, contact: POD Network, c/o Teaching
and Learning Center, University of Nebraska, Lincoln NE
68588-0623.)

BOTTOM LINE

What's good teaching? There are hundreds of books and
thousands of articles out there — if you have the time and energy. But several years ago the AAHE, the Education Commission
of the States, and The Johnson Foundation summarized the essentials in their "Seven Principles for Good Practice in Undergraduate Education" (*Faculty Inventory,* Milwaukee: The
Johnson Foundation, Inc., 1989).

Good practice:

- encourages student-faculty contact
- encourages cooperation among students
- encourages active learning
- gives prompt feedback
- emphasizes time on task
- communicates high expectations
- respects diverse talents and ways of learning

These principles provide excellent guidance; keep them in mind
from the moment you begin planning your courses until you
turn in your final grades.

CREATING A NEW COURSE

STARTING FROM SCRATCH

If you have the opportunity to do something in an area that interests you, great! Maybe the department hired you specifically to open up a new area. If so, then you probably have some ideas about what you should offer in your course. Most likely, however, you'll have to identify and colonize a niche that doesn't overlap other courses excessively — or step on any toes.

POLITICS AND PRAGMATICS

You may want to consider this opportunity not only in terms of what you can bring to students but also in view of your situation in the department. (Few faculty actually enjoy the politics of academia, but wherever there are people there are politics.)

A former colleague was in the minority in her department: most of her colleagues were involved in areas of interests apart from hers — and sometimes in competition for department resources and personnel decisions. So she decided to create a course that bridged between her interests and the interests of the majority of her colleagues. The course was a hit with the students, it scored points with her colleagues — and it developed into a major career area that offers opportunities for teaching, publications, contacts, and service. Don't sell out for politics, but be aware of the politics in whatever you do.

Consider the merits of creating a course for a single credit. It's an easy way to test out a new offering — and you're less likely to step on toes, because a one-credit course generally won't draw students away from your colleagues' established courses.

You'll probably need to justify your proposal and parade your credentials before a jury of your peers, particularly as the outcry for better quality in higher education may rightly make deans and chairs skittish about any course that smacks of an ego trip, that might be motivated by selfish academic interests.

When you prepare your proposal for the review committee to consider, you should find the following headings a useful guide:

- Introduction
- Purpose of the Course
- Rationale
- Scope
- Content
- Objectives
- Relationship Within the Curriculum
- Summary
- List of Readings and Other Materials

WORKING WITH STUDENTS OUTSIDE THE CLASSROOM

ADVISING INDIVIDUAL STUDENTS

What else does a good instructor do outside the classroom? What else might a department and dean expect from faculty?

You may need to counsel individual students, especially at smaller colleges, where it may be one of your major responsibilities. Several points merit at least brief mention here.

The campus service perhaps the most maligned by undergraduates is advising. Why? Many students expect not only answers to their questions, but solutions to their problems. Act as a guide, not as a parent. Give them information and show them that you care — then leave the rest to them.

(This can be particularly difficult for female faculty, as students seem more likely to expect nurturing from them. This may also be the case when a minority student seeks out a faculty member of the same race or ethnic origin. It's only natural to feel sympathetic and want to lend a hand. But the best advice is still to help the student help himself or herself.)

Keep in mind that the world is getting more difficult for students in the '90s: they have more varied backgrounds and abilities, more academic requirements, more career choices, and more family and financial responsibilities. If students come to you, try to be sensitive to their reasons and needs — which they may have trouble expressing. Sometimes they may need a straight answer, just the facts. Or maybe an interpretation of policies or regulations. They may need help sorting out their lives — or even just someone to listen to them sorting things out.

Know your stuff. Be knowledgeable about current requirements, for your department, your division, and the institution as a whole. Keep information handy on campus counseling centers and support groups, including addresses and phone numbers. (Centers and groups may be happy to provide you with brochures and other documentation for your students.) Some students like "one-stop shopping": they may ask you questions about virtually anything. Of course, nobody could reasonably expect you to know every campus policy and regulation. If you don't have an answer, offer to check into the matter. Then follow up, preferably by calling somebody in the know while the student is there in your office.

Keep up to date. For students who major or minor in your field, you should be familiar with employment trends and career opportunities.

If your department has a graduate program, you may also have a chance to mentor grad students. Many faculty truly enjoy working with these "junior colleagues," but there are no roses without thorns.

As a colleague warned Bill, "You've got to be ready to work with the whole student. They're into their studies, they're intelligent, but they've got lives outside the classroom and library and lab — and there's lots of pressure on them to be cool and professional — especially around faculty." So, be attentive to "chinks in their armor" and help them make the most of their years in graduate school.

While a graduate student at the University of Georgia, Bill had worked closely with two professors. They'd discussed his projects and opportunities to turn his work into papers and articles. One had invited him to several professional conferences, where she introduced him to other faculty working in his field of interest. The other mentor had helped Bill earn a two-year post-doc assignment with the Chesapeake Bay Commission. And they both kept in touch with Bill, by mail and by phone, when he was applying for tenure-track positions. Bill appreciated all their efforts and hoped that he could be as helpful a mentor for budding botanists at Midland.

Many faculty dread advising: it takes time, energy, and patience — and may offer virtually no reward toward tenure. For a beginner it's particularly tough: there's a lot to learn about being a student on your campus. But some people claim that students may be shaped less by what you do in the classroom than by your activities outside. If advising is part of your job, you should consider it an important responsibility.

P.S. Advising isn't necessarily labor in obscurity. Colleagues are sure to take note of students hanging around your door and walking away, content or complaining. And every colleague carries a mental dossier with your name on it.

It may be useful to maintain a log or files to keep track of the students you advise: names, class level, major, dates of sessions, and any decisions. Don't trust your memory for details. If you keep track, you can advise students more effectively — and they'll appreciate the individual attention and effort. Of course, such records are also good documentation for your tenure dossier.

Finally, be careful about developing social relationships with students you advise, whether undergraduate or graduate. If you feel attracted to a student, fight the feeling: sexual harassment can cause very serious damage. If a student expresses interest in you, discourage him or her; keep your relationship strictly professional. And if the feelings are reciprocal, if you become romantically involved with a student, you run the serious risk of being ostracized by others in your department. If you find

yourself in that situation, it's generally wise to keep things cool
and wait until that student receives his or her degree. To quote
a popular advice columnist: "If it's real, it will last. If not, then
it's not worth the risk."

ADVISING STUDENT ORGANIZATIONS

You may also have the opportunity (perhaps thrust upon
you) of advising a student organization. Remember high school?
Remember the teachers who were in charge of the school paper,
yearbook, debate team, pep squad, Spanish club? Some did it
out of interest, some out of a sense of responsibility, and some because they had no choice. What's the situation in your department? Are you free to choose or do your colleagues expect you to
get involved? If you're acting out of interest or departmental expectations, do it. Otherwise, leave that area of involvement to
those who share the interest of the students.

(This is often a problem for female faculty in particular. In
some departments advising student groups is considered a "pink
collar" responsibility. If you find yourself under pressure to do
more than your fair share of service, discuss the situation with
an ally in the department. Sometimes that sort of discrimination is just viewed as "tradition." A few probing but tactful questions might put it to rest. If you accept every advising responsibility they hand you, you're not likely to have the time and
energy to make tenure — and you'll be accepting second-class
citizenship in your department.)

If you become involved in any way in a student organization
or special program, keep track of what you do — title, responsibilities, role in any particular activities. Later you'll need to
sort these things out for your dossier and you won't want to forget anything. Remember: you get involved in student activities
for the sake of the students, but evidence of your commitment to
the students and the campus should be duly recorded — and
rewarded. Of course the rewards vary from department to
department and campus to campus. Again, you've got to know
your territory.

KEEPING TRACK OF ALUMNI

When are your students no longer your students? After the
term ends? After they graduate? Actually, your students may be
a part of you — and you may be a part of them — for life. Good
teachers should have a lasting impact on their students.

And you may well want to keep track of your "alumni" as
they make their way through the world. Such relationships can
help you remember what some faculty seem to forget — that students are people too. It can also be very rewarding to know that
you're part of a success story. Share their stories with your

colleagues, who may remember some of those students. Again, an enthusiastic and devoted instructor leaves a definite impression on his or her colleagues.

TAKING YOUR TEACHING OUT INTO THE WORLD

When it comes to teaching, it pays to think big. Too often good teaching gets little recognition because it's confined to the classroom and the office, documented only through student evaluations. You should also consider your teaching efforts in terms of research, presentations and publications, and community service.

PRESENTATIONS AND PUBLICATIONS

Although presenting and publishing are extensively covered in Chapter VI, "A Bottom Line: Getting Published," they merit a few words in this chapter on teaching. Teaching and publishing don't have to be adversarial pursuits: many "teaching professors" consider it a vital part of their vocation to contribute to the idea network through conferences, articles, and books.

Maybe a classroom experience might draw your attention to something interesting. Or maybe you can apply some aspect of your research to your courses. If your research has raised any questions in your mind, consider posing them in class, in the form of problem-solving and case studies. Have your students apply their knowledge of the field and of research methodology. Outline the problem and then let them approach it, providing guidance only as needed. Focus on the process, not the product: your students don't need to find answers, just the right questions.

But you may gain some interesting insights for your research activities — and you may want to present a paper or publish an article to share such classroom experiences with others teaching in your discipline. Remember: if you're putting a lot of thought and energy into your teaching, you're probably learning things of value and interest to others in your discipline.

In addition to general publications such as *College Teaching* and *The Teaching Professor*, there are many discipline-specific teaching publications, such as *Journal of College Science Teaching, Teaching Psychology, Engineering Education, Journal of Chemical Education,* and *Teaching Sociology*. They can provide an excellent forum for your classroom experiments.

OUTREACH OPTIONS

But what if your area of research and your courses don't match very well? A French professor specializing in Eustache Deschamps may not be able to share research with an introductory language class, and a physics prof engaged in the study of quarks may not be able to bring that area of endeavor to first-year students in a required general science course.

Check with colleagues who teach courses more relevant to your research interests. (Don't neglect extension courses.) Offer to visit their classes as a guest lecturer on specific topic or, more generally, on research methodology and problem-solving.

Is your research of interest to local business or community groups? Maybe you could be of service to a high school teacher or counselor for career days. Be creative. And remember that such activities aren't necessarily one-way: you're bringing your skills and experience to others, but you may gain insights when you consider your work from their perspectives.

Here again, keep track of what you do. Such activities can mean points in your tenure dossier under "Community Service." And you may be inspired to write an article about bridging the gap between the college and the community.

These possibilities can open attractive opportunities, especially for faculty at smaller institutions, with more limited research facilities. And they can be alternative research: presentations and articles on teaching can supplement other research, broaden your perspectives, encourage you to invest more energy and thought in your classroom activities, supplement student and collegial evaluations of your teaching, and give evidence of a greater range of interests.

Finally, you might want to find out what campus committees and/or publications are devoted to teaching. Consider serving on a committee and publishing articles based on those activities. A small investment of time and energy might help improve the quality of education and draw attention to the importance of that institutional mission — as well as providing you with some valuable attention among your colleagues.

Caution: "Extracurricular" teaching activities may take a lot of time and energy and carry little weight in your tenure decision. Depending on the climate of your department and division, you may have to put off some time-consuming yet undervalued opportunities until after tenure. As we stress throughout this manual, you've got to know your territory.

IN A NUTSHELL

If what you're doing to combine research and teaching or research and service is worth doing, it should be documented in your dossier and it may be worthy of a presentation or article.

DOCUMENTING YOUR TEACHING ACTIVITIES

INSTITUTIONAL CRITERIA

OK, this is the bottom line for most readers: How do you get proper credit for your teaching activities? It's also one of the hottest questions in higher education.

Leaders call for greater commitment to quality in education, but at many institutions the story remains the same. Recently at a major state university a new dean was appointed for the school of education. The chancellor reported being "absolutely delighted to attract such a well-known scholar who has continued to be a productive researcher along with his broad experience in university administration." But what about the teaching of this new dean of education? Not a word. Even at institutions that traditionally stress the importance of teaching, candidates for tenure should document their instructional activities as completely and carefully as they document their scholarship and service. Remember: you can't trust your tenure to mission statements. It's not what they say about the value of teaching; it's how they reward it.

The value placed on teaching in institutions of higher education is inversely related to the highest degree an institution offers. In our research, 96% of the deans in colleges offering no graduate study at all reported that teaching was the most important factor in tenure decisions, as did 91% of the deans in institutions that offer both bachelor's and master's degrees. Doctoral institutions ... often conceal a very different set of priorities which guide internal decisions. Deans rated teaching as a secondary or tertiary factor in tenure decisions in slightly more than half (56%) of those universities.
— J. Richard McFerron, David M. Lynch, Lee H. Bowker, and Ian A.C. Beckford, "The Importance of Teaching in Tenure Decisions," *The Department Chair*, Winter 1992, p. 17.

It's essential to know what your department and division use as criteria for weighing the value of your teaching in tenure decisions. The possibilities include:

- Evaluation by chair
- Opinions of colleagues
- Systematic student evaluations
- Committee evaluation
- Informal student opinions
- Evaluation by dean
- Content of course syllabi and exams
- Popularity (i.e., enrollment in elective courses)
- Self-evaluation

- Teaching improvement activities
- Student performance on exams
- Ratings by colleagues (classroom visitations)
- Opinions of course alumni
- Long-term follow-up of students (performance in subsequent courses)
- Videotape of classroom teaching

These 15 criteria were used by John Centra in his survey of 453 department heads in 1976. Respondents ranked the importance of these criteria in the order shown, reporting that only the first six were of *major* importance. How much has changed in 15 years? How do your department, division, and institution compare? Once again, it's essential to know your territory.

When Bill arrived at Midland University, he checked the faculty handbook and learned that "documentation of teaching quality and effectiveness can include but is not restricted to":

- Evaluation by colleagues and department administrators, particularly if based on class visitations or the results of the candidate's teaching in courses prerequisite to those taught by the evaluator.
- Evaluations by students.
- Exit interviews of graduating seniors by the department chair.
- Evidence of innovation: teaching techniques, content, materials, and evaluative procedures (tests).
- Development of new courses and programs.
- Publications and presentations pertaining to teaching.
- Invitations to consult or lecture on teaching.
- Opinions of graduates who have achieved notable professional success.
- Numbers and quality of graduate students attracted to the department because of the candidate's professional reputation, and the number of those guided through master's and doctoral degrees.
- Authorship of textbooks, audiovisual materials, software.

DOSSIER/PORTFOLIO

Traditionally the P&T dossier contains lists of presentations, publications, and work on campus and in the community, together with copies of all materials, as evidence of research and service activity. In recent years, however, faculty and academic associations have been promoting the importance of documenting teaching activity as well.

Your portfolio should contain evidence of the following general areas of your teaching activities:

- Subject area mastery
- Curriculum development and innovation
- Course design: goals, content, methods, assessment
- Delivery of instruction: methods, skills, and materials
- Assessment of instruction: assignments, tests, grading practices
- Availability to students
- Administrative requirements and expectations

These areas are outlined in greater detail, with suggestions for appropriate documentation for each area, by William E. Cashin in "Defining and Evaluating College Teaching," IDEA Paper No. 21 (Manhattan KS: Kansas State University Center for Faculty Evaluation and Development, 1989). You might also consult *A Guide to Evaluating Teaching for Promotion and Tenure*, by John A. Centra, Robert C. Froh, Peter J. Gray, Leo M. Lambert (Littleton MA: Copley Publishing Group, 1987), *The Teaching Portfolio: A Practical Guide to Improved Performance and Promotion/Tenure Decisions* by Peter Seldin (Bolton MA: Anker Publishing, 1991), and *The Teaching Portfolio: Capturing the Scholarship in Teaching* by Russell Edgerton, Pat Hutchings, and Kathleen Quinlan (Washington DC: AAHE, 1991).

So, what can you put into your teaching portfolio? Here are a few suggestions:

- **Student evaluations.** It's probably policy or hallowed tradition that your department put the evaluations into your file. If not, it's up to you. If the department doesn't provide a summary of each set of evaluations, you probably should do so yourself, including a copy of the course description and any other details that would help your colleagues better understand the evaluations.
- **Evaluations by visitors** — colleagues or instructional development staff.
- **Self-assessments.** Whether you've completed forms, maintained a journal, or simply written down your reactions to each course, these documents are evidence of your interest, commitment, and attitudes.
- **Course outlines and syllabi.** You may want to attach a commentary sheet, to explain what thoughts and considerations went into putting the course together. List and describe your goals, both primary and secondary. Your commentary should include your reading and other

preparation, to show your professional development —
How are you better for having taught the course?

- **Ancillary materials** you've prepared: handouts, review
  sheets, bibliographies, overhead transparencies, and so
  forth. You don't need to include everything, but you
  should give evidence of variety and depth. Again, a commentary sheet may be useful: Why did you decide to
  develop the materials? How did they facilitate learning?
  How would you grade them? What might you do differently?

- **Documentation on activities outside the classroom.** Did you organize a field trip, an exhibition of student projects, or any other "above and beyond" learning
  activities?

- **Audio- and videotapes.** You'll need to briefly outline
  the context of the segments recorded: course, level and
  background of your students, stage in the syllabus,
  preparation, type of activity. You should also describe
  your reactions — How would you judge the class or
  specific activities? What were the ups and the downs?
  What would you do differently? (When you put together
  your commentary, remember that your colleagues may
  not all review the tapes, unfortunately, so your comments should be able to stand on their own as evidence
  of your teaching.)

- **Student projects.** These might include exceptional
  term papers or essay exams, descriptions of special
  group activities, photographs of three-dimensional crea-
  tions, videos of student debates or role-play or skits.
  Remember to attach a brief explanation of the instructional circumstances.

- **Records of your advising activities.** If you maintain
  a log or files, include these as evidence of your interest
  and commitment beyond the classroom.

Teaching portfolios are valuable not only as documentation
but also as guides to improvement. When you develop your
portfolio, you focus on what you consider important. Then you
take note of your weaker areas and work to strengthen those
areas.

Teaching portfolios have been in use on some campuses
since the early '70s. Faculty development specialists estimate
that 50 to 75 institutions use them at present. With the AAHE
promoting their value and the quality of undergraduate instruction attracting greater attention nationally, the use of teaching

portfolios should rise considerably in the '90s.

HEART AND SOUL

Your academic career may emphasize research and publication, focus on discovering knowledge and advancing your discipline: this may be what most impresses your colleagues and the dean. But teaching is traditionally the heart and soul of faculty activities. You should take your teaching responsibilities seriously, as opportunities to make a significant contribution to our future.

You may spend months, even years, to provide a small step for a few specialists in your field — or in those same months help your students to make giant strides. Whatever they become, you become a part of their success.

Be idealistic, but keep a grasp on reality. Know the value of good teaching in terms of tenure in your department and division. Many new faculty find it easy to become so committed to teaching, so devoted to their students, that they forget to wear their two other hats, research and service. They neglect their responsibility to present and publish and to otherwise serve the campus community — and they risk losing their chance to make an impact through teaching.

Higher education leaders and associations are progressively insistent that institutions recognize the importance of effective teaching, particularly for undergraduates. If you believe that your teaching responsibilities are vital to your professional life and if your department and division encourage and support more effective teaching, then you should promote your activities in your tenure dossier.

FURTHER GUIDANCE FOR YOUR JOURNEY

In meeting and mastering the teaching challenge, you'll find invaluable the following guides:

Eble, Kenneth, *The Craft of Teaching: A Guide to Mastering the Professor's Art*, 2nd ed. (San Francisco: Jossey-Bass, 1988).

Ericksen, Stanford C., *The Essence of Good Teaching: Helping Students Learn and Remember What They Learn* (San Francisco: Jossey-Bass, 1984).

Fink, L. Dee, *The First Year of College Teaching* (San Francisco: Jossey-Bass, 1984).

Fuhrmann, Barbara S., and Anthony F. Grasha, *A Practical Handbook for College Teachers* (Boston: Little, Brown, 1983).

Lowman, Joseph, *Mastering the Techniques of Teaching* (San Francisco: Jossey-Bass, 1984).

Magnan, Bob, Ed., *147 Tips for Teaching Professors* (Madison WI: Magna Publications, 1989).

McKeachie, Wilbert, *Teaching Tips: A Guidebook for the Beginning College Teacher*, 8th ed. (Lexington MA: D.C. Heath, 1986).

Newble, David, and Robert Cannon, *A Handbook for Teachers in Universities and Colleges: A Guide to Improving Teaching Methods* (New York: St. Martin's Press, 1989).

Weimer, Maryellen and Rose Ann Neff, Eds., *Teaching College: Collected Readings for the New Instructor* (Madison WI: Magna Publications, 1989).

References

1. Abbott, Robert D., Donald H. Wulff, Jody D. Nyquist, V.A. Ropp, and Carla W. Hess, "Satisfaction With Processes of Collecting Student Opinions About Instruction: The Student Perspective," *Journal of Educational Psychology*, 83:2 (1990), pp. 201-206.
2. Altman, Howard, "Syllabus Shares 'What the Teacher Wants,'" *The Teaching Professor*, May 1989, p. 2.
3. Bogen, Iver, "Shadow Messages," *Instructional Development*, 7:4, Instructional Development Service, University of Minnesota-Duluth.
4. Brinko, Kathleen T., "Visioning Your Course: Questions to Ask Yourself as You Design Your Course," *The Teaching Professor*, February 1991, pp. 3-4.
5. Cashin, William E., "Student Ratings of Teaching: A Summary of the Research," IDEA Paper No. 20 (Manhattan KS: Kansas State University Center for Faculty Evaluation and Development, 1988).
6. Centra, John A., "Evaluating College Teaching: Some Reflections," *Department Advisor*, 5 (Winter 1990), pp. 1-5.
7. *The Chronicle of Higher Education*, Aug. 28, 1991 (Almanac), Jan. 22, 1992, pp. A33-36, and Jan. 29, 1992, pp. A1 and A21.
8. Clarke, John H., "Designing Discussions as Group Inquiry," *College Teaching*, Fall 1988, pp. 140-143.
9. Corder, Jim W., "Traditional Lectures Still Have a Place in the Classroom," *The Chronicle of Higher Education*, June 12, 1991, p. B 2.
10. Dressel, P., "Grades: One More Tilt at the Windmill," *Bulletin*, Memphis State University Center for Study for Higher Education, 1983.
11. Erickson, Bette LaSere, and Diane Weltner Strommer, *Teaching College Freshmen* (San Francisco: Jossey-Bass, 1991), p. 124.
12. Glassman, E., "The Teacher as Leader," in *Learning About Teaching*, John F. Noonan, Ed. (San Francisco: Jossey-Bass, 1980).
13. Hanna, Gerald S., and William E. Cashin, "Improving College Grading," IDEA Paper No. 19 (Manhattan KS: Kansas State University Center for Faculty Evaluation and Development, 1988).
14. Janick, Jules, "Crib Sheets," *The Teaching Professor*, June/July 1990, p. 2.
15. Johnson, Glenn Ross, *First Steps to Excellence in College Teaching* (Madison WI: Magna Publications, 1990), pp. 9-10.
16. Johnson, Glenn Ross, James A. Eison, Robert Abbott, Guy T. Meiss, Kathy Moran, Joyce A. Morgan, Thomas L. Pasternack, and Ernest Zaremba, *Teaching Tips for Users of the Motivated Strategies for Learning Questionnaire (MSLQ)* (Ann Arbor: National Center for Research to Improve Postsecondary Teaching and Learning, 1991).
17. Kolb, David A., *The Learning-Style Inventory* (Boston: McBer, 1985).
18. MacGregor, Jean, "Collaborative Learning: Shared Inquiry as a Process of Reform," in *The Changing Face of College Teaching*, Marilla D. Svinicki, Ed. (San Francisco: Jossey-Bass, 1990), p. 23.
19. McMullen-Pastrick, Miriam, and Maryellen Gleason, "Examinations: Accentuating the Positive," *College Teaching*, 34:4 (1986), pp. 135-139.
20. Melvin, Kevin, "Rating Class Participation: The Prof/Peer Method," *Teaching of Psychology*, October 1988, pp. 137-139.

21. Muller, Thomas E., "Assigning Students to Groups for Class Projects: An Exploratory Test of Two Methods," *Decision Sciences Journal*, Summer 1989, pp. 623-634.

22. Pintrich, Paul R., Wilbert J. McKeachie, David A.F. Smith, Robert Doljanac, Yi-Guang Lin, Moshe Naveh-Benjamin, Terence Crooks, and Stuart Karabenick, *Motivated Strategies for Learning Questionnaire* (Ann Arbor: National Center for Research to Improve Postsecondary Teaching and Learning, 1988).

23. Pintrich, Paul R., David A.F. Smith, Teresa Garcia, and Wilbert J. McKeachie, *A Manual for the Use of the Motivated Strategies for Learning Questionnaire* (Ann Arbor: National Center for Research to Improve Postsecondary Teaching and Learning, 1991).

24. Rowe, Mary Budd, "Getting Chemistry Off the Killer Course List," *Journal of Chemical Education*, November 1983, pp. 954-956.

25. Shulman, Adley M., in "When They Don't Do the Reading," *The Teaching Professor*, December 1989, p. 3.

26. Smith, Page, *Killing the Spirit: Higher Education in America* (New York: Viking, 1990), p. 214.

27. Svinicki, Marilla D., and N.M. Dixon, "The Kolb Model Modified for Classroom Activities," *College Teaching*, 35:4 (1987), pp. 141-146.

28. Weimer, Maryellen, "Tips for Productive Classroom Climates," *The Teaching Professor*, March 1990, p. 4.

29. Weinstein, Claire E., A.C. Schulte, and D.R. Palmer, *Learning and Study Strategies Inventory (LASSI)* (Clearwater FL: H. and H. Publishing, 1987).

IV
THE RESEARCH PARADIGM

Unless you're in a college devoted exclusively to teaching, you'll be expected to engage in research. Particularly at a prestigious research university, productive scholarship is the *sine qua non* of the faculty role. Even in a "wannabe" institution, at least a modest level of research publication is a criterion for retention and promotion. (Of course, unless you're wedded to the institution, you'll want to consider your own career goals and interests as well.)

Why is research held so highly in academia?

A university is pre-eminently a place of learning. If it is to teach by example, a university must have faculty members who themselves perform the learning process with distinction. If it is to serve, it must constantly supply an expectant society — with everything from smart armaments and biotech zygotes to archeological digs and Zoroastrian prophesies — from a reservoir of knowledge that is constantly being refilled. If it is to be dynamic and inspiring, a university must be more than a repository of what others have said and discovered. If it is to be of the 21st century, it must continuously be pushing forward and outward its scholarly frontiers. The university is an anachronism if it puts its graduates into the modern world with only the information of yesterday.

So to display intellectual curiosity, to investigate at the boundaries of your discipline, to advance those very boundaries, will be a key measure of your worth as a professor, of your being *of* as well as *at* a university.

To help you grasp this crucial role of yours, to set your sights high, let's look first at what a representative research university might tell its applicants for tenure.

REPRESENTATIVE STANDARDS

You should have demonstrated the ability to conduct research that reflects original scholarship and makes a contribution to knowledge. Your competence may be manifest in one or more of these categories:

- To conduct research with appropriate methodological technique and rigor;
- To conceptualize and theorize in an original way, with logical and mathematical formulation as appropriate;
- To synthesize, criticize, and clarify extant knowledge and research;

- To innovate in the collection or analysis of empirical data;
- To relate research to the solution of practical problems of individuals, groups, organizations, or societies.

Evidence of research performance and of your standing in a discipline includes:

- Articles published or accepted for publication in scholarly or professional journals;
- Scholarly books, monographs, chapters, bulletins, and so on;
- Reviews and other evaluations of your publications or manuscripts;
- Citations of your work, if particularly frequent and laudatory or by distinguished scholars;
- Research awards, grants, and proposals;
- Evaluations by authorities, especially those from other major universities, in your field of specialization;
- Papers read at professional meetings, invited lectures at other universities and learned societies, invitations to participate in professional meetings, editorial positions with major professional honors, awards, and consultations.

You will be expected to accompany your record of past achievement and current projects with a succinct statement about your future research plans; say, over the next five years.

Such standards will vary from institution to institution, of course, and from discipline to discipline. Scholars in the arts, for example, can substitute a record and prospectus of creative activities for research narrowly defined.

For example, here's what Midland University has to say in its "Criteria and Procedures in Promotion and Tenure Decisions" (p. 4):

> In certain fields, such as art, architecture, dance, music, literature, and drama, distinguished achievement may be considered in addition to distinction in scholarly analysis involving the particular branch of creative endeavor. In evaluating artistic creativity, an attempt should be made to define the candidate's merit in the light of such criteria as originality, scope, and depth of creative expression. It should be recognized that in the fine arts distinguished performance, including conducting and directing, is evidence of a candidate's creativity.

The semantics are different from conventional research criteria, but the vector is the same — excellence.

Does this all sound tough? It is. As Midland's guidelines
(p. 1) make explicit:

> Attaining tenure at this institution is very difficult ....
> Every effort is made to ensure that tenure is awarded only
> to already productive, hard-working faculty who give solid
> promise of the ability and attitude necessary for a produc-
> tive **lifetime** career.

Tough as the research regimen is, assistant professors make
tenure all the time. You can, too. What does it take?

WHAT RESEARCH IS AND ISN'T

When the senior author (**ACS**) first entered academia in
1948 as assistant to a president, early on he was adjured to
draw a sharp distinction between scientific research (both basic
and applied), productive (humanistic) scholarship, and artistic
activity. At the time it was important to do so because the National Science Foundation was supporting only the first, and
there were no comparable funding sources for the other two.

Today it's customary in academic circles to use the general
term **research** to cover all three activities. Yet each is distinctive.

Spanish professor Howard Mancing, head of foreign languages and literature at Purdue University (IN), explains (4):

> Research in the biological and physical sciences often re-
> quires teams of investigators and large sums of external
> grant money.(5) It is what much of the public thinks of as
> research, although field research in the social sciences is
> steadily gaining recognition both off and on campus.
>
> Humanistic scholarship — the research engaged in by most
> professors of languages and literatures — tends to be car-
> ried out by individuals whose major resources are extensive
> libraries rather than laboratories.
>
> Artistic creativity, of course, includes the literary, visual,
> musical, and theatrical works that are performed for or
> presented to the public. (Poets, sculptors, and actors may
> feel downright uncomfortable when their work is described
> as research for shorthand purposes, but such is often the
> nomenclature these days.)

Just as it is valuable to distinguish among the three
categories of research, so is it important to distinguish **process**
from **product** in research.

Mancing has some strong words to say on the subject:

> Professors who read to keep current with developments in
> their fields but do not add to existing knowledge in ways
> that are useful to others (generally by reading papers at
> scholarly meetings and publishing articles and books) are
> not doing research but are merely maintaining their profes-
> sional competence.

Similarly, professors who generate grant or contract money for their institutions and do not publish the results of the work carried out with that support are not engaged in research.

Research is not a **process** or an activity but a finished **product**. That is why publication (or, for artists, performance or showing) is crucial. The products of original research — the published books, articles, or short stories, the concerts or exhibitions — become, in turn, teaching tools, and they extend an institution's teaching mission beyond the campus.

Ernest L. Boyer, of the Carnegie Foundation for the Advancement of Teaching and author of the 1991 book *Scholarship Reconsidered*, might not totally agree with Mancing about the primacy of publication. It's a judgment call with site-specific ramifications.

RESEARCH PREREQUISITES

INSTITUTIONAL CONTRIBUTIONS

In your quest for excellence as a productive scholar, you're not alone. Your college or university, to a greater or lesser degree, can provide a starting gate. If you didn't negotiate varieties of support before accepting your appointment, negotiate them early on.

Freedom

You have every right to expect your institution to:

- Employ a fair promotion system that ensures you a decent opportunity for steady advancement based on scholarly merit;
- Provide a climate of academic freedom — the privilege, derived from the very nature of democracy, to study, discuss, and write about facts and ideas without restrictions, other than those imposed by conscience and morality;
- Rely not upon regimentation but upon the free play of intellectual curiosity;
- Encourage professors to follow indications of truth wherever they may lead, with no thought but to gain a deeper insight into the order of the universe and its denizens;
- Remind the powers-that-be, in the words of a university president, Charles R. Van Hise, that "all human values are the legitimate field of sober inquiry," that "knowledge is ever incomplete, never reaching a final goal";

- Resist the siren blandishments of tainted private monies;
- Keep alive a sense of adventure, encourage imagination, and boldness of thinking, and revive enthusiasm when it flags.

You have every expectation as well that you'll be allocated clock and calendar freedom to engage in research — through considerate teaching loads, acceptable service chores, sabbaticals, summer subventions, and other means of releasing your time to pursue the most productive scholarship of which you are capable — all assuming your own time-management skills permit you always to salvage the unforgiving moment in your day.

Facilities

When he was a graduate school dean, E.B. Fred used to say all a good scientist needed was a coil of bailing wire and a hank of string. That was in the 1930s. While it is true that even today a philosopher may make do with a loaf of bread and a jug of wine, for most scholars the trappings of research can be staggering — dedicated buildings, laboratories, libraries, equipment, instrumentation, computer software and hardware, research assistants, logistical and secretarial sort, and so on. Universities with an expectation that their faculty produce new knowledge are constrained to provide the wherewithal, and you have every right to expect your share.

Does this mean, however, that without massive accouterments there can be no research? Hardly. The scholar with less apparatus and fewer books can still perform that invaluable function of drawing to a magnetic mind the steel filings out of dust of papers. The interrelationship of natural phenomena that may escape the molecular biologist peering into a high voltage electron microscope may be vouchsafed to an ecologist on a vacant lot. The formula hidden in the synchrotron radiation center of a physicist may come crystal-clear to a mathematician in an attic. Main currents in American thought undetected by a political scientist with a computer may be revealed by a professor of literature with personal insight.

The senior author of this manual (**ACS**), for example, drafted his first scholarly book on scratch paper by gaslight in a pyramidal tent while on an enforced "sabbatical" in Korea in 1952 — although admittedly he polished the MS once he got back to a campus carrel. It won a publisher's prize, thanks in part to the perspective that tent provided on *The University and Its Publics* (New York: Harper & Brothers, 1954).

Funds

Research costs money, and a university is at pains to provide it. With luck your university will have internal fluid funds you can tap in a variety of ways — released time, RAs, computer support, and so on. Your institution, too, may be of such repute that it is the regular recipient of block grants from federal, state, and local government agencies, from philanthropic foundations and individuals, from business and industry, from regional compacts — some of which can come your way.

But you'll be encouraged to attract some of your own support. To that end your institution will undoubtedly maintain reference directories of funding sources by discipline and topic, help in writing proposals, and a business office skilled in bookkeeping — knowing full well that it is the creative mind of the individual professor or team of professors, not the president, that lures the most research dollars.

Department chairs report that they take these types of actions to help faculty with their research agendas:

- *Provide resources — start-up and short-term travel money, RAs, and equipment, as well as information about publishing outlets, grant sources, and seminars.*
- *Adjust teaching loads and committee assignments.*
- *Act as "promoter" for faculty who become productive.*
- *Personally mentor faculty.*
- *Actively encourage and support faculty.*
- *Collaborate with faculty, by suggesting research goals and activities and by linking faculty on research projects.*
- *Actively challenge, confront, and prod faculty, as befitting the situation.*

— Adapted from John W. Creswell and Martha L. Brown, "How Chair- persons Enhance Faculty Research Careers," *The Department Chair*, Winter 1992, pp. 19-20.

TUNING UP FOR RESEARCH

Before launching any research effort, consider putting down on paper a tentative objective and scheme of maneuver. Such an exercise will markedly clarify your thoughts about your research question and the feasibility of answering it — research design, scope, needed evidence, and so on. A written plan will also give you a "talking paper" for bouncing your idea off colleagues.

Your schema might contain the following elements, looking

ahead to the research grant proposal you'll probably be writing:

<u>Title</u>. A brief, clear, specific designation of the subject of the research, providing a concrete idea what the project is all about.

<u>Content and Justification</u>. You conduct research in either a theoretical or conceptual setting, as you know. Describe briefly the relationship of your area of inquiry to broad disciplinary issues. For example, a focused study of "damages" in civil libel is part of the larger context of First Amendment issues which intrigue mass communication scholars, just as a study of mass media political content may be in context of economic structure, of democratic political theory, or of the psychology of persuasion. Similarly, a study of the effect of "clean" fencerows on the gray and fox squirrel population in Michigan farmlands is an aspect of the larger issue of the ecology of the wild squirrel in a modern agricultural environment.

The justification for a piece of research is the knowledge it contributes to the context. The research may fill a gap in existing knowledge, draw out and test fresh inferences from existing theory, propose and test a new theoretical position, revise conventional wisdom, solve a significant practical problem.

In general, remember, research answers questions about relationships and yields information not previously known; research is not just a compilation of data.

<u>Literature Review</u>. Summarize and evaluate pertinent previous research. (Note *"pertinent"*; yours is not to compile an exhaustive disciplinary bibliography.)

<u>Objective</u>. Compose a clear, complete, and logically arranged statement of your specific objectives, featuring the major question(s) to be answered or hypotheses to be tested.

<u>Procedure</u>. Explain your design, your methods, and the data to be gathered — all of which must obviously relate to your objectives. Pay attention to these components: sources of evidence and how available; definitions of the concepts you're employing; any special problems of design and analysis you foresee and how you propose to assail them.

<u>Calendar</u>. Make a realistic estimate of the dates for completing the various phases of your project.

<u>Cost</u>. How much will your project cost, and who will pay for it?

<u>Outline of Report</u>. To the extent you can at this stage of the game, draft clear versions of the section headings in any eventuating report. Contemplate a minimum of four chapters: introduction, methods, findings, conclusions.

Topics and their order in any such research plan can vary, of course, with the nature of your discipline and your specific subject matter. Don't let a format hamstring you; after all, this is only a training exercise. But do congeal your thoughts on paper; it will give you a big leg up on writing what may well be a necessity — a request to a funding source for a subvention.

SOME SPECIAL RESEARCH CONCERNS

IN ARTS AND LETTERS

As we've indicated, many arts and letters faculty don't really fit the laboratory or empirical investigation paradigm, so promotion-to-tenure criteria need to be adjusted accordingly.

Here's how one university lists such criteria:

> Faculty members who excel in artistic activities engage in creative work that is appropriate to their area of specialization and is respected by their colleagues and peers, both within and without the university. They disseminate the results of their work through means appropriate to their specialty, such as publications, lectures, performances, and exhibits; and by participation in appropriate technical, professional, and scholarly societies that reflect their artistic reputations. They are aware of new developments and strive to broaden and deepen their knowledge and understanding of their specialties and, where relevant, related fields.

That isn't exactly a specific road map, but it's livable.

Actually, arts and letters faculty can have certain advantages:

First, at least in the case of the languages, society's new fixation on the global marketplace has vaulted foreign language departments into a prominence not enjoyed since the sputnik era. Ditto for area studies consortia.

Second, the emergence of the National Endowment for the Humanities has given arts and letters a federal government cachet which, while it's nowhere near the scope of NIH and NSF, has at least demonstrated a public commitment institutions can't ignore.

Third, as Derek Bok, emeritus president of Harvard, has pointed out, the arts and letters fit a time-honored history of higher education — as the custodian of the preservation and enhancement of culture. This tradition explains "why most universities will struggle to maintain excellent programs in French literature" while allowing some plebeian pursuits to languish.

Fourth, many arts and letters departments have a natural constituency in the form of the lovers of art, dance, drama, music, and literature in their institution's patron community. In many cities across the country, their college or university is the prime purveyor of culture through exhibits, plays, concerts, and readings, and hence local aficionados of arts and letters display a very proprietary and potent interest in the health and long life of their professors.

So if you're an arts and letters assistant professor, you've got a lot going for you even in a research environment. But there's a flip side.

As a university president once said, "It is not the purpose of a university to question carelessly or disturb recklessly the current traditions, customs, or morals."

But that was in 1904. Today his strictures are exactly what arts and letters professors are bidden to do by the very nature of their calling. As French professor and former Yale dean Georges May pointed out recently, "There are no ivory walls to our tower. The world outside the university is divided, and that division is reflected on campuses." Consequently, in any given season, except for a losing football team no campus activity can give an institution's president so many public relations headaches as a "lascivious" art exhibit, a "scandalous" play, a "heavy metal" concert, or a "politically unacceptable" poet.

Yes, you do live dangerously as an arts and letters profession — unless you're fortunate to be on a campus that extends you the same measure of academic freedom enjoyed by its biochemists.

But whoever said life should be fair?

It has only been in the last decade or so that institutions have recognized that all faculty, not just those in the "hard" sciences, need start-up funds for research. A new biochem assistant professor might require hundreds of thousands to get a lab started, but a comp lit professor only a word processor, library acquisitions, and some travel money. But while the new comp lit faculty member's needs require less money, the biochemist is more likely to get the funds. Why? The biochemist will in all probability replenish the money someday out of grant overhead, but it's unlikely the comp lit professor can. So it behooves the humanist assistant professor to bargain hard before even signing on, because the chances may be slim of getting that computer later on.

IN THE SOCIAL SCIENCES
Basic vs. Applied

Research in the social sciences is often deeply involved in the ordering of public values and public goals — in education, in crime prevention, in health care, and so on. Some people like to say such a role is either too controversial or too nonacademic.

Unlike natural scientists whose objectivity as scholars is not

often questioned, social scientists are often criticized for displaying greater subjectivity and hence less scientific rigor. The
critics claim that the tendency of social scientists to compromise
objectivity is a natural byproduct of their goal of social reform,
that the very desire to produce useful knowledge impairs the
ability to approach research "scientifically."

Rather than seemingly being led astray through utilitarian
investigations — instead of being willing to try to help reshape
society — some social scientists feel safe only in studying it, es-
chewing any concern for the political or ideological environment.
It is on unexamined concepts that these experts literally depend
for their professional lives. Asked to render a pragmatic judgment on an issue, they march right up to the moment of decision
and then turn and run. Yet the long-term value of social science
research is likely to rest quite heavily on the ability of scholars
to recognize and analyze the societal implications of their investigations, other scholars contend.

Some social scientists as well, adept at building theoretical
models, tend to regard with some scorn the applied researches
that constituent agencies seek. Preferring fundamental questions and gross problems universal in scope, they shun what
they call "manhole counting" or "brush-fire fighting." Administrators are caught between their responsibilities to their supporting publics and their esteem for the new basic researchers
they've fought so hard to recruit.

Stung by the charge that social science research has little
practical value, other social scientists are willing to go into the
streets with the aim of improving the utility of their product.

Cosmopolitan vs. Community

Those social scientists willing to perform research that
"makes a difference now" increasingly are cosmopolitan rather
than community-oriented. To professors contemplating advancing their careers on a world stage, local and state research has
to some extent gone out of style. As one department chair recently put it, "The question is now, not how do you get colleagues out
of their ivory towers, but how do you keep them at home?"

In short, in the social sciences a gulf is increasingly appearing between global, theory-oriented and generic, problem-
oriented studies — a dichotomy that may make career-building
difficult for new assistant professors. If you are one such, assess
carefully the tilt in your department and its impact on the
reward system you're operating under. Recognizing the problem
may be at least part of the solution.

Interdisciplinary vs. Departmental

Whereas the social sciences today are a congeries of

disciplines and sub-disciplines, once upon a time there was only "political economy." Yet today there continue to be scholars in the social sciences who see modern habits of thought and institutional configurations inadequate to address real-world problems that don't come packaged along departmental lines. However, coordinating the efforts of researchers from diverse fields runs hard up against the inertia of a departmentally based structure of promotions and rewards. Promising as interdisciplinary studies may be, grass-roots social science faculty and administrators tend to be biased against extra-departmental research that demands a reallocation of power and resources.(7)

Here again, junior faculty members must tread circumspectly. If you believe that individuals working within a disciplinary setting are handcuffed by narrow intellectual frameworks that militate against producing research attuned to contemporary social problems, check signals before you shove off all alone onto an interdisciplinary sea.

"No Study Is Immune to Criticism"

Another pervasive problem for new social science researchers lies in the simple fact that the methods and results of their research can closely resemble conventional wisdom and hence be subject to popular trashing.

As higher education researcher Alexander Astin writes:(1)

> Finding flaws in any piece of social science research is like shooting fish in a barrel. Thus decision makers who want to undermine the results of a particular study can always find an expert to argue that the results can't be trusted because of deficiencies in the research method, the variables, or the sampling. No study is immune to criticism.

When faced with such flak, the scholar can seek out an honest and meaningful appraisal that would "try to assess whether, and by how much, the results may have been distorted by the defects, and what the odds were that the key findings and conclusions would be different if the defects could be remedied."

Young social science researchers can take heart from Astin's belief that in a non-adversarial climate, when studies are used objectively to inform planning and policy making, "social science research can improve our understanding of how institutions function, suggest alternatives to existing policies, and help administrators anticipate the likely consequences of alternative courses of action."

IN EXTENSION/CLINICAL

To what level of productive scholarship do you hold a young assistant professor with an extension appointment? Institutions have been wrestling with that question for years.

As a partial answer, some institutions have created extension divisions, outreach faculties, colleges of continuing education, or similar instrumentalities with more or less autonomous tenure criteria which do not include conventional research performance at all, in effect running the risk of housing what some might view as a sort of second-class citizenry.

Land grant universities, on the other hand, habitually employ integrated departments, particularly in agriculture, in which the person with an extension appointment is a full-fledged member, cheek by jowl with regular teaching/research colleagues, subject technically to regular promotional criteria. In actual practice, however, such departments have come to recognize the peculiar nature of extension work and hence weigh the attainments of an extension appointee in custom scales.

In the words of one such document:

> Faculty with extension appointments have significant responsibilities to utilize their professional expertise to disseminate information outside of the traditional faculty-student interactions to help improve the knowledge and skills of their clientele or the environment in which their clientele live and work.

Or another:

> In evaluating the record of candidates with extension responsibilities, the evidence must show that the candidate's work has significantly contributed to the translation and dissemination of the results of scholarly inquiry in his or her discipline to the benefit of society, and that this work has extended the knowledge base of the university to the citizens of the state.

The fact that the chair of an integrated department himself or herself is paid in part with extension monies affords some assurance that the department will factor in specialized extension requirements in arriving at tenure decisions.

If you're one of those assistant professors with a partial or full extension appointment, make doubly sure that the criteria for promotion against which you'll be measured are clearly stated — and then hope that any resident professors in your institution's quality-control structure understand and appreciate the outreach mission.

A clinical assistant professor in a medical school is in much the same boat as an extension assistant professor in a college of agriculture — by what promotional criteria will he or she be measured? A solution: besides consulting all available sources of essential guidance, seek out a helpful mentor.

IN SCIENCE AND ENGINEERING

While the research paradigm fits neatly if you're an

appointee in a science or engineering department, you nonetheless have some special research concerns that warrant attention.

Mushrooming Fields of Inquiry

While the humanities and social sciences are by no means static fields of scholarship, at any given moment they are probably not so explosive as the physical and biological sciences and their engineering applications. For example, rapidly growing, important areas of biology include neuroscience, cell biology, immunology, developmental biology, biotechnology, sustainable agriculture, and biological aspects of environmental impact remediation. Keeping an individual young professor — and an institution — at the growing edge of such mushrooming fields of inquiry calls for more than ordinary alertness, particularly when traditional department lines may work to stifle the interdisciplinary teamwork that is often essential to progress in research in areas of study that don't fit neatly into existing organizational patterns.

If you're in a research area that transcends current configurations, you might start early to push for facilities that could bring together groups with related research missions and provide a focal point for coordinated investigations. Don't ever assume that a dean or provost who dates from another generation is necessarily on top of all the possibilities inherent in interdisciplinary configurations. And don't assume that he or she will necessarily defend rigid campus walls and yesterday's programs when confronted with documentation of emerging needs.

For example, *alter ego* Bill Campion in the Midland University department of botany and applied ecology is at least as apt to find willing research collaborators in Midland's School of Forestry and Environmental Studies as in his home department. But working out joint funding and facilities may take some fancy footwork in tune with Midland's current stance *vis-à-vis* interdisciplinary research programs in emerging fields of investigation.

All this exciting activity in science and engineering research may cause Bill and you to rethink your position on SCIENCE in capital letters. Do you believe that *knower* and *known* are separated, that *theories* are distinct from *facts* and *facts* from *values*? That subjectivity plays no part in the gathering of objective knowledge? That natural laws are inferred from experience, involving confirmation and verification — scientific empiricism? Or do you concede that sociological, historical, economic, and philosophical points of view impact on you and other researchers, that we cannot identify *science* with *truth*, for we think that both Newton's and Einstein's theories belong to science, but they cannot both be true, and they may be false?(2)

It is, indeed, a conundrum. Just so you realize that fact (pardon the expression) and to your own self be true.

----

*No nation can afford to neglect basic research, since
it is the source of knowledge from which come the great
forward steps — in weapons, medicine, agriculture, and
technology in general. It is a university responsibility, in
accepting federal support, to work out an appropriate
balance between applied and basic programs, so that
basic research and the training of young scientists will
not suffer.*

*To build the structure of modern science has required
patience and vision, imagination and discipline, cooperation and honesty. To study it and to add to it will foster
those qualities. If we lose them we lose science and we
lose freedom. If we strengthen those qualities, we shall
have strong science. More important, we shall have such
independence and vigor of mind and heart that no power
on earth can take our freedom from us.*

— Henry D. Smyth, Member, U.S. Atomic Energy Commission,
"The Place of Science in a Free Society," address given at
Amherst College, March 23, 1950, pamphlet, p.4.

Patenting Procedures

So you believe you may have a patentable idea. What do you
do?

The first step is to determine whether the idea may in fact
be patentable (as opposed to being a copyrightable piece of
software or literary, musical, or artistic expression).

There are three types of patents: utility, design, and plant.
Ordinarily you'll be concerned with the first, utility patents.

To be considered for a utility patent, an invention must be a
machine, a process, a composition of matter, or a manufacture.
Further, the invention must be useful, new, and non-obvious.
And, of course, the person who seeks a patent must be the inventor; nobody but the inventor can apply for a patent.

Patent lawyers sometimes refer to a technical field as an
"art." Let's say your contribution to an art seems to meet the
basic tests we've just outlined. The next question: do you own
this piece of what is called "intellectual property"?

The inventor must be the applicant for a patent but may be
obligated to hand it over to someone else. Your college or university policy may state that all rights to a faculty member's discovery reside with the institution. If federal funds supported the

research, the government reserves certain rights. Or a non-government funder of the research involved — industry or foundation — may have a contract reserving rights to any discovery. Also, one or more colleagues or graduate assistants may have a partial claim as joint inventors.

But if you or a group of joint inventors do in fact own an invention free and clear, what are your options?

- You can simply give it away to the world by publishing the idea and making no attempt to patent it. But then you lose control of its application.

- You can turn entrepreneur and attempt to commercialize the idea. But that takes forms of business acumen and amounts of venture capital ordinarily beyond the reach of scholars.

- For a share of any royalties to be earned, you can seek the services of your institution's in-house patent management office, or of one of the national corporations that make patent management their business.

A frequent question is this: if my idea is of such great potential value, do I risk losing it to the public domain via publication in a scholarly journal? And publication is vital. Unless you want to violate that sacred code of scientific conduct — the norm of commonality — you are absolutely obliged to share your concept with the world of scholarship. To do otherwise would seriously tar your reputation.

Fortunately, sharing an idea via publication need not mean allowing just anyone to commercialize it. By being prompt, you can both publish your research and seek a patent. Simultaneously with submitting your paper for publication, arrange to apply for a patent. In a normal time-frame, a patent application can be written by an attorney and filed before the journal article comes out. To preserve patent rights overseas, it's usually necessary to file a U.S. application before first public divulgation of the invention. The requirement is often inflexible. U.S. patent law is more generous: you have a one-year grace period after publication in which to file a patent application.

Now if all this sounds complicated and enervating, it is. Few subjects are so arcane as patent law and management. So the best advice we can give you is: see a good patent attorney as early as possible. Most universities will have at least one in house or on call.

Research Record-Keeping

If only to buttress a patent claim, it behooves any scholar to follow commonsense rules of record-keeping. A researcher's success in obtaining and defending a patent may depend as much on how carefully he or she has kept a research notebook as on how original and patentable the discovery. And even if a patent isn't in the picture, meticulous record-keeping is simply good scholarly practice.

So you should follow these basic mechanics:

- Record all research in a bound notebook to demonstrate that pages have not been added, subtracted, or substituted.

- Leave no blank spaces on a finished page; draw an "X" through any unused portion to prevent adding later entries.

- Number and date every page; begin each day's work on a new page.

- Use pen, not pencil; use the same pen throughout the day.

- To correct an old entry, enter the correction on the current day's page, citing the earlier page and noting why the original record required change.

- **To verify the legitimacy of data, have your notebooks witnessed on a regular basis by an impartial party, such as a colleague who can understand but is not participating in your work: have the reviewer sign off in writing. This is vital.**

To these basic rules, add these refinements:

- Record events as they happen, not as they are recalled.

- Record what you are thinking as well as what you are doing; a researcher can spend months on experiments, but if her or his notebook fails to indicate awareness of eventual potential, that person may have a hard time later answering challenges to the prior ownership of the resulting discovery.

- Arrange with someone else to witness and archive the work of your graduate students or lab assistants.

- Archive your own work by having it photocopied, the copies stamped "received" with a date and locked in a department file cabinet not accessible to you.

- Lock your notebook up at the end of the day in a fireproof cabinet.

- Collect the notebooks of graduate students or temporary workers when their terms are up; they may keep photocopies.

- If you keep your research records on a computer, use a "time stamping" program that automatically dates all

entries into the system and would detect any late
entries into already complete work.

There is no precedent in patent case law where computer-
based data have been used to establish priority of a claim; hence
there's no proven substitute yet for a permanently bound, handwritten research notebook. And that notebook should be more
than a repository of static data with no hint of your evolving
thoughts that are driving the research.

Quite apart from anticipating a patent matter, keeping an
articulate notebook provides a useful personal reference, helps
maintain workplace continuity when a long-term project passes
from one lab assistant to another, provides evidence of where
your ideas came from, documents compliance with a research
grant, and facilitates responding to any allegations of scientific
fraud.

In the final analysis a professional notebook is the quintes-
sential hallmark of the careful scholar.

(A very good review of research notebook practices you can
find in *Writing the Laboratory Notebook* by Howard M. Kanare,
American Chemical Society, 1985. The Society also offers a 1990
free pamphlet, "Electronic Record-Keeping: Cautions and Pitfalls." The Society address: 1155 16th Street, NW, Washington
DC 20036.)

The University-Industry Relations Quandary

While it was popular in the 1980s to promote university-in-
dustry research arrangements to help make American corporations more competitive, both academic and business
administrators are having second thoughts about a strategy
that has been something less than effective.

For example, Professors Richard Florida and Martin
Keeney,(3) authors of *The Breakthrough Illusion* (New York:
Basic Books, 1990), have this to say:

> It is a mistake to push universities into becoming the re-
> search-and-development units of American corporations.
> Universities have other very important missions — educat-
> ing new generations of scientists, providing space for the
> free interchange of ideas, and generating powerful new con-
> cepts. American industry is losing out to foreign competi-
> tion because we don't have the product-development and
> manufacturing skills needed to turn innovations into the
> products the world wants, not because overseas universities
> are better at developing commercial technology.

So think twice about participating in any short-term-horizon
applied research alliances with an industry that (a) separates research and development from manufacturing, (b) fails to nurture innovation among factory workers, and (c) emphasizes

military applications of technology. That's the advice of Florida and Keeney, the former a management and public policy expert in Carnegie Mellon's School of Urban and Public Policy, the latter an applied behavioral scientist at UC-Davis.

On the other hand, what do some of America's industries see when they peer into the groves of academe? As reported recently by *Washington Post* columnist Michael Schrage, they see many university officials who tend to have an inflated view of the importance of university research efforts in innovation, according to an industry-sponsored study on "Industrial Perspectives on Innovation and Interaction with Universities."

Of course numerous science and engineering deans and corporate executives disagree with both propositions. Check signals with the graduate research dean on your campus for a sense of direction.

IN EVERY DISCIPLINE
Your Students

Unless you bore them with too minute a travelogue, sharing your research odyssey with your undergraduate students can be as refreshing for you as it is stimulating for them.

But that sensation can be eclipsed when you walk down the commencement aisle with your first Ph.D. recipient.

To a degree you probably never recognized when you were one of them, graduate students can just about make or break a researching professor, so care in recruiting them and consideration in nurturing them are now a prime concern of yours.

Not only can grad students save you mountains of physical and mental labor, their insights can lift the caliber of your productive scholarship while under your one-on-one tutelage. What's more, their future accomplishments and their proffered assessments of you will come into play when your P&T committee evaluates you.

You'll feel this subtle symbiosis markedly when you preside over your first Ph.D.'s orals. With its probing questions, the committee will be testing you quite as much as the candidate — even more so, you may think as you sweat out of experience.

Hence the time and attention you lavish on promising grad students can be rewarding in more ways than one, even though at times they may seem almost a distraction.

The colleague who says, "A university would be a great place if it weren't for the students" is not only making a crass joke but missing the whole point.

Your Research Proposals

The tender, loving care you devote to your students is equaled in importance only by the attention you bring to conceiving and writing research proposals.

While what we say in Chapter VI about how to develop a research paper is directly relevant to developing a research proposal, there are some differences in degree between the two.

At the very outset, of course, you must satisfy yourself that your idea is sound. Face the fact that a proposal based on shoddy conceptualizations and procedures isn't going anywhere. As one foundation reviewer has complained, "The avalanche of utterly unintelligible thinking dumped out in research proposals each year is ghastly."

Assuming you've surmounted that evaluation, you can then turn to the task at hand.

To help you, Carolyn Saarni, professor of counseling in the Center of Teaching and Professional Development at Sonoma State University (CA), has put down some apt "Tips for Developing a Basic Research Grant Proposal":(6)

Before you start to write —

Study successful proposals in your field, looking particularly for organization, buzz words, and strategies.

Prepare to cite scholars who are likely to review your proposal.

Run your idea past colleagues in your field to test its currency.

As you scan articles in learned journals, check the acknowledgments to see who supported what sort of research.

Face up to your status and/or credibility in your field. If you're relatively unpublished, it's probably wise to shoot for a relatively small grant yet one that will yield at least two publications and two conference presentations.

When you attend society meetings, seek out the grant administrators there and ask them what's the cutting edge of methodology and topic these days.

Sitting down in front of your computer —

Reassure yourself that your mind is indeed creative, original, and alert.

Using the organizational format of successful research proposals, begin to sketch an outline, making sure you don't put "method" ideas under "objectives," and so on.

When you're on top of your subject, go to the campus office that maintains directories of research-funding agencies and

match your idea to the current thrusts of likely sponsors and to the size of their pocketbooks.

Revise your tentative outline in the light of funding agency requirements.

Now flesh out your outline into a draft proposal and circulate it for review among fellow professionals whose savvy you respect and whose time you can draw on.

Revise your proposal to reflect reviewer comments, suggestions, and criticisms of value.

If you're confident you're sufficiently prepared to discuss your research plan coherently over the phone, call the staffs of your target funding agencies to "dry-run" your proposal.

Final planning and writing —

Assemble a file of "trimmings" such as vita revisions, probable appendices, recent relevant references, budget items, and so on.

Back up with hard copy everything you enter into your computer.

Remember whose approval you may have to have before you can formally submit your proposal: a campus committee for the protection of human (or animal) subjects? an office for sponsored programs? your department chair or college dean?

Whether the funding agency wants one or not, make yourself a time-line to keep on track the sequential steps of your project.

Write very clearly and explicitly. Your reviewers will be busy people, not mind-readers.

Write and revise, write and revise, write and revise.

If you submit your proposal simultaneously to several agencies, acknowledge the fact, probably on a "concurrent support" page.

Mind-set —

Steel yourself for rejection.

If that is indeed the outcome, take seriously but not personally the negative comments — and revise your proposal for another try.

Show the criticisms and your revision to a colleague for his or her feedback.

Be persistent and of good heart.

Your References

Along with staying abreast of the literature of your discipline, check as well into the literature of researching in general.

For example, scholars of higher education have this new reference: *By Design: Planning Research on Higher Education*, by Richard L. Light, Judith D. Singer, and John B. Willet (Cambridge MA: Harvard University Press, 1990).

Or any researcher will find delightful reading in *Craftways: On the Organization of Scholarly Work*, by Aaron Wildavasky

(New Brunswick NJ: Transaction Publishers, 1989).

For a look at the big picture, you can scan *Research Universities and Their Patrons*, by R.N. Rosenweig (Berkeley: University of California Press, 1982).

Other suggestions from Charles C. Thomas, Publisher, Springfield IL:

Wadarski, John S., *The University Research Enterprise*, 1989.

Perlman, Alan M., *Write Choices*, 1989.

Carver, Ronald P., *Writing a Publishable Research Report*, 1984.

Westmeyer, Paul, *A Guide for Use in Planning and Conducting Research Projects*, 1981.

Gardner, David C., and Grace Joely Beatty, *How to Prepare a Research Proposal and Get It Accepted*, 1980.

Your campus librarian can help lead you to similar books or monographs you'll find insightful.

Your Perspectives

Research vs. Teaching. You'll meet some peers — natural-born teachers — who bridle at the requirement that they do research. You'll meet other peers who fight the problem of teaching obligations eating into their research time. As if teaching and research were somehow at war with each other.

A healthier perspective may be the recognition that in a very fundamental sense they are mutually supportive, even though they may be carried out by different actions under different forms of motivation. Your teaching is kept creative by means of scholarship; your scholarship gains impetus from the instructional demands of your students. Which is precisely why campuses are home to both — and why you're doing what you're doing.

Being professors, not all of them agree. As Page Smith puts the counterargument bluntly: "The first fact to be established is that there is no direct relationship between research and teaching. The notion that research enhances teaching, although thoroughly discredited by experiences **and** by research, is one that lingers on and is often trotted out ... as a justification for the publish-or-perish policy."

How could the author of a Book-of-the-Month eight-volume *People's History of the United States* hold to such a point of view? Had he held it as a candidate, perhaps he wouldn't have made tenure. As a university provost emeritus, he has more elbowroom.

Perhaps Jaroslav Pelikan, author of *Scholarship and Its Survival*, has it about right. While he holds that teaching and research belong together, he recognizes that the combination "is not always for anyone, not at all for everyone, and not in the same proportion for every university."

Heredity vs. Environment. The classic approach to the history of science has been one of charting the intellectual feats of individuals who have fought and overcome the chains of past folly and ignorance.

As Mark Solovey(5) points out, historians increasingly focus today on such issues as the political economy of scientific research, the ways in which scientific theories reflect cultural concerns and function as social ideology, the processes of disseminating scientific information, and the social, organizational, and institutional factors that influence the practice of scientific research.

These approaches highlight features of scientific development that seem to reveal inadequacies in the traditional stories of the march of scientific progress — science as wholly objective and as progressing ever closer to eternal verities. The newer insights tend to demonstrate a variety of considerations that shape scientific knowledge, of which intellectual merit is only one. They suggest that if the impetus driving the growth of scientific knowledge owes its strength to political, social, and cultural forces as well as to professional powers, then scientists themselves are constrained to understand their environment that bears on scientific practice.

Young assistant professors of science and engineering take heed: add to your perspective of your calling the requirement to appreciate struggles other than those that are ostensibly intellectual in character. You'll find them alive and well in most departments.

Your Program

New faculty in a research-oriented department have to know they're expected to:

- Develop a **program** of research wherein there is maturation in ideas and methods over time on a single topic or a small group of related topics, and

- Extend this research beyond that done for the dissertation.

In other words, a promotion-and-tenure committee will want to see growth beyond graduate school and a sense of direction that will carry a young assistant professor into associate professor years. Creating such a program requires a commitment to scholarship, hard work, and mentorship. The hard work and commitment are up to the candidate; the mentorship is a responsibility the department should assume, but you may have to seek it out.

(Unfortunately, you may need to pass up some interesting research paths, to return to them after tenure. As one reviewer notes, "On my campus people sometimes are denied tenure for lack of 'programmatic' research, meaning that they flit from topic to topic, instead of marching from one research question to the next.")

Looking ahead to your tenure review — which, after all, is a major consideration — be cognizant of the crucial need to turn your research program into published papers and, as another reviewer points out, "of the eventual need for letters from scholars of associate or full professor rank, exhibiting geographical distribution around the country or beyond, and the need to go out and meet such future writers of testimonials early in your career and to keep them aware of the fruits of your research program."

(For full details on "A Bottom Line: Getting Published," see Chapter VI.)

If we are absolutely honest about it, we must admit that the over emphasis on research has ... meant a lot of useless activity, a lot of publishing that serves no purpose beyond expanding the authors' CVs .... A faculty member in the sciences recently compiled what he called an "index of uncitedness." His purpose was to show how many scholarly articles are never cited again. And he found it to be the case that within four years of publication, 37% of the papers published in physics remain uncited and 47% of the papers published in medicine. In the social sciences, the rate of uncitedness rose to 75% and in the arts and humanities to 98% .... It seems to me critical to acknowledge that while there are fine and important things happening [in research], there are foolish and insignificant ones as well. And if we aren't willing to try to discern the difference, why should anyone trust us with the public's money?

— Lynne V. Cheney, Chair of the National Endowment of the Humanities, at the annual meeting of the American Council of Learned Societies, June 1991.

A FINAL RESEARCH CHECKLIST

At Midland University, "documentation of research quality and quantity may include but is not restricted to":

- A record of ongoing scholarly production in refereed journals, including information on the relative contributions of multiple authors and the rejection rates of the journals involved.

- Review papers written for professional journals if they reveal the scholarly knowledge and judgment of the reviewer. (Thoughtful synthesis when accompanied by the ideas of the synthesizer can and often does lead to the creation of new knowledge.)

- A record of success in obtaining research or performing-arts funds from competitive outside funding sources.

- A record of publication in monographs, proceedings of professional meetings, extension bulletins, and other non-refereed outlets.

- Presentation of research and other scholarly work at conferences of professional organizations, especially when the presentations are invited and the conferences are national or international in scope.

- Frequency of citation and critical appraisal of research, scholarly work, or artistic activity, especially when the appraisals are sought independently by evaluators.

- Recognition and awards received for research and scholarly contributions or artistic performance.

- Evidence of work in progress, including manuscripts, grant proposals, and draft scripts.

- Invitations to be visiting lecturer, scholar, scientist, or performer, if that invitation relates to research, scholarship, or the fine arts.

- Evidence of national or international reputation as a researcher and/or scholar.

References

1. Astin, Alexander W., "VMI Case Dramatizes Basic Issues in the Use of Educational Research," *The Chronicle of Higher Education*, July 24, 1991, p. A 36.
2. Donmoyer, Robert, Arthur L. White, and Michael H. Klapper, "The Knowledge and Pedagogical Base of Science Eduction: An Overview," *Teaching Education*, Spring 1991, pp. 11-16.
3. Florida, Richard, and Martin Keeney, "Universities Should Not Become Research Units for Corporations," *The Chronicle of Higher Education*, July 10, 1991, p. B 1, 3.
4. Mancing, Howard, "Teaching, Research, Service: The Concept of Faculty Workload," *ADFL Bulletin*, 21.1 (1990), p. 45.
5. Parker, Glenn, *Team Players and Teamwork* (San Francisco: Jossey-Bass, 1990).
6. Saarni, Carolyn, "Tips for Developing a Basic Research Grant Proposal" (Rohnert Park CA: Center for Teaching and Professional Development, Sonoma State University, May 1990) pamphlet 1-3.
7. Solovey, Mark, "Shattered Dreams and Unfulfilled Promises," MA thesis, University of Wisconsin-Madison, 1991.

V
THE SERVICE SYNDROME

It is the rare American institution of higher education, if any at all, that doesn't list in its triad of faculty missions that of **service** (as if teaching and research weren't themselves services). But what the term encompasses for an assistant professor depends vastly on the character of your discipline, your department, the unit "home" of your department, and your institution as a whole. In the lights of an English department in a bucolic liberal arts college, for example, service will have quite a different connotation from that of a school of communication in an urban university.

"Service" is too narrow a term and too often relegated to third place. I change this third dimension [of faculty roles] to "citizenship" — citizenship in an interactive, contributory sense ... administration, curriculum development, evaluating candidates for advanced degrees, service on campus committees, outreach to professional organizations, and more .... Rather than picturing scholarship and teaching as hierarchically superior to or separate from collegial citizenship, I propose that we look at them as a triangle.

— Susan Rava, Washington University, in a paper presented at the Third National Conference on the Training and Employment of Graduate Teaching Assistants, at the University of Texas-Austin, Nov. 8, 1991.

Institutional documents describing faculty promotion criteria generally talk about three separate categories or dimensions of service: (1) public, (2) institutional, and (3) professional — not always in that order.

Again, to help you grasp your service role and to set your sights high, let's look at what a representative state university might tell its applicants for tenure.

REPRESENTATIVE STANDARDS

PUBLIC SERVICE

"The university of the people has the responsibility of taking the university — the professors, the books, the skills, the findings of research, the interpretations, the insights, the forums, the publications — to the people ... to make all the resources of the university available beyond the college walls." So did Frank

Graham characterize the dimensions of public service when he
was president of the University of North Carolina.

Not all institutions share this massive a commitment, of
course, but all subscribe to the principle to one degree or
another.

You can participate in various ways in carrying out your
institution's obligation to serve the public at large. Your public
service might include membership on committees and boards,
preparation of popular articles and booklets, testifying at public
hearings, speaking to or consulting with public bodies or clientele groups, participating in or organizing workshops and conferences, speaking to lay gatherings, and so on.

(You'll find more about this important outreach function —
as public service is increasingly being called — in a succeeding
section.)

NOTE: Participation in your capacity as a private citizen —
outside the realm of your academic expertise — will not usually
constitute public service in the eyes of your reviewers, who will
rather want to evaluate your **real** public service in terms of
your level of skill and success in communicating and applying
the knowledge in your own field of professional competence to
public needs and problems.

---

*Junior professors need a minimum involvement in
campus service to permit their responsibilities in this important aspect of collegiality to be assessed, to initiate
them into a significant area of professorial responsibility,
and to combat the sense of anomie and helplessness that
many junior professors battle. Department chairs should
carefully supervise junior faculty involvement in service
however, to ensure that each individuals's situation and
personality is matched by the right amount and type of
activity. Women and minority faculty members need to be
particularly encouraged to examine sensibly well-mean-
ing requests that could result in overcommitment.*
— Donald K. Jarvis, *Junior Faculty Development* (New York:
Modern Language Association of America, 1991), p. 73.

INSTITUTIONAL SERVICE

The effective operation of any institution requires a high degree of faculty participation in faculty government, departmental and campus committees, advisory functions, administrative
roles, and similar tasks. While a P&T committee will recognize
that a heavier burden may and should fall on the shoulders of

more senior and already tenured faculty, it will not excuse you for playing hookey. You're simply expected to accept an appropriate role in institutional service as your vital contribution to the functioning of your campus.

The situation may be different in many departments and divisions if you happen to be a woman or a member of a racial minority. You may be invited to serve on every committee, to represent the perspectives of your gender or race. Obviously you'll need to find tactful ways of dodging most of these "honors" or you'll burn out and fade away long before you can come up for tenure. Do whatever it takes to be "good citizen" in your department and division, but no more. And, as long as you have a choice, choose appointments to high-profile committees.

PROFESSIONAL SERVICE

As a professor you're a professional, with all that word implies in terms of relating to all other professionals engaged in your calling. Service to your profession or academic discipline can occur at local, state, national, or international levels.

Recognized activities typically include service as an officer or member of a board, committee, or task force of a professional group; on-site program evaluation visits; reviewing research proposals or manuscripts; and organizing or participating in professional meetings such as training institutes, workshops, conferences, and continuing professional education.

Peer judgment will distinguish your contributions that should be rated as **real** service from those activities that reflect mere membership.

OUTREACH STRATEGY AND TACTICS(3)

PHILOSOPHY

The embodiment of the concept of public service, outreach is fundamentally an institutional state of mind which views the campus not as a place but as an instrument. Translated into an operational philosophy, outreach asks faculty members individually and collectively to make themselves as available as possible to the whole of society, or at least to the constituency from which an institution draws its inspiration and support.

In actual practice, outreach leaders seek to identify public problems and public needs, to interpret those concerns to the campus, to focus institutional skills and resources upon them, and thence to translate campus insights into educational activities throughout a state or region.

As a corollary, the outreach function brings back to the campus those essential public impulses that enliven teaching and stimulate research. What is more, outreach helps to build those public appreciations that keep open the doors to free inquiry and broad educational opportunities, to reinforce the support of the constituency that nourishes the institution, and to continue the acceptance of college and university as the highest order of free institutions of learning.

The outreach mission, in essence, is to bring campus and community into fruitful juxtaposition, thereby immeasurable, enriching the life of both. In so doing, an institution seeks to be both responsible for traditional academic standards and responsive to current public issues.

Manifestly, outreach has public relations overtones. As a pioneer outreach-oriented university president put it: "The purpose of extending an institution should be simply that of educational service. But utilizing the opportunity to carry out knowledge to the people will be a practical advantage to the growth of the institution along all other lines."

As has been said, a true American college or university should have "both open gates and cloistered libraries, both practical messengers and theoretical scholars." Hence has emerged this third university function, a role in which the campus, freely and without perversion, lends its knowledge and skills to all the people in their communities and regions for the solution of everyday problems of living and for intellectual and spiritual enrichment of lives.

METHODS

Outreach methods are manifold. Perhaps not on your or every campus, but as a whole they may encompass specialized residential instruction, evening classes or colleges, short courses, field studies, staff experts on loan to government agencies or private industries, centers for continuing professional education, exhibits, radio and TV programs and stations, educational TV networks, off-campus undergraduate installations, area agents, touring orchestras and theater groups, correspondence study, lectures, concerts, newspaper and magazine columns, summer-school seminars, library services, film and other visual aid distribution, manuals and bulletins, demonstrations, formal consulting services, and a wide range of informal instructional liaisons with individuals, institutions, agencies, and groups.

In other words, in accomplishing your public service responsibilities, you have a wide range of options.

ORGANIZATION

While you can, of course, perform public service duties independently, you will likely have on your campus an administrative officer charged with energizing and coordinating institutional outreach.

What that person will be called on your campus is anybody's

guess: dean, director, coordinator, or even vice president of extension, outreach, continuing education, adult education, public service, or educational services. His or her unit will be variously
called a division, center, office, bureau, university college, or
some such.

For assorted reasons, not all of them logical, some forms of
institutional outreach may not be under the domain of this instrumentality, such as the campus TV station, for example, or
the evening college. As we've said, you've got to learn your own
territory.

Almost certainly, if yours is a land-grant university with a
cooperative extension service, that unit will be set up separately
from other outreach configurations, befitting its charter in
federal legislation "to aid in diffusing among the people of the
United States useful and practical information on subjects relating to agriculture and home economics, and to encourage the application of the same."

Unless you hold part or all of an appointment in co-op extension, you normally will engage its clientele by invitation only,
since deans of agriculture and home economics are zealous guar-
dians of their turf.

A handful of institutions have attempted to arrive at some
sort of organizational entente among "ag extension" and "general outreach," but with indifferent success, so disparate are the
traditions and mechanics of the two entities. More than one
president has stumbled at the chore, so it behooves you to step
with caution.

This is not to say there's a shooting war on. Both organizations subscribe to the proposition that "the essential motivating
force behind a university's work in all times and places when
universities have flourished has been the connection between
the scholar's activities and the burning issues of the day."(1)

GETTING DOWN TO YOUR SPECIFIC OPTIONS

Again, what service expectations hold for you will vary with
the situation and the terrain.

This is a good time to check in with your *alter ego* Bill in the
Midland University department of botany and applied ecology to
see how he's handling the service syndrome.

Bill is uncertain about exactly what should be the scope and
depth of his service role, particularly in his first couple of years
on the Midland faculty, so he seeks counsel from his assigned
mentor, who happens to be the senior plant ecologist in the
department and the chair of Bill's search committee -- Professor
Donald R. Gray.

"Don," Bill said (it's an informal department), "I've read the

Midland P&T guidelines on service expectations *(see last page of this chapter)*, but I still need advice on what my options are."

"I'm glad you've come to me, Bill," Don said, "because it's tricky balancing your civic service duties against your teaching and research obligations. What I'm going to do is tick off some of the service activities I've engaged in during the past 10 years so you can see how you can exploit your professional strengths in a service mode without getting in the way of your teaching and research, and in fact reinforcing them. But it's with the proviso that you take it slow your first couple of years. Do what comes naturally in terms of service, but save your heavy hitting for a while until you're on top of your research program and your new courses. OK?

"University service —

- I chaired the **department curriculum committee** that set up our new biological conservation/sustainable development master's.

- I was a member of the college **student life and interests committee.**

- I served on an all-university **ROTC program evaluation panel.**

- I substituted for Amanda Perkins' predecessor as **acting department chair** one summer when he went to China.

- I advised the president on university **arboretum management.**

- I represented the department on an **interdisciplinary Ph.D. team.**

- I advised the **botany student group** observing the 20th anniversary of E-Day.

"Disciplinary service —

- I served on a state public school **science teaching advisory commission.**

- I held a **contributing editorship** on *Plant Ecology.*

- I was president of the regional **plant ecology society.**

- I was a member of the **AAAS plant ecology committee.**

- I helped develop a **national conference** on the role of plant ecology in the environmental era.

"Public service —

- I advised the **state natural resources board** on land acquisition issues.

- I was a **consultant** to the Ramgo Oil and Gas Pipeline Company — for pay, by the way.
- I served on the Midland city **park commission**.
- I coordinated the department's revised **state outreach program**.
- I worked with school administrators, teachers, parents, and pupils on a **science curriculum**.
- I gave innumerable **public lectures**, particularly after my African trip.
- I appeared occasionally on University **radio and TV** station programs.
- I wrote a **popular brochure** on back-yard prairie restoration.
- I **testified** at a capital hearing on endangered plant species legislation.
- I prepared a **report** for the Midland Lake Protection Association on the long-term effects of agricultural runoff in the lake basin on lake eutrophication.
- I chaired an **on-site team** evaluating the Weyawega Technical School science department.

"That's about what I recall at the moment. As you can see, a lot of what's called service is really a form of teaching or research. For example, that consulting I did for those oil and gas people led to a modest research grant, and that eutrophication paper became a teaching tool in one of my seminars.

"Remember, that's a decade-long track record. Give you any ideas, Bill? You take it from there — and take it easy, but without copping out."

You take it from there, too.

SOME SPECIAL SERVICE TOPICS

Before you even think, "I didn't bargain for any of this," and start trying to figure out how you can get out of "busy work" and "Mickey Mouse" service obligations, consider a couple of factors. First, you may be performing service without knowing. Second, each form of service can bring you a brawny bonus.

FUZZY DEMARCATIONS

The lines between teaching, research, and service are not particularly distinct. For example, as one institution says:

> Textbooks, reports, newsletters, circulars, semi-popular articles, and similar publications are normally considered evidence of teaching ability or public service and will be considered creative work or productive scholarship only when they

present new ideas or incorporate original scholarly research.

Or again:

> Extension activities should not be confused with service;
> they should be evaluated as teaching or research.

Some institutions list "Consulting Activities" as a separate and distinct category in their criteria for promotion; others lump consulting under public service or even occasionally under research (without saying whether paid consulting counts or not; cynics will say that depends on the character of the client and the size of your stipend!).

In the face of all this logomachy, it behooves you to find out exactly what means what at your institution, and how you can perform valued public service without knowing it — or not.

BIG BONUSES
Public Service

The alumni association secretary is always hard up for reunion speakers. The director of admissions pleads for faculty participation in high school career days (a campus euphemism for recruiting trips). The downtown Rotary Club wants somebody to talk about something. An outstate civic group wants a forum leader. A municipal research bureau needs help. The dean of continuing education importunes for evening adult class instructors. Your own dean hears you'd be a fit expert at a legislative hearing in your subject area. The chancellor invites you along on a fund-raising soirée.

Before you get on your high horse and turn your back on all such requests with the excuse you're too tied up teaching and researching, think again. What some dismiss cavalierly as nothing but an institution's "cheap public relations" is actually part and parcel of that matrix of activities that go into generating public and private support for institutional wherewithal — and your salary.

What's more, your institution's administrators are keeping little black books with the names of faculty earning brownie points as "good university citizens." While your name in their books won't protect you from inept performance in teaching and productive scholarship, it won't do any harm either — and may someday be just the difference between promotion and a pink slip.

Institutional Service

In the luck of the draw, you'll wind up pretty quickly assigned to a department committee of one kind or another, and as the junior member you'll likely be appointed secretary. Don't bridle; look on it as a signal opportunity. There's nobody like a committee recorder to make an impression, because with the chore often goes the requirement that you draft the ultimate committee report.

Keep your eye on that prize. Your trouble will lie in the fact that committee deliberations can be elaborate and extended, and hence that the final report be something less than clear and concise, yet complete. So don't even attempt to be a court reporter inscribing each and every entry in the conversation. Capture the essence of who moved what to which effect.

<u>Committee Report Crafting</u>. In drafting the report, apply the 30/3/30 formula. What's that? you ask.

Well, the first number (30) means that many readers will stay with you for only about 30 seconds or so, no matter how compelling you think the subject. What you don't get across in 30 seconds of perusal, you won't get across at all.

So your report title can't be simply a label, like "Annual Report of the Department Library Committee." The title must give the gist of your total message in a strong declarative statement, like "In a Period of Fiscal Austerity, Faculty Are Obliged to Exercise Restraint in Requisitioning Fugitive Serials." That either satisfies or intrigues your 30-second readers.

For your 3-minute colleagues — those who take long enough to leaf through your report — you're adjured to distill your principal subpoints down to strong declarative statements, and display them as bold lines throughout the document, like mini-chapter headings. Either that or consolidate them in a one-page preamble to the report as a whole (sometimes called an "executive summary").

Then, for any 30-minute readers, you can give them the full treatment in condensed type.

You'll recognize there's nothing unique in the 30/3/30 formula. It's the basic pattern of newspaper makeup: headlines for scanners, lead paragraphs for leafers, longer copy for avid readers. And it's the basic scheme for a half-hour TV newscast: first you get the headlines, then the main stories one by one, interspersed with commercials.

The 30/3/30 technique carries a big plus. There's almost no limit to the amount of discourse a faculty committee will insist on including in its statement. Applying the formula will produce a cogent report and preserve peace in the bargain.

Provided, of course, your recording is accurate. There's no fury like a colleague who thinks he or she has been misquoted or, worse, left out of the transcript. Political pitfalls abound for the committee report writer who's careless.

If you want to add a real touch of institutional-service professionalism to your report, apply the doctrine of completed staff action: affix to the report a draft of the memo

the department chair is to issue if he or she accepts the committee's recommendations.

<u>Chairing a Committee</u>. There's only one trouble with becoming recognized as a competent committee secretary: you get named to **head** a committee!

Take that in stride as well. Here's a tip: a lot resides on your timing.

Regularity is important, in order that your department colleagues can arrange their schedules accordingly. So your call should always be for the same day at the same time, at least during any one term.

What day? What time? Your choice will perforce be dictated by the teaching schedules or other unavoidable commitments of fellow committee members. You certainly don't want to pick a day and/or time when one or more professors simply can't attend. With luck you'll have several options. (You have to throw your own needs into the equation, of course.)

Choosing the day of the week can be an interesting exercise, assuming you have a choice: in the fresh of a Monday? a TGIF finale? Your venue may require T, W, or R. Or the weight of departmental tradition may simply dictate day and time.

Chances are your choice of time will ordinarily be limited to early morning, noon, or late afternoon. Sunrise seances can be popular with some colleagues, a plague to others. Bag lunches can be an effective solution, particularly if you can arrange a choice of beverages. Late-afternoon meetings can work if you don't let them drag on and on. A sure way to avoid tedium is to pass out an agenda in advance, along with a synopsis of past discussion.

The meeting of a committee you chair doesn't have to be dull and forbidding; it can actually be a looked-forward-to collegial get-together. Picking a favorable day and time can contribute mightily.

Your reward? A favorable impression on your department colleagues — and an assignment to a college or university committee! Here's a big payoff in institutional service: you get to mingle with the very faculty members, or their associates, who may ultimately be on your P&T assessment committee. There's nothing like being known, if only in a limited way, as somebody other than a listing in a telephone directory. On a more substantive level, extra-department contacts, as we've said earlier, can energize both the scope of your teaching and the depth of your research.

Professional Service

"The department chairperson is expected to supplement the opinions of colleagues within the department

by critical appraisals from distinguished scholars at other universities."

That's a typical directive from a divisional P&T committee to a department chair about how he or she can best "sell" the department's recommendation regarding your promotion potential.

Now if you want to live dangerously, you can rely on whatever prestige your byline on "X" number of research papers has generated. But if you really want to get into the flow, you'll start attending meetings of the most appropriate learned societies or professional organizations in your field.

Yet just attending won't be quite enough. You've got to start finding your way around your calling. While rendering proper obeisance to the big wheels there, concentrate on acquiring acquaintances with the peers in attendance of your own status. It's often best done, not in a seminar, but at the bar. You'll all agree the old fogies in charge of this menagerie ought to be put out to pasture, and you're just the Young Turks to do it. As indeed you will, in fairly short order. Meanwhile you're cultivating just the sort of liaisons you can pull out of the hat when later your department chair says, "To document your case for promotion, we need the opinions of scholars around the country who can attest to your contributions. We have our own sources, but whom would you like to suggest as references?"

Cynics may call it "the buddy system," but don't knock it.

There can be an added bonus in playing the convention game — a family affair. While some learned societies meet in the stuffy confines of a DC Dupont Circle hotel, others assemble in campus dormitories off-season where parents sleep barracks-style and kids run rampant. To get there you perform a cross-country tour that can be as exhilarating for your family as it is enervating for you. No matter. You've made it to Valhalla — the convention.

Once there, regardless of the accoutrements, you can start making professional contributions and personal ties. It's a terrible thing to say, but 40 years or so from now, when you're a retired emeritus, you may look back on those early convention experiences as being almost more satisfying than anything that ever happened back home, what with forming fast friendships, conquering society politics, and challenging disciplinary thinking.

However, to be perfectly frank, we have to admit not everybody is as enthusiastic about conference-going as are we. For example, this diatribe on the subject by Camille Paglia, associate professor of the humanities at the University of the Arts in Philadelphia, in the May 1991 issue of *Arion*:

The Modern Language Association convention sessions ... splinter the profession into political special-interest groups like Washington PAC lobbyists; they encourage the midget form of the "talk," which is simply a vehicle for cozy relationships and networking ... and cram the moneychangers into the Temple instead of driving them out.

Attendance at conferences must cease to be defined as professional activity. It should be seen for what it is: prestige-hunting and long-range job-seeking junkets, meat-rack mini-vacations. The phrase, "He or she is just a conference hopper," must enter the academic vocabulary.

I look for the day when conference-hopping leads to denial of employment or promotion on the grounds that it is neglect of professional duties to scholarship and the institution. Energies have to be reinvested at home. The reform of education will be achieved when we all stay put and cultivate our own gardens instead of gallivanting around the globe like migrating grackles. ...

Excessive contact with other academics is toxic to scholarship. The best thing for scholars is contact with non-academics, with other ways of thinking and seeing the world. ... Instead of schmoozing with other academics at conferences, faculty should be required to acquire a sense of the general audience.

Paglia's meat axe draws some blood, but we believe you follow her dictum at your own risk.

MULTIPLIERS

"Why don't you tell your readers how to title talks and articles to make them look different on a CV and to appear scholarly?" one reviewer suggests.

OK. Examples:

When the senior author **(ACS)** was asked to update his research on 1970 Earth Day leaders for a 1990 North American Association of Environmental Education panel presentation, he spoke from notes on the subject of "Those Original E-Day Leaders: Where Are They Now?" Turning the material into a submission to the *Journal of Voluntary Action Research*, he titled the paper "Long-term, Correlates of Volunteerism: Eco-Activists Revisited."

In reverse, when he was asked to update his 1981 research monograph, *The Environmental Information and Education Ecosystem*, for a 1992 conference on the public relations of environmental management, he again spoke from notes on "The Environmental Management/Mass Communication Mix."

In other words, tailor your title to the occasion at hand, and you'll automatically have varied entries for your CV — some scholarly, some more colloquial.

(For much more on how to make appearances and get published, see Chapter VI.)

CLOSE ENCOUNTERS OF THE FOURTH KIND

Along about now we can hear some of you saying, "All this teaching/research/service trilogy is well and good, but isn't my institution interested in the real me — my character?" Of course! But most don't say so in so many words.

Some do quite precisely, however:

Personal Criteria

> A faculty member (1) displays those marks of character and personality which ensure his/her contributing to the missions of the University, (2) maintains a respectful attitude toward the religious beliefs of others, (3) observes respectfully the rule of law as the basis of constitutional government, and the fundamental human and political rights of others.

That from the "Essential Appointment and Promotion Criteria" of a midsize Midwest urban university (of church affiliation).

If you don't find that frame of reference in the documents of your institution, don't assume character doesn't count; it may be all the more stringent a requirement for being unstated — a basic assumption by one and all.

Certainly an unprincipled person won't last long in academe, particularly under the increasingly close scrutiny by critics of academia in the '90s — unless he or she is a super con-artist or crook.

The exceptions are just few enough to prove the rule.

A FINAL SERVICE CHECKLIST

At Midland University, "documentation of service activity can include but is not limited to":

- Evidence of participation on committees, including chairs held and dates of service (especially demanding committee assignments should be identified).

- Evidence of coordination of programs, seminars, symposia, workshops, etc.

- Description and appraisal of work as advisor to student organizations.

- Description and appraisal of contributions made to professional organizations, especially offices held, committee assignments, task forces, etc.

- Evidence of work as a consultant on disciplinary matters, on editorial boards, as a reviewer or referee for scholarly publication and/or funding agencies, and as a

referee for faculty members under review at other
universities.

- Recognitions and awards for service.
- Evidence of presentations before community organizations.
- Evidence and appraisal of professional contributions made to agencies, industry, and public service organizations.
- Publication of reports, guides, handbooks, newsletters, circulars, etc.

"But," as a Midland mentor cautions, **"don't trivialize
your service activities by including too much. I've seen
some faculty folders that indiscriminately contain so
much padding that the more noteworthy activities are
buried."**

References

1. Jaschik, Scott, "Political Activists Working to Change Land-Grant Colleges," *The Chronicle of Higher Education*, March 20, 1991, p. A 1.
2. Paglia, Camille, "Academe Has to Recover Its Spiritual Roots and Overthrow the Ossified Political Establishment of Invested Self-Interest," *The Chronicle of Higher Education*, May 8, 1991, pp. B 1-2.
3. Schoenfeld, Clay, *The Outreach University*, (Madison WI: UW-Madison Office of Inter-College Programs, 1977), pp. ii-iv.

VI
A BOTTOM LINE: GETTING PUBLISHED

"The Payoff for Publication Leaders" read the title of a **Trendlines** report in a recent issue of *Change: The Magazine of Higher Learning.*(4)

Looking at the characteristics of faculty who are most prolific in journal publications, researchers at the Carnegie Foundation for the Advancement of Teaching identified some rather striking distinctions between productive scholars and all other faculty responding to a 1989 CFAT national survey.

Among other traits, publication leaders:

- Receive higher salaries and rate their compensation "excellent."
- More frequently have outside income from consulting.
- Garner financial support for their research from a range of sources.
- Display consistency over time in the rate of publication.
- More likely teach graduate courses and for fewer hours.
- Have a positive view of the academic stature and environment of their institution.
- Are satisfied with their choice of profession

(Incidentally, these same publication leaders don't shirk their other duties; out of a reported average 50-hour work week, they spend 20 hours on teaching preparation and in-class presentation, 15 on research, the balance on service assignments and other unspecified activities.)

Why not join the club?

IN THE BEGINNING WAS THE WORD

THE WHY

A professor is, literally, in Webster's words, "one who professes," that is, "one who openly declares his beliefs, sentiments, etc." So publishing is simply a hallmark of your profession. Not to publish in some form may seem a denial of your calling.

But by expanding the dimensions of knowledge, by fulfilling your responsibility to interpret, you do more than merely satisfy standards of the professoriate; you gain that tremendous sense of satisfaction that comes from reaching out and touching someone.

Quite apart from these noble ends, of course, there's the bottom-line fact that, in order to meet the requirements for promotion to tenure — in most departments in most colleges in most universities — you must present for review by a designated authority the evidences of your productive scholarship in such form, of such quality, and in such quantity as the laws of your Medes and Persians dictate.

THE WHAT

Manifestly there are many forms of professing. With the exception of the arts and some professional schools, however, the universal academic coin of the realm for purposes of evaluating scholarship has been for centuries and continues to be the printed word (although computer data bases on floppy disks may be the coin around the corner).

Again, there are many forms of the printed word. For purposes of this manual we're going to concentrate on the three broad forms professors most commonly employ in disseminating the fruits of their scholarship:

- the standard research paper or professional book,
- the interpretive article, essay, or monograph,
- the textbook.

Each of these major forms has certain permutations. The orthodox research paper for a scholarly journal, for instance, is readily adaptable to a technical report for practitioners, or expandable to a monograph or book-length treatise. The interpretive article can be made to fit the periodical of a learned society or a semi-popular magazine, or expanded to a university press or trade book. Textbook chapters can be submitted independently as scholarly or popular articles, or the whole book condensed as an monograph.

While all three forms have much in common from the viewpoint of communication principles, each is distinct enough in its intended audience, development, construction, and submission to warrant the separate treatment we'll give them.

THE WHERE

Since your goal is not merely to get published but to get promoted, **where** you publish is a crucial consideration, because in the groves of academe one printed word isn't equal to every other printed word in terms of inherent prestige. Indeed, like a scholar's Gresham's law, "bad words" can even drive out the "good."

In general, a sort of academic "Nielsen rating" for your publication "wheres" will look something like this, in descending order:

- Refereed scholarly journal, the more prestigious the better.
- Refereed professional journal or book.
- Book chapter.

- Non-refereed semi-professional periodical or textbook.
- Conference proceedings, essay collection.
- Semi-technical general-circulation magazine.
- General-circulation magazine or newspaper.
- Radio or TV documentary.

There are many subtleties and exceptions to this "for instance" pecking order, depending on your discipline, department, college, institution, and the expectations of colleagues.

For example, it's one of the anomalies of academic life that if you were to appear in one of the toughest-to-crack, most widely read, highest-paying periodicals, *TV Guide*, it wouldn't count for nearly as much as if you were to appear in an obscure, esoteric journal that charged *you* composition costs — *unless* you're in a professional communication arts department at an institution that values public service highly.

In other words, humanities scholars in liberal arts colleges usually enjoy a smaller range of options than do practitioners in professional schools in public universities.

On the other hand, professors in four-year colleges are more apt to be applauded for publishing papers on disciplinary teaching methods than are professors in research institutes. (That may be unfortunate, but it's likely the truth.)

Again, solicited works can carry different values. Sometimes colleagues may rate them higher than unsolicited work, since they show you've established a reputation. Others may give less credit, since there's the possibility the solicitors may have outlined the papers or even quietly collaborated.

If all this "where" business seems grotesque, grin and bear it; it's the name of the game.

THE WHO

Whatever its form, wherever it appears, writing for publication starts with **you**. You pick the subject. You select the medium of publication. You provide the data or lend the point of view. Writing for publication is inevitably a direct expression — an extension — of you. So before you start researching and writing, look in a mirror. Yes, that's right.

What do you see? What motivates you as a would-be publishing author? What are your publishing goals? What are your strengths and weaknesses as a scholar/writer? The more sharply and frankly you analyze yourself before you even try to set words to paper, the better the odds you'll get into print.

What are some qualities that mark a good publishing author?

Curiosity, about the realm of your subject matter, about your intended audience, about the breadth and depth of media of publication;

Craftsmanship, putting one word after another with clarity or flair, as the case may be;

Conscience, a basic regard for truth and honesty;

Confidence, the will to keep going in the face of rejection slips. As Sinclair Lewis once said, "Be egotistic as the devil, but don't tell anybody about it. It's not the will to be great that's offensive, it's the telling of it."

Want some help in measuring yourself against these attributes? All right, try answering these questions as honestly as you can:

Do you have scholarly talent? Do you have a passion to profess? Will you work diligently at tailoring your writing to the demands of a particular publication? Can you take advice? Will you rest on initial laurels? Will you always research and write your very best?

Assuming you can give yourself at least a B+ in most regards, then you're ahead of the game. Now just watch out about the company you keep and whom you consult.

CHOOSING ROLE MODELS

If you feel you need help in scholarly writing for publication, choose your sources of advice **very** carefully.

Donald K. Jarvis(recently surveyed a small sample (117 people at eight institutions) about their scholarly writing habits.(9) His results were shocking. Here's how they answered these questions:

- *"How do you generate ideas?"* Only 7% said they "test out ideas as papers." (Maybe that's why a journal editor has said submissions are typically "hackneyed, hastily conceived, turgidly written, deficient in clarity and perception.")

- *"How do you plan and protect time for a project?"* Some 66% admitted they try to use "small blocks or fragments of time." (That could account for commentator George S. Fichter going on record to state that too often "dissertations are void of all the vigor and enthusiasm with which the scholars pursued their research.")

- *"What sort of resources do you usually need?"* Only 3% used "papers circulated to attract feedback from others." (Perhaps that explains a publisher writing in *Daedelus* about manuscripts with "a lack of grace and wit and lucid style.")

- *"What is your style of researching?"* Only 8% replied that they "try to collect the needed books to have on hand."

- *"How do you get your outline into publishable form?"* Only 7% said they "make an outline." (No wonder engineer John M. McCullough has commented on "the amount of disconnected discourse dispensed each year as research.")

- *"How do you select a publisher?"* Only 9% "send a letter of inquiry with outline or abstract."

You can do a lot better than all of that if you use as your mentor what follows in this chapter.

As Jarvis concludes in his *Junior Faculty Development* handbook, you must establish the habit of research-and-writing early if you ever expect it to be established.

In his utilitarian guide, *Professors as Writers*, author Robert Boice agrees that you can acquire sound work habits — setting and meeting reasonable goals for editing, rewriting, and submitting manuscripts — if you work at it.(3) Editors Mark Zanna and John M. Darley have much the same to say in the chapter on publishing in their *The Compleat Academic*.(19)

So let's move ahead to a consideration of key common denominators in all written communication.

THE ECOLOGY OF YOUR MANUSCRIPT

A principal reason why some scholarly papers fail to communicate — and hence fail to get into print — is simply because their writers fail to invest a decent amount of time and talent in organizing their facts and expressing their thoughts.

Fortunately the professoriate is coming increasingly to accept responsibility for the effective interpretation of productive scholarship. As *Scientific Monthly* has observed, "There is a growing recognition that if philosophical and scientific ideas cannot be explained in plain language, it is due in plain terms to the ineptness of the writer."

One of the first concepts to recognize at the outset is that there is no such thing as good writing in an abstract sense. There is good writing for one occasion, good writing for a special purpose, good writing for a particular audience, good writing for a certain medium, and so on. The first task of any writer, then, is not to start *writing* but to start *thinking* — thinking clearly and objectively about the "ecology" of his or her manuscript, that is, about the interrelationship of the manuscript and its environment. For example, to answer the question, "How long should my article be?" you have to ask in turn, "What subject, for what purpose, in what journal, when?"

Look at it this way: Robert Louis Stevenson once said a

writer is like a juggler trying to keep a bunch of balls in the air at once. What he meant was that you as a writer must be conscious of a number of "ecological factors" as you go about translating thoughts into words on paper.

SUBJECT

Given any writing chore, it's essential to reduce your message to a paragraph or two that represents the absolute gist of what you want to communicate. Now is when it's a mistake to think in terms of global problems, projects, or programs. The pertinent question is whether your topic boils down to a nub that somebody wants or needs to know about.

During the many years that Manning Pattilla has been reviewing extended manuscripts, he's discovered that in each case he could usually summarize the essential facts in one or two pages, and that the best articles could be reduced to one paragraph. If your theme seems to require a large amount of paper, your lack of brevity may indicate either that you can't yet see clearly the essentials of your article, or that you are bogged down in muddy details, or that you are using verbiage to make up for lack of substance.

Distilling your message has great utility. You can transfer it directly to your completed manuscript — as the covering abstract, as a part of the introduction, or as the summary, depending on the requirements of your chosen medium. But the biggest value of your "nutshell statement" to you will be as a compass azimuth, lending a sense of direction to your total writing task.

AUDIENCE

Having decided in general what you want to say, another step is to come to grips with your audience. For whom exactly are you writing? Fellow scholars in your field? In related fields? Practitioners? Administrators? Students? Laypeople? The more sharply you can delimit your audience, the easier will be your task and the more effective your presentation.

It will help if you picture in your mind's eye a specific individual, the better to conjure up the backgrounds, experiences, intellects, prejudices, and needs your intended readers will bring to a consideration of your paper. Associated Press reporters, for example, are told to "write for a milkman in Omaha"; *New Yorker* writers are reminded that magazine is not for "a little old lady in Dubuque"; while contributors to *The Elementary School Journal* are advised that "our readers are exclusively K-6 teachers and principals."

Your primary aim, remember, is to be *understood* and not necessarily to be *appreciated.* When you begin to contrive how your ideas will be received, not with the most efficiency by the reader, but with the most advantage to yourself — it is precisely then that you will run the risk of becoming confusing. For this affliction the very best antidote is to select an intended reader and write for that one individual.

MEDIUM

Where do you intend to publish your paper? The choice of a journal — even though it may be a tentative choice — should always precede the writing of your article, because no two journals are identical in their requirements. The ideal article is so constructed that it is suited for only **one** publication. Probably more scholars falter here than at any other stage in communicating. They persist in writing first and searching for a periodical afterward.

In analyzing why a religious publication had rejected her manuscript, a comp lit professor thought perhaps it was because one of her quotes contained some four-letter words. She rewrote the article, cutting out the offensive terms, and sent it back to the editor. Once again the paper was returned. This time there was a message scribbled on the margin of the rejection slip: "We do not wish to appear irreverent, but if you cut the hell out of this manuscript we still wouldn't accept it."

It is the matching of manuscript to medium that is the essence of consistent publication. No other aspect of writing is so frustrating — and so intriguing. That is why to it we devote a coming segment of this chapter exclusively to the topic.

PURPOSE

Why are you writing your article? To report new facts or insights? To elucidate a complicated concept? To comment on current trends? To synthesize a number of findings? To propound a novel theory? To entertain? Your purpose will help dictate your audience and your means of reaching it.

Wilbur Schramm, pioneer mass communication scholar, reduced the communication phenomenon to four elements:

1. The individual with a message to transmit.
2. The individual for whom the message is intended.
3. The message itself.
4. Unifying experiences, backgrounds, or goals that enable a message to be coded and de-coded efficiently and effectively.

Element four is crucial. By capitalizing on known common denominators, you can lend to your message those aspects of appeal, clarity, force, and tone that go a long way toward guaranteeing that your reader will willingly receive and accurately interpret your communication.

OCCASION

The "when" of article writing is another factor on which some scholars stumble. Rarely is it possible to make a manuscript do double duty effectively. The piece of work composed originally as a convention address will have to be re-tailored if it is to become a journal paper, assuming it was an apt speech in the first place. The seminar term paper or graduate thesis is seldom (if ever) in proper shape for publication. This doesn't mean, of course, that materials can't be put to different uses. They can. But considerable carpentering is invariably essential.

TYPE

There are various types or forms of writing. As we've said, we deal with three of the more common in this chapter. The exact format you choose will emerge from a consideration of the ecological factors we've just outlined — subject, audience, medium, purpose.

Incidentally, think of that list as forming a wheel, not a ladder. In other words, you don't have to start with a subject; you can enter at any spoke. In reconnoitering media, for example, you may identify a subject. An occasion may suggest an audience. And so on. Whatever your starting point, in constructing your manuscript you can profit from a firm grasp of that key communication strategy — marrying manuscript and medium.

MARRYING MANUSCRIPT AND MEDIUM

"A house," said Frank Lloyd Wright, "should be a circumstance in nature, like a rock or tree." Had the dean of American architects been talking about writing for publication, he could not have defined any more aptly the principle of marrying manuscript and medium. For that's all we mean, that each piece of writing be a natural circumstance in the publication in which it's contained.

How do you perform the ceremony? You begin by selecting a promising subject.

CHOOSING A COMPELLING SUBJECT

The most likely source for subject ideas will naturally be your own discipline in general and your specialty in particular. On one topic or another you have a near-monopoly.

On occasion, your background will suggest a topic. For example, during Desert Storm some cytologists as well as classicists who were Middle East natives wrote interpretive articles based on their personal experiences and insights.

Sometimes an avocation may provide a fertile field for subject matter.

Actually, subject ideas are all around, if you make a practice of looking for them — your classrooms, laboratories, libraries, museums; journals, magazines, newspapers, radio, TV; conventions and symposia; memories, chance observations, personal contacts and colleagues; house and home; history; the calendar; even your true loves and pet peeves.

You're a scholar, of course, not a media reporter, so to any potential subject you're expected to bring a high level of expertise as a principal investigator, performing artist, practicing professional, interpreter with more than ordinary insight, commander of cogent argument, connoisseur of rhetoric, master of technical detail, or some other specialist.

Testing Your Idea

In picking a subject to work on, then, look first in that mirror again. Can **you** handle the project? Is your idea really within your grasp, or is it outside the range of your experience, expertise, ability, or stature? Don't sell yourself short, by any means; but on the other hand, it's probably foolhardy to tackle a champagne project on a beer capacity.

Assuming you've picked a subject within your scope, put it to these tests:

- Does your idea have **utility** for your intended readers, or is it merely a means of self-expression for you?
- Is it **salient**? Does it make a difference now?
- Is it **timely**? A fresh entrée or a warmed-over casserole?
- Does it have **substance**, based on well-documented data or inspired insights, or is it sophomoric?
- Does it contribute something **new** to the profession?

And now the $64 question: Do you know a publication into which your subject will fit?

To answer that question, there's no substitute for a thorough and continuous study of your options.

What About Your Thesis?

The first subject idea to put to these tests could very well be your thesis, about which you're rightfully proud.

What do you do with it?

One option, of course, is to evaluate it in terms of turning the whole thing into a book — with considerable tailoring, no doubt. If you honestly believe that approach has possibilities, adapt the tactics we outline in the forthcoming section on getting a textbook published.

A second option is to extract any experimental data as a research paper, adapting the tactics we outline in the forthcoming chapter on getting research findings published.

A third option is to convert one or more of the chapters into an interpretive article or essay, adapting the tactics we outline in the forthcoming section on getting that form of productive scholarship into print.

Let's face it: a fourth option is to forget it. It's no criticism of a thesis that it has no exploitative value. After all, it's served its purpose.

(If you had known then what you're learning now, you might have crafted a book under the guise of a thesis. It's done all the time. For example, Roderick Nash's Ph.D. thesis in intellectual history, "Wilderness and the American Mind," was in print as a book by that title within a year after his graduation. You might bear that possibility in mind as you advise your own grad students, albeit warning them that thesis criteria and book criteria can be comparable only in their principles, not in their mechanical details.)

Assessing the "market value" of your thesis — as of any subject idea — demands a thorough command of intelligence about the publishing world, to which we now turn your attention.

RECONNOITERING THE PUBLICATION WORLD
Casting About

There's no better place to begin your search for suitable publication outlets than your department reference room with its selected shelvings. It may be your good fortune to find an annotated bibliography of periodicals in your particular discipline; for example, a new (1991) annotated list of over 300 international journals accepting articles in the field of education: *Publication Sources in Educational Leadership: A Compilation of Publication Outlets for the Creative Exchange of Information in Educational Administration and Supervision* (Lancaster PA: Technomic Publishing, 1991).

But don't stop with visiting your reference room; its resources may be limited, or your best bets may lie in journals in collateral fields. So branch out to the campus library. There you're practically sure to find some excellent reference aids:

- For scholarly journals, *Ulrich's International Periodicals Directory, Standard Periodicals Directory, Serials Directory*, and/or *MLA Directory of Periodicals*.

- For publishers of trade books and magazines, *Writer's Market*.

- For publishers of scholarly and textbooks, *Literary Marketplace*.

- For news media, *Gale Directory of Publications and Broadcast Media* (formerly *N.W. Ayer's*), and *Editor & Publisher International Yearbook*.

Don't hesitate to ask your friendly reference librarian for clues to other aids. For example, of signal help in finding out what current American general-circulation magazines are carrying is the *Reader's Guide to Periodical Literature*, a monthly index (later bound in semi-annual volumes) of articles by author, title, date, and publication, categorized under topic headings based on Library of Congress nomenclature.

There's one catch: the LC and hence *RG* can be slow in adopting newer classification options. For example, when a new breed of environmental scholars went to *RG* in the mid-'60s, the only articles they could find under "Environmental Management" referred to heating and air conditioning. What they were looking for they could locate only under assorted forms of "Conservation" — water, soil, forest, and so on. Today, of course, environmentalism has its own multiple *RG* categories.

Fortunately, activist college librarians are creating new subject headings every month to keep up with the *zeitgeist*, and pressuring the Library of Congress to step up its cadence in reflecting changing times. In the past decade the LC has added over 400 new headings, from "Anti-smoking movement" to "*Glasnost*" and "Tex-Mex music." But you're apt to find *RG* headings still lagging behind avant-garde scholarship. So, hunt.

And don't forget about the young and hungry journals that have appeared since the latest bound directory was published. Fortunately, *The Chronicle of Higher Education* regularly carries a valuable listing of new scholarly periodicals as they emerge from the womb, together with a succinct description of what each one is looking for in the way of manuscripts.

Journals in your discipline may also offer occasional summaries of projected collections of invited papers.

Professors seeking to expand articles into specialized books should pay particular attention to the more than 70 university presses that serve scholarship in effective and imaginative ways. In the wake of changes in commercial publishing brought about by corporate mergers, university press lists may assume increasing relevance through the growing practice of commissioning or contracting in advance to sign up promising and desirable authors. The University of Tennessee Press has recently published Professor Paul Parson's book, *Getting Published: The Acquisition Process at University Presses*.

However, university press publishers themselves are by no means in agreement on how to proceed in an era clouded by financial and cultural upheaval. At their July 1991 convention, some argued for going after the best scholars, seeking wider audiences outside academe, and publishing serious general-interest books that commercial publishers overlook. Others saw such a diversion of resources as a threat to what's supposed to be the lifeblood of university presses, the scholarly monograph.

Yet all could coalesce in honoring the Johns Hopkins University Press for bringing out a book that 49 commercial presses had turned down and which then sold 100,000 copies in 1989 alone— *Staying Dry: A Practical Guide to Bladder Control*, by academicians Kathryn L. Burgio, K. Lynette Pearce, and Angelo J. Lucco. Of course it didn't hurt that Ann Landers endorsed the book in her syndicated newspaper column.(5)

Do you have such a "Golden Fluke Award" book in your repertoire?

Another excellent source of up-to-date information on the world of scholarly publishing is the bimonthly review of academic life, *Lingua franca*, which regularly carries an "Inside Publishing" column. For example, in a typical issue you could have learned what Duke University's *South Atlantic Quarterly* is up to; that the Princeton Series of Contemporary Poets is in limbo; that Basil Blackwell is expanding its journals division; that the University of Pittsburgh is working on a series of original-language critical editions of 120 20th-century literary works from 22 Latin American and Caribbean countries; that the University of Virginia was seeking manuscripts for a new series, "Knowledge: Disciplinarity and Beyond" — books that track the histories, rhetorics, methodologies, and "institutional topographics" of academic disciplines; that the Ecco Press is inaugurating a new series of book-length essays on artists; and how the formative field of film studies has editors and publishers in a quandary about how to proceed. All good grist for the mill of the scholar seeking outlets.

Nobody seems to know exactly how many scholarly journals there are, but most estimates place the number published in the U.S. alone in the tens of thousands. The Institute for Scientific Information, a reference data bank in Philadelphia, tracks articles in 7,000 scholarly journals, including foreign publications — probably only about 25% of what's actually out there. The Modern Language Association's most recent *Directory of Periodicals* lists some 3,200 journals dealing with literature, linguistics, language, and folklore alone.

Then there are 5,000-plus general-circulation periodicals and an estimated 500 book publishers as well for you to analyze — and consider.

Not only is the number of periodicals in circulation at one time known imprecisely, new journals and magazines are born seemingly every day, as disciplines expand and/or fractionate and as differentiated audiences arise. As we've said, *The Chronicle of Higher Education* carries a listing of new scholarly journals just about every week, and *Writer's Digest* keeps track of new (and deceased) general-circulation magazines. It pays to keep abreast of such developments because young periodicals tend to be hungry for manuscripts.

Keep your eye as well on developments in the field of electronic journals — periodicals that are distributed over computer networks. At present they're held in low repute by most academicians, but they could stimulate a major shift in the nature of scholarly communication. At present there are six such peer-reviewed journals available on Bitnet and Internet, all in the humanities and social sciences, and the American Association for the Advancement of Science is thinking about experimenting with a journal in either chemistry or math.

Zeroing In

Unless the screen you used was too fine, your casting about should net you upwards of a couple dozen publications that would find your subject compatible. From your years as a grad student, you're no doubt abundantly familiar with several of them. All you know about the others is what you read in an annotated directory of periodicals. In such a case the best way to get a line on what a journal is accepting is to consult its "Guidelines for Contributors" which habitually appears on the inside back cover. If none's there or elsewhere, don't hesitate to write for one.

Here's what you might get from a hypothetical journal:

Guidelines for Contributors

THE JOURNAL OF AUSTRALIAN STUDIES

Submit to: The Pacific Rim University Press, 164 West Coronado Avenue, La Jolla CA 01293.

Style Guide: University of Chicago Press *A Manual of Style*, or consult the "Note to Contributors" on the masthead of any issue of *Journal*.

Type of MS: Accepts original typescript, double-spaced research papers, interpretive essays, technical reports, book reviews related to Australian history, culture, public issues, demographics, geography, trends. Particularly interested in aborigine studies, genealogy of today's leaders, impact of U.S. media, endemic gambling, Anzac traditions, environmental hazards, economic strategies. Usual length: 2,500-3,000 words, with a maximum of 4,000-5,000. Average of six articles per issue.

Mechanics: Submit original on white opaque paper (8 1/2" x 11") plus three copies with a self-addressed stamped envelope and a covering letter. Author(s), give full name, rank,

department, and university, or any other pertinent identifying information. No cost or pay for articles published.
Covered reprints available at a cost varying according to
length. Author(s) receive(s) two copies of *Journal* and six
offsheets free.

Disposition: Receipt of MS acknowledged within a week if
accompanied by a self-addressed postcard. Decision of Editorial Board in four to six months. Published approximately
a year after acceptance. Rejected manuscripts are sometimes criticized for possible reconsideration.

Such a guideline gives you a pretty fair idea of what you
might submit and how, but changing times and editors may
have passed by a guideline the publishers haven't adjusted since
it was set in type a decade ago. In any case, there's really no substitute for analyzing a half-dozen current issues of your journals
of choice.

What do you look at? The table of contents; the masthead
slogan; the cast of characters — editors, editorial board (anybody you know?), authors; departments; advertisements; and, of
course, the articles themselves in some detail.

What do you look for? Range of subject matter; style, treatment, organization, length; evidence of audience type and level;
proclivities of the editors; mechanics — charts, graphs, tables, illustrations; title and citation format; in short, all the increments
of intelligence that can help you answer the question, "How can
I best marry my MS to this medium?"

Picking a Target Publication

Sooner or later you've got to pick a publication of first
choice. What should be your criteria?

Prospect: Which publication offers the most likelihood of interest in an article on your subject matter — submitted by you?
No matter how compelling your topic or your treatment, some
media simply deny their pages to other than "name" authors.

Prestige: In which publication will your byline return the
most in the way of brownie points toward tenure? As we've
pointed out, in every discipline and institution there's a pecking
order.

Balancing these two perspectives is a crapshoot. A journal
with a high rate of acceptance may be at the bottom of the pecking order, while one at the top probably has a scandalous rate of
rejection. Everything else being equal, it probably makes sense
to go for the gold initially and then accept tin later if necessary.

Tailoring to Fit

Now you're ready to tailor your MS to fit your journal of
choice. What do you tailor? First, the subject. Then your treatment of it — general style, approach, details you include and

details you exclude, length, title, beginning and ending, phraseology, attributions, rhetorical devices, data presentation, illustrations — in short, everything except your facts.

The simplest sort of example:

When biochemist Karl Paul Link first announced the synthesis of a new rat poison in the research notes of a journal of analytical chemistry, he titled his brief paper "3-(1-phenyl -2-acetylethyl)-4-hydrox-coumarin as Hemorrhagic Agent." A more elaborate succeeding article for *Chemical Industries* was titled "Warfarin: A New Anticoagulant as Rodenticide." Describing the discovery and its discoverer for a newsmagazine, a national science writer headlined his piece "Karl Paul Link: Pied Piper of the Test Tubes."

That's marrying manuscript and medium in a nutshell. We'll have more to say about this essential technique later in this chapter as we discuss those three principal forms of disseminating productive scholarship.

THE "BUSINESS" SIDE OF WRITING

LEGAL AND ETHICAL CONSTRAINTS

It's a free country, but for writers, not that free. It would take a book, and then some, to cover all the ins and outs of press law. All we'll do here is outline key aspects a scholar ought to be conscious of.

Copyright

While facts as such can't be copyrighted, only the specific expression or wording of information, the intent of copyright law is clearly to protect the original writer, so acknowledgments are always in order, even if you don't use exact quotations. (Besides, what better way to demonstrate your scholarly diligence?)

When and how you can use such materials depends on whether a source is "free." You can quote freely from a source said to be in the public domain: your own interviews, works on which the copyright has expired, public documents, giveaway materials.

It's best to assume that any printed material not clearly in the public domain is copyrighted material. You can still quote from such material provided you do three things: (1) acknowledge the source fully, (2) obtain permission of the copyright owner, and (3) adhere to the doctrine of "fair use." The last is a thorny issue. The rule of thumb is 300 words or less, but that has no standing in the courts.

Since the specter of plagiarism shadows every scholar, the best thing to do is to cite everything and get permission for every direct or indirect *extended* quote. To do so, record the following data as you take notes from printed material: (1) from

a periodical or newspaper — writer, headline, name of publication, address of publisher, date, volume and issue number,
page(s), (2) from a book — author(s), title, date of publication,
name and address of publisher, date of copyright and name of
copyright holder, page(s).

To get permission to use a quote, you write letters to the
copyright owners. Each letter should indicate exactly how the
material is to be used, the precise passage(s) to be quoted, the
context it will be quoted in, and the bibliographical acknowledgment you propose to use.

If all this sounds like work, it is. But remember, the law that
makes it necessary is the same law that should protect your own
work from word thieves.

Usually you'll be granted permission to quote gratis, unless
an author has some reason for not wishing to be associated with
your work. If you and/or a publisher stand to make money from
your project, then the copyright owner will probably want a
piece of the pie. Writers of song lyrics are particularly voracious.
You'll just have to decide how big a bite you can afford.

It's ordinarily your responsibility as a writer to get all necessary clearances and file them with the publisher. When an editor accepts your manuscript he or she wants to be assured the
title is clear.

Libel

If you have a hand in publishing something that injures
another identified individual, you may be subject to suit for
libel. If it is something that would be highly offensive to a
reasonable person, you may be subject in some states to a suit
for invasion of privacy. To be sure, it's highly unlikely that an
academician would be subject to such hazards, if only because
the deep pockets of a publisher are the more lucrative target.
But it has happened. When in doubt, consult an attorney.

Ethics

A more likely hazard for a scholar is the slippery slope of
questionable data or of breathing implications into those data
that simply aren't there. Even in academe, there are different
strokes for different folks, as the saying goes. The best advice we
can give is just this: in the final analysis you have to live with
yourself. If you can honestly rationalize behavior that might be
cause for professional concern, OK. But if you know in your
heart that what you're doing is alien to the better angels of your
nature, don't do it. As Hoagy Carmichael once said, "Don't ever
play anything that ain't right."

YOUR METHODS OF WORK

Stake Out a Territory

In animal species it's a congenital habit to delimit a territory to facilitate reproduction. Your needs are the same. Your office will do admirably, so long as you continue to maintain rigid office hours for students. And provided it's within reasonable commuting distance from your residence. If the latter doesn't apply, then carve out a sacrosanct niche at home — in the basement, in the attic, in a corner of the master bedroom — wherever. You simply must have a previously prepared position of retreat.

Earmark Time

"Oh, I write when the spirit moves me." Forget it. Unless you reserve a set time each day or so for applying the seat of your skirt or pants to the seat of your chair, you'll never do it. Known for his prolific writing, the senior author of this manual (ACS) was frequently asked by colleagues, "When in the world do you ever find the time?" His invariable answer: "What were you doing last Sunday morning at 5 a.m.?" A dawn patrol may not be your dish, but find one you can live with.

Line Up Your Tools

What they are will depend on your field — applicable references, manuals, dictionaries, thesauri, and so on. The one common tool today: a word processor/computer. Tablets and typewriters are as out as the kerosene lamp — unless, of course, your retreat is a cabin without electricity. Nothing has so revolutionized the mechanics of scholarship as word processing. In fact, some publishers may even require that you do the whole composing process for them: you send them floppy disks of your final version, done according to their specs, and they translate them right into page-proofs. Today a computer-illiterate scholar is an anachronism.

Composing on a word processor or computer can present a hazard, however. Computer-literate professors can become afflicted with what newspaper editors call "screenitis" — a tendency to polish whatever is visible on one screen and ignore overall coherence. The result can be a "clean" but disjointed article. As one journal editor has noted, "At the level of the individual paragraph, the writing can be very good, but there is no train of thought linking paragraphs together. Some authors will even repeat an early sentence later on in an article, as if they had never read the paper through as a whole."

An antidote: print out an entire draft of hard copy and edit that, to make sure you've connected the knee bones to the thigh bones.

Have Your Theme Well in Hand

A broad topic doesn't make an effective paper or article. You've got to define sharply in your mind a particular aspect or theme or angle.

For example, let's say you're an American historian in a liberal arts college in mid-Illinois. For a special February edition, the editor of *The Illinois Magazine of History* is soliciting contributions on "Abe Lincoln in Illinois." That's too broad, too unmanageable, too fuzzy a subject for a journal — for a book, maybe, but not for a journal. If you say, "I'll do a paper on Captain Abe Lincoln's brief career as a soldier in the Blackhawk War," now you're beginning to arrive at a subject with a handle, but you've still got some focusing to do. Let's say your topic will be how Abe was like many GIs before and since — a reluctant volunteer who spent more time fighting boredom than Indians and who looked back in later years on his days of soldiering with both loyalty and loathing. Now you've got a true theme.

Always distinguish between subject as generality and subject as specificity — and cling to the distinction. That's your lodestar as you work.

Another example of narrowing a topic:

Under the broad rubric of "black women," you could begin by picking one of such options as these:

- A specific place — New York City, for instance
- Person — Maya Angelou
- Time period — Depression
- Type — Politicians
- Aspect — Teenage mothers
- Relationship — Employment
- Event — Assassination of Martin Luther King, Jr.

But you haven't sharpened your thinking enough yet for an article. Now you want to mix and match to distill a true journal report. For instance:

- Civil rights cases involving black women during World War II.
- Black parent involvement in school desegregation efforts.
- Female black Olympic athletes.
- History of the National Council of Negro Women.
- Shirley Chisholm's influence on the feminist movement.(8)

Now, give your chosen topic a news peg or a seasonal slant and you're off and running.

Make an Outline

If you don't make an outline, the piles of notes you have scattered around on desk or bedspread will show up just as scattered in your manuscript. What form your outline takes is unimportant. It can be just a list of key sequential facts scribbled on a scrap of paper. Or it can be a fully developed affair, following all the niceties of an English composition class assignment. Use whatever form best serves you. You may need a detailed outline in order to ensure unity, coherence, and emphasis. Or you may find a more fragmentary outline permits you to write with more spontaneity. Whatever the form, make sure you have some sort of article "map" in hand or in mind before you set to work.

As one commentator recounts, "For what it's worth I take notes, let it gel, then outline one day and write the next. If I let the outline sit too long, I lose the cohesion."

Get Away From It All

Well, you say, I've done extensive research, I've got a hideaway and writing time, I've lined up my tools, I have a theme well in mind, and an outline. Now do I write?

No. Get away from it all.

We're not kidding. Store your notes and take a break for mental digestion. You're too close to your subject. If you start writing now, you'll tie yourself in a Gordian knot. So let your ideas rest. Your unconscious mind will take over and contribute to your paper a logic and a flair that you can never achieve if you move directly from note-taking to writing.

In short, what we're saying is that all writing — even a laboratory report — is creative writing. "The light that never was, on sea or land" can shine on a research paper quite as much as on a poem.

But don't let your voluntary sabbatical run on and on. Procrastination is the enemy of productivity.

Field-Test

Now let's jump ahead to the stage where you have a first draft in hand. What do you do? Field-test.

First, a really tough job — look at your own work with an eye sufficiently jaundiced to spot your own flaws. There is perhaps no aspect of writing so difficult as objectively judging your own MS. You're so close to your work that you can't see it as others will see it. The trouble arises from your frequent failure to recognize that what you have so well-rounded in your mind you have simply not conveyed completely and clearly on paper. Looking over a draft, you are all too prone to read into it what is not there for the reader who does not know what you know.

The remedy? Steel yourself and submit your draft for critique by valued colleagues with varied talents: someone familiar with your subject matter, someone expert in quantitative or qualitative research, someone representing your target audience, someone qualified as a connoisseur of the English language — and then sit back and take it.

Some comments will be so complimentary as to be worthless, some so savage as to be devastating. Pay particular attention to suggestions about what you say, less to quibbles about how you say it. And then revise accordingly.

A word of advice: don't use a friend, a relative, or a spouse as a critic. You want to improve a manuscript, not break up a relationship.

That Final Polishing

Sometime in the process of field-testing your MS, it will be well if you take a hard look at it from the mundane viewpoint of good old-fashioned grammar and sheer readability. Not that we don't think that after 20-some years of schooling you aren't skilled in the basics. It's just that scholars in any discipline can fall prey to some nagging habits.

Seven Deadlies. So called because they can kill the soul of your writing:

The Verbose. The use of a whole phrase when a single word will do, the long word instead of a short one — displaying your vocabulary instead of trying to get an idea across. Example: "A recent study has shown that leaf reflectance of infrared light is dependent mainly on the nature of the cell wall/air space interface of the chlorophyll-containing spongy mesophyll cells and, to a lesser extent, on the cytological features of other tissues within the leaf." If you think you have to indulge in such verbosity for the sake of scientific respectability, at least supply a translation for the uninitiated, like this: "Depending on their makeup, different plant and tree leaves reflect infrared light in different ways to produce different colors on infrared photos."

The Hackneyed. Certainly you want to avoid expressions that through overuse have lost all their freshness. Studying writing burdened with clichés and redundancies, three Marquette University scholars found 10 in one 500-word book review: "stink ... state-mandated ... boost ... watered-down ... stamp of approval ... flawed and inaccurate ... accepted and widely used ... vigorously opposed ... complied with at any cost."

The Passive. "It was determined that ...." Why, oh why scholars can never say, "I discovered" or "We found," we simply don't know. Perhaps it's simply a dodge to escape responsibility or an inculcated modesty. The debility shows up in other ways: "The reason he left college was that his health became impaired," instead of "Failing health compelled him to leave college."

The Convoluted or Run-on Sentence. At its best, such construction impedes understanding; at its worst, it can trap you into comical inaccuracies in word usage, as in these varied examples dredged up by Columbia University composition detectives:

> In 1992 it will be exactly five centuries from the date when it is said Italian mariners whom the decline of their own republics had put at the service of the world of adventure, one of the group being Christopher Columbus, seem to have discovered America while seeking for Spain a legendary passage to the Indies to offset the achievement of Portuguese discoverers who had carved their names in the history books of the westward expansion of European culture and Christianity unless to be sure the heathens had triumphed instead of succumbing to the pernicious diseases and firearms that were obviously manifest evidence of the spirit of God moving on the waters of the new open seas stretching from Occident to Orient interrupted only by new continents of immense natural resources that were to sustain the emergence of hitherto undreamed of civilizations.

* * * * *

> The Mormon Church has no doctrinal position on when life begins but takes a hard line against abortions performed for reasons other than to save the life of the mother or in cases of rape and incest after counseling with a bishop.

Accent on the Negative. In other words, addiction to tame, colorless, hesitant, noncommittal language. Example: "*The Taming of the Shrew* is rather weak in spots. Shakespeare does not portray Katharine as a very admirable character, nor does Bianca remain long in memory as an important character in Shakespeare's works." How much better to say, "The women in *The Taming of the Shrew* are unattractive: Katharine disagreeable, Bianca insignificant."

Dangling Modifiers. Among the most common, the participial phrase at the beginning of the sentence that doesn't refer to the grammatical subject: "A soldier of proved valor, residents entrusted him with the defense of the city" should be "A soldier of proved valor, he was entrusted with the defense of the city." "As a young and inexperienced assistant professor, the assignment appeared easy to me" should be "As a young and inexperienced assistant professor, I thought the assignment appeared easy." Violations of this rule can be ludicrous: "As a mother of five, with another on the way, her ironing board was always up." And a final example, from a recent news report:

"Beatitude," a student art exhibit that uses religious images
to support abortion rights, is at the center of a controversy
at Grover Whelan Community College. Students charged
the college had engaged in censorship when officials, in
response to complaints from other students and politicians,
covered the display with black paper. After being kept
under wraps for a day, college officials reviewed their decision and ordered it to remain on display.

The Dreaded "This." Technically called a demonstrative
pronoun with an indistinct antecedent, **this**, referring to the
complete sense of a preceding sentence or clause, can't always
carry the load and so may produce an imprecise statement:
"Visiting dignitaries watched as the ground was broken for the
new high-energy physics laboratory with a blowout safety wall.
This is the first visible evidence of the university's plans for mod-
ernization and expansion." **This** doesn't make clear what the
"first visible evidence" is. Correction: "Visiting dignitaries
watched as the chancellor broke ground for the new high-energy
physics laboratory with a blowout safety wall. The ceremony af-
forded the first visible evidence of the university's plans for mod-
ernization and expansion."

Traffic Control. If you've gotten into the habit of strewing
punctuation marks around indiscriminately, reconsider that
habit and think of them in terms of their value as ways to control the flow of your words for greater impact and readability.
Here are some simple rules:

- **Use a comma before a conjunction introducing an
  independent clause:** "The early records of the city
  have disappeared, so the story of the first years can no
  longer be reconstructed."

- **Use a semicolon to join independent clauses:**
  "Smith's theories are compelling; they command attention."

- **Use a colon after an independent clause to introduce a list, an amplification, or an illustrative
  quotation:** "Today's headlines remind you of a classic
  line: 'These are the times that try men's souls.' "

- **Use a dash to set off an abrupt break or interrup-
  tion and to announce a long summary:** "Violence —
  the kind you see on TV — is not honestly violent. There-
  in lies its harm."

We could go on and on about all of this (Is "this" indistinct
here?), but after all, this (Whoops, we did it again!) is not supposed to be a refresher course in grammar. Better that you buy,
read, and put on your nightstand a little paperback,

The Elements of Style, by William Strunk, Jr. and E.B. White. First printed in 1935, it's a little out of date now: for example, it frowns on the common fare of TV announcers, breaking sentences in two; and it contradicts several newer style books by saying that in a series of three or more terms with a single conjunction you use a comma after each term except the last. But it's still a classic guide to making your words count. As *The New York Times* says, "It's as timeless as a book can be in our age of volubility."

The Importance of Writing Well. In an excellent paper by that title in a University of Iowa *Graduate Bulletin*, Ralph Frasca makes the telling point that "the quality of your thoughts are perceived to be only as good as your ability to express them."(7) That proviso should be tacked to your bulletin board.

Now let's quote along with Frasca from a master of sideline language, Bobby Knight: "All of us learn to write by the second grade, and then most of us go on to other things."

The acerbic Indiana University basketball coach was commenting on sports writers, but may as well have been referring to professors. Regardless of the field of study, all professors are called upon to write, and writing ability is simply assumed to be part of the intellectual repertoire they've mastered over the years. Yet publication editors complain vociferously and often about the turgid and garbled prose of their would-be contributors, Frasca says. It's an unspoken maxim in most periodical offices that editors are more likely to hold lucid, concise, and technically correct papers in higher esteem than those that are poorly constructed. (Just think of how you probably react to student term papers and essay exams.)

The clarity and technical precision of your writing inevitably influence editorial decisions, particularly in the case of scholarly journals:

"The paper that needs less work, less language repair, is more likely to get an acceptance," according to Don McComb, editor of *The Journal of Communication Inquiry*. "If you submit a poorly written manuscript, we just find we can't work with it, because unless we find a reviewer who will take up the challenge of trying to get it into shape, we'll send it back and tell you it needs to be revised because the language is a problem."

Although you may be tempted to discount writing skills in favor of your capacity to think and reason, it's by your ability to communicate that such attributes are most often judged, Frasca points out. A professor may have a brilliant mind, but the value placed on that mind will be considerably diminished if the scholar demonstrates an incapacity to translate its contents into effective prose.

Writing is a public act to attract the attention of others, so it's just plain insulting to tax their time and effort with a tortuous, vague, and incompetent display of putting one word after another.

Mastering good writing isn't "busy work," a distraction from your other responsibilities. It's a powerful tool you as an assistant professor need to communicate the contents of your mind and to influence judgments made about it. It takes practice and conscientious dedication.

Preparing Your MS for Submission

And now let's jump ahead still further to the stage when you're ready to prepare a final draft.

You've written enough themes, term papers, and theses to know in general what to do — type or print out double-spaced on 8 1/2" x 11" single-sided numbered sheets of white bond (no crude dot matrix printing and no spreadsheets). The rest isn't that complicated.

Cover your MS with a letter to the editor that makes clear your status. (A professional letterhead adds aplomb.) Add on separate sheets any charts, graphs, tables, or illustrations, properly captioned. Include a large, self-addressed stamped return envelope. Add cardboard stiffening. Mail first-class in a 9" x 12" envelope, addressed to the editor by name. As a courtesy you can enclose a couple of extra copies of your MS, but in an age when photocopy machines are ubiquitous, it's not absolutely necessary to do so.

Rules for submitting magazine articles or book proposals vary somewhat from this procedure; we'll take them up in sequence later.

Keeping Records

Writing for publication requires organization, notably that you keep a record on each MS: stage(s) in preparation, date of periodical, date of acknowledgment, date of rejection or acceptance. You can make notations on a 3" x 5" card; you can keep an elaborate journal; if you want to be dramatic you can post the data on a bulletin board in your office for all to see. The format isn't important; keeping track is — if only to avoid the embarrassment of sending the same article to the same magazine twice.

Here's a "bookkeeping form" suggested by Professor William Moore of the University of Kentucky:

    MS Title

    First Draft

    Final Copy

    Expenses Incurred

Sent to

Date

Rejected Date

Accepted Date

Publication Date

Some Standard Procedures

Don't (repeat, **do not**) send a manuscript simultaneously to more than one publication. (Exception: textbooks can be submitted to several publishers at once.) First of all, if properly tailored, your MS will fit only one periodical anyway; second, your submission is a tacit guarantee that you are offering uncontaminated goods. For example, if you submit a paper to the higher ed journal *Change*, you'll get back a card saying, "It is our assumption that your manuscript has not been concurrently submitted to any other journal or magazine; if it is under consideration by another publisher, please let us know immediately." The clear implication being, "Don't play dirty pool with us."

If you're a nervous type and want to make sure right away that your MS has been received, enclose a stamped, self-addressed postcard that says something like, "We have received your paper, *Surviving in the Urban Wilderness* and have it under consideration."

Once you get that card back, don't hound the editor. Particularly in the case of refereed journals, review can take months as your MS makes the rounds of busy fellow professors. If you think it's really time to check up on an article, wait another week. Then send off a friendly tracer letter on the long shot that your MS has actually gotten buried in somebody's in-basket.

Don't ever send off an MS without keeping a copy, either a hard copy or a floppy disk, properly sequestered.

Don't give up after one rejection. Re-tailor and re-submit to another likely journal. (After multiple rejections, of course, a strategic withdrawal may be the better part of valor; put the MS in a bottom drawer until you can approach it with renewed vigor and a fresh perspective.)

Don't wait too long to start your next project. To be a consistent published scholar, there's no substitute for keeping manuscripts in the mail.

Practicing Public Relations

And now comes that halcyon day when your paper appears in print. Don't bury your light under a bushel. Distribute reprints among appropriate colleagues, both on and off your

campus, particularly those who reviewed your MS. Send a copy
to the campus information office; the professionals there can
judge whether it has any news value. Some relatives and friends
may also appreciate knowing of your accomplishment.

Then anticipate your paper being cited by other scholars.
There's no greater satisfaction. (Unless, of course, it's reaping
book royalties — or getting promoted to tenure.) And then move
on to other publication projects.

As you accrue a list of citations to your work, keep a running
list (preferably in your computer) so you don't have to hunt
them all down when you need to produce them.

Mark of Distinction

Correctly conceived, reporting about scholarship can be as
challenging and rewarding in its own way as scholarship itself.
As you walk the golden road to tenure, you can join the growing
ranks of scholars adept at both research and communication.
"These intergrades in human taxonomy," ecologist Aldo Leopold
wrote of such scholars, "are perhaps more important than those
which so perplex the mammalogists and ornithologists. Their
skulls are not yet available to the museums, but even a layman
can see that their brains are distinctive."(12)

THE STANDARD RESEARCH PAPER

The lines we've drawn among types of scholarly writing are
flexible and interdisciplinary. While what we're calling the
standard research paper is most at home in the sciences and
professional schools, humanities scholars on occasion may
employ the format. Likewise, while the interpretive article or
essay is the format of choice for humanities scholars, its use is
not uncommon on the part of professors in the sciences and
professional schools. Textbooks are interdisciplinary.

Each form of discourse takes its signals from the requirements of a particular type of publication; the research paper, for
example, from the scholarly journal. The researching professor
and the scholarly journal are symbiotic; neither could live without the other. Scholars necessarily, then, learn all they can
about learned periodicals.

UNDERSTANDING LEARNED JOURNALS

Learned journals have as their mission the dissemination of
the fruits of research and productive scholarship. Few of them
make money, or at least not much. If they at least break even,
they're content. They're "kept" by learned societies, by universities, by publishing houses, by editors laboring gratis, by
librarians, by scholar/subscribers paying high subscription
rates. Their survival hinges on keeping up with the times, by

publishing the works of known savants, by somehow defeating rising publication and mailing costs. A common fear: that they'll be rendered irrelevant by scholars who "break" results of their research in the press before their papers appear. That's why some journals will yank a paper if it's been upstaged, and why scientists are increasingly timing their public announcements to the appearance of their papers in refereed journals.

The thing to remember is, learned journals need you just as much as you need them. Without a flow of publishable manuscripts their editors would be bereft. So be a good sport and meet their needs.

RECOGNIZING YOUR OPTIONS

Let's say you're an assistant professor of educational psychology in the school of education at California State University-Sutter's Mill. Your research emphasis is child development, and you have some interesting data and theories to communicate. You're reconnoitering for scholarly journals in your field that seek "reports of original research, especially empirical studies making contributions to theory."

If you cast your net widely enough, you'll find a whole range of options:

- *Journal of Applied Psychology,*
- *Journal of Counseling Psychology,*
- *Journal of Educational Research,*
- *Journal of Experimental Education,*
- *Journal of Experimental Psychology,*
- *Journal of General Psychology,*
- *Journal of Social Psychology,*
- *Peabody Journal of Education,*
- *American Educational Research Journal,*
- *California Journal of Educational Research,*
- *Child Development,*
- *Educational and Psychological Measurement,*
- *Harvard Educational Review.*

And probably some others that haven't made it into the directories yet.

Which journal you pick as your initial target will depend on an astute analysis of how well the thrust of your subject meets the thrust of a particular journal, on a comparison of rejection rates, and on a frank recognition of that well-known pecking order.

THAT PECKING ORDER

Determining the ranking of journals has become important to scholars and those who evaluate their performance, because although all journals seem to be created equal, in fact some are more equal than others.

Three techniques stand out when it comes to ranking professional journals: the **reputational** approach, in which a panel of scholars votes subjectively on which journals in a particular field are the more prestigious; the **citation analysis** approach, in which librarians determine the number of times a journal's articles are cited or quoted elsewhere; and the **rejection rate** approach, in which the easier it is to get into a journal, the lower its "Nielsen rating."

Each method is relatively crude. It's probably an ecological fallacy that the quality of an article can be determined solely from the ranking of the journal in which it appears. In fact, at least one study suggests greater variation in the intrinsic quality of articles appearing within than among journals.

Sociologists Ralph A. Weisheit and Robert M. Regoli advise scholars to "rank journals in sets or clusters rather than by assigning artificially precise indicators of rank."(18)

Be that as it may, the important pecking order for **you** is the one employed by **your** evaluators, assuming you can figure it out with any certainty. When in doubt, ask your librarian for an assessment.

Variety is also an important consideration. As one reviewer notes, "If all your articles appear in one journal, even in the most prestigious, people may suspect you have an 'in' there."

Regardless of your journal of choice, the organization of your paper will follow a stylized outline common to almost all research journals, similar to the outline you used in planning your work and in writing a research proposal.

ORGANIZING YOUR PAPER

A research paper can be based on either qualitative or quantitative paradigms. At least in the physical, biological, and social sciences, it will usually include the following components, more or less in this order:

Abstract

Say, a hundred words or so, in which you summarize clearly and concisely the whole of your paper, from A to Z. Don't just say what you did; say what it means.

Problem Statement

A theory to be tested, a practical issue to be resolved, a question to be answered.

Review of the Relevant Literature

Without going back to the Punic Wars, it's better here to err on the side of inclusion rather than exclusion, lest you inadvertently leave out just the reference a reviewer may be looking for.

Description of Your Research Methodology

This section should be precise and complete enough that another scholar could replicate your research without stumbling.

Report of Results

Hew to the facts objectively; let the chips fall where they may.

Discussion

A frank recognition that your results did not support your hypothesis may be just as valuable as a positive outcome. Speculation about *why* you got what you did and *how* to direct future investigation may be the most significant aspect of your paper.

Summary

For those readers who'll only read your summary, give them both barrels. Where you draw conclusions, support them with appropriate research methodology and documentation. You can indulge in recommendations and/or conjecture so long as you identify them as such.

ABOUT STYLE

Not so long ago, a classics professor had some fun in a point-of-view piece in *The Chronicle of Higher Education* under the title, "Semantics and Symbioses: How to Write an Article to Impress Your Peers." Among other recommendations, Marleen Boudreau Flory said: (1) in the title, try to hide the subject from the readers; (2) lavish attention on your footnotes because all readers will read them, only a few the article itself; (3) when it comes to style, protect yourself by writing everything in the passive voice and by inventing new terminology nobody knows; and (4) keep before you at all times a mental picture of a board of review counting pages.

Flory was only half-kidding. Unfortunately it's true that some scholars "impose upon themselves a certain technical lingo as a mark of professional respectability," as *Scientific Monthly* has complained: "The specter haunts these scholars, not of a frustrated reader, but of a tart review accusing them of superficiality." As a matter of fact, the senior editor of this manual once got back a manuscript with this notation:

> This work is so interestingly written we are persuaded it is not sufficiently scholarly."

(Schoenfeld changed all the active voice to passive voice, all the

first and second person to third person, most of the monosyl
lables to polysyllables, and sent the MS to a sister journal —
where it was happily accepted.)

If you think this sort of advice is an aberration, here's more
in the same vein:

> Be very careful when choosing a title for your article. Promo-
> tion committees never read papers, but they do see titles.
> The more pedantic, the better; scholarly work isn't sup-
> posed to be interesting. I almost called my articles on dic-
> tionary usage in last year's *French Review* "Practicing Safe
> Lex," until I realized that promotion committees would see
> them. Of course, don't make the titles so pedantic that no
> journal will want to publish them.

> Be sure to cite as many sources as possible. A long bibliog-
> raphy has come to represent thoroughness of research. It
> helps get articles published in the first place. Even col-
> leagues who do not read your work may flip to the back of a
> reprint to look at the bibliography.

> Avoid first-person articles or simple reports on how you do
> things [in the classroom]. Some colleagues do not even con-
> sider this research, no matter how useful it may be .... By
> comparing one's own program with what has been described
> in the literature, one can accomplish the same thing, but
> not make it look like memoirs. Thus, "TA Supervision in
> French at State University" becomes "Alternative Models
> for Supervision."

That's advice from Joel Walz of the French department at the
University of Georgia, writing in the November 1991 *AAUSC
Bulletin*.

It doesn't have to be that way. And indeed scholarly journals
are increasingly asking you to break away from the straitjacket
of scholasticism. So let your thoughts flow out naturally and
simply, as if you were speaking to a colleague or leading a seminar. In other words, talk to your keyboard; and talk to say something, not to show off.

This approach will help you use straightforward English,
with a minimum of gobbledygook, tortured construction, and Ed-
wardian prose. Strive always for the phrase that most strikingly
imparts meaning, even if it borders on the colloquial. Professor
Edward Schten, for example, lifted a scholarly article in *Public
Administration Review* out of a scholarly rut by writing about
"good guy" public servants vs. "bad guy" pressure groups. In a
recent *Journal of Higher Education*, reporting on reasons for a
national decline in the number of transfer students from community colleges upward, Professor W. Norton Grubb said the
answer was not a single stab in the back but a concatenation of
a large number of causes — what he called "death by a thousand

cuts." Observing the 500th anniversary of that fateful voyage of Columbus in 1492, historian David Gelman wrote, "Over the centuries, his reputation has tended to expand and deflate like some unruly Thanksgiving Day parade balloon." In the same vein, historian David Gates spoke to Columbus: "You started out with the best intentions. You were going to get rich *and* save the world. You didn't see any contradiction there. You were the first American."

It must be admitted, of course, that in some disciplines there may be a certain risk attached to sounding too "popular," particularly on the part of an assistant professor. If that's your situation, adjust accordingly.

ABOUT DATA PRESENTATION

In "The Science of Scientific Writing" in a recent *American Scientist*, Judith Swan of Princeton and George D. Gopen of Duke(16) offered some excellent advice on how to choose from a variety of formats in presenting your data:

- A list of data sets is easier to interpret than a line of data separated by semi-colons, especially when the data sets may also contain other symbols, such as equal signs (=) or Greek letters.

- Presenting the data sets in columnar form with clear column headings would be better.

- Numerous columns of data are best presented in tables.

- Data columns or tables should flow exactly as we read, with contextual material on the left in a pattern that produces an expectation of regularity, and clarifying or statistical information to the right, in order of greater and greater detail. It might be easier to think of it as "an outline lying down."

TAILORING TO FIT

In making an initial evaluation of how well you've married your research paper to the requirements of a particular journal, editors and reviewers are drawn inevitably to two inescapable components — your title and your citations.

The Title

While an editor may edit your title or change it all together, it's the mark of the pro to propose as suitable a one as possible. And you should be able to do so accurately and with feeling, since learned journal formats, typography, and metier change very little from issue to issue. In structure, style, and even letter-count, strive for an exact fit.

If your journal of choice prefers stark labels, use one, like "Weight Gain Investigations Revisited" for *American Journal of*

Clinical Nutrition. For *Science News,* a paper on the same subject might be titled, with more flair, "Fat and Fiction: Calorie for calorie, the thin gain more — and other weighty findings."

In the same vein, writing for *American Heritage,* William L. Rivers titled a historical profile thus: "Thurlow Weed: Back Room Strategist." For a more scholarly journal he might have called it "A Study of the Influence of Thurlow Weed on the Election of John Quincy Adams."

What you don't include in your title can be just as diagnostic of its fit as what you put in, and vice versa. For example, take this title/sub-title in *Journalism Quarterly*:

> ### The Press and NEPA: The Case of the Missing Agenda
> With respect to "the most sweeping environmental law ever passed by a United States Congress," neither the daily press nor specialized periodicals played an agenda-setting role. Congress constructed its own social reality.

The author could use the terms "agenda-setting" and "social reality" freely because they're in the lexicon of every professor of mass communication, but the National Environmental Policy Act (NEPA) had to be explained as "the most sweeping ... law."

A similar example: In the title of this manual, the terms "mentor" and "tenure" are apt, since their meaning is familiar on any campus; in a manual for another profession, you'd have to substitute alternate terms familiar to that audience.

Signature

The signature (byline) for journal articles is likewise all-important as a proof that a potential author has studied the journal in question and therefore is worthy of serious consideration: type style and location (beginning or end; left, right, or center) of author's name, academic affiliation, rank. There are dozens of combinations — yet only one for each journal.

Clean Copy

Misspelled words, triple letters, missing copy, repeated lines, grammatical errors, and so on can only suggest that the author takes neither his/her work nor the audience seriously. (And don't trust your computer's spelling and grammar checking programs to do it all. Even the best programs won't catch every sort of mistake.)

Citations

Next to — if not before — your title/abstract and signature, editors and reviewers will look at your footnotes/references/ bibliography.

For one thing, they'll check to see how current your MS is. If your dates are all three years or more old, you're passé.

Then they'll look for names of authors known to be crucially pertinent to your subject matter (perhaps even their own). If you've ignored relevant papers, you're in trouble.

Finally they'll inspect the style of your references, because nothing is so diagnostic of the degree to which you've tailored your MS to the specifications of the journal in question. A miss is as good as a mile.

If you've seen one reference you've seen 'em all? Guess again. There are more than two dozen formats in common use today, sometimes even within a single discipline — AGU, AAA, APSA, MLA, Chicago A, Chicago B, AIP, ASM, ANSI, CBE, LSA, GSA, ACS, APA, ASA, Cambridge, UP, AIBS, AMA, ICMJE, RAI, Praeger, SSSA, Turabian, Wiley.

For example, a so-called standard humanities footnote style (carried at the bottom of each printed page in a journal; in a book, at the end, chapter by chapter; in each case, preceded by a serial number superscript clued to a corresponding number at the appropriate place in the text):

> [9]Clay Schoenfeld, "Communicating Research Findings," in Robert J. Griffin *et al.*, *Interpreting Public Issues*, (Ames: Iowa State University Press, 1991), p. 269.

Or a so-called standard hard sciences reference style (carried alphabetically at the end of the paper or book, with the date appearing after the cited author's name in the text):

> Schoenfeld, Clay 1991
>
> "Communicating research findings," in Griffin *et al.*, Interpreting Public Issues. Ames, Iowa: Iowa State University Press. 490 pp. 269.

A common variation, in which the cited references are listed alphabetically at the end of the paper or book and assigned a serial number, that number then appearing in association with the citation in the text:

> 21. SCHOENFELD, C., 1991, Communicating research findings, in Griffin *et al.*, Interpreting Public Issues, (Iowa State University Press, Ames), 269.

Some journals may employ both footnotes and references, the former to indicate source of research funding and/or prior presentation at a conference, to acknowledge the assistance of any collaborators, and to pay the inevitable homage to a significant other "without whom the pursuit of my career would be dust and ashes." Other journals may call for a bibliography in which you include source materials not specifically cited.

And so on and on through picayune variations. The variations may seem slight to you, but they're significant in an editor's eyes.

Don't (repeat, **do not**) adopt any of these styles — or any other — unless it's the one in current use by the journal at which you're aiming. Which means, of course, that you've got to consult a current issue and/or its "instructions to contributors."

If you get rejected by your journal of choice and are readying your MS for an alternate submission, don't forget to adjust your reference format accordingly. To fail to will only suggest that your research may be as sloppy as your conformity to convention.

Fortunately, if you use a computer, there's at least one citation program that will do all the work for you, once you've entered information in the data file. Just call up the journal-specific style you want and press the proper keys. An Einstein or a Dewey never had it so good.

PERSPECTIVES

At least by implication, any research paper can well express basic tenets of scholarship. The essence of science is its trying, testing, and trying again. Viewed in this fashion, science becomes a determined, never-ending search in every nook and corner for knowledge of the way things really are and usually operate. The scientific method is a way of investigation which relies on rigorously exact testimony. The aim of research is objective verification. The techniques themselves are varied. And each project is always a gamble.

Let's let those two previously quoted *American Scientist* authors have the last word:

> Although scientific data, analysis, and concepts can be complex, their expression need not be incomprehensible. The goal of scientific discourse is, after all, communication. The intent of scientific writers, therefore, as with all writers, should be to produce clarity in communication without oversimplifying the issues.(16)

THE INTERPRETIVE ARTICLE OR ESSAY

When she was a young Wesleyan University professor, Sheila Tobias decided "to do what a lot of scholars can't bring themselves to do — write about their work for a wider audience. Research is done and reports are written, but somehow I didn't feel the people were reading them. I asked myself, How do you get people to read things? I concluded the answer was, You use a narrative writing style." The result was a best seller, *Overcoming Math Anxiety*, and over 100 articles from *Atlantic Monthly* and *Family Circle* to *Harvard Educational Review*.

"Those articles gave me an opportunity to reach more readers," she says. Now the College Board has published *Breaking the Science Barrier*, written in collaboration with her husband, Carl T., a physics professor at the University of Arizona, based on an earlier report, *They're Not Dumb, They're Different:*

Stalking the Second Tier, about students who did well in high school but then drop out of college chemistry "because they find it dull." Tobias is a much-in-demand consultant for the Science Foundation Research Corporation.(17)

Tobias' work exemplifies the fascinating range of exposition types and publication opportunities covered by the article/essay rubric: a philosopher's sermonette, a humanist's familiar essay, a historian's interpretation, a sociologist's analysis, a bio-chemist's commentary, a lawyer's argumentation, a political scientist's point-of-view article, a publisher's editorial, a journalist's news feature, an engineer's manual, an outreach specialist's bulletin, a business professor's prediction, and so on.

These variations may differ in degree, but not in kind; so we can say some things in general about writing articles and essays for publication. In fact, in the sense that a book is simply an extended article or an articulated assembly of chapter-essays, this discourse is applicable to book writing as well. (However, we do devote a later separate unit to the special case of textbook writing.)

CATEGORIES OF ARTICLE/ESSAY OUTLETS

There are six categories of periodicals you can contemplate as outlets for the fruits of productive scholarship in the form of the interpretive article or essay. In order of scholarly "prestige," they are:

I. The Scholarly Journal that does not carry reports of investigations in the form of the standard research paper but does carry statistical studies in discussion mode, as well as issue-oriented essays. Published by a learned society, a professional association, or a school/college/university. Refereed.

II. The Professional Journal interested primarily in the application of knowledge to practitioner problems and issues. Published by a professional association or a government agency. Usually refereed.

III. The Technical Journal carrying "how to" articles and provocative essays for the field. Published by a commercial house. Not refereed in the academic sense, but the editors are no pushovers.

IV. The Semi-Scholarly Magazine published commercially yet with very high standards of sophistication and exposition. Its sophisticated subscribers want the best in contemporary literature and commentary, particularly when the author's credentials contribute to the impact. Not refereed, but carries great prestige in most circles.

V. The Consumer Magazine, happy to translate syntheses of new research written in terms a layperson can understand and appealing to his or her need to know. Published by a commercial press. Not refereed in the academic sense, but professional editors put manuscripts through a fine screen.

VI. The Extension/Outreach Bulletin that translates the results of campus research and scholarship into utilitarian information for an institution's lay constituency. Can be edited, illustrated, published, and distributed by campus specialists, or contributed by the author to a citizen group or government agency. A valued activity for extension and professional school professors.

RECOGNIZING YOUR OUTLET OPTIONS

Let's say you're again that assistant ed psych professor at California State University-Sutter's Mill. You've scored with a research paper in *The Journal of Educational Research*, and now you're casting about for other means of communicating your child development findings in the form of articles or essays. By dint of diligent reconnoitering you can identify a surprising number of options in each of these six categories (we'll list only three periodicals each here):

I. *Teachers College Record, Catholic Educational Review, Educational Theory*

II. *Journal of Teacher Education, National Elementary Principal, Phi Delta Kappan*

III. *Scholastic Teacher, Teaching / K-8, The Instructor*

IV. *Atlantic Monthly, Harper's Magazine, New York Times Sunday Magazine*

V. *Gifted Children Monthly, Parents Magazine, Teaching Families*

VI. *Home Education in California, School Activities for Elementary Teachers in California, Sutter's Mill PTA Pre-School Childhood Education Guidelines*

UNDERSTANDING THOSE COMMERCIAL MEDIA

At the outset, you have to recognize that you're dealing here, not with a kept enterprise like a learned journal, but with a **business** whose primary mission is making a profit by selling a service, that service consisting largely of news, entertainment, self-help for readers. Only by helping a magazine or newspaper stay solvent and flourish can you expect to appear in its columns.

Second, the commercial print media bear a legal and ethical responsibility to perform in the **public interest.** By tradition and statute they are common carriers of uncensored information. Don't expect a magazine or newspaper to become a consistent, exclusive purveyor of your point of view.

Third, **time and space factors** are crucial. A MS that isn't timely or that runs on and on page after page has little chance of making it.

Fourth, each of the media is really a collection of media. A newspaper, for example, has a variety of sections or pages. So does the typical magazine. The more sharply you can tailor your article to the requirements of a particular **sub-medium,** the better. For instance, our ed psych professor aiming at *Better Homes and Gardens* would tailor his or her article for its "Health and Education" section.

Fifth, each representative of the commercial print media has **a particular character.** It may be a philosophical bent, a geographic focus, a topical emphasis, a concentration on a certain public, a technical specialty, and so on. Marrying MS and medium is at least as important here as in the case of the research paper.

Finally, while the commercial print media are well-staffed with professionals, their editors are nonetheless on a constant prowl for what the trade calls free-lance writers, particularly new talent. As *Time* said recently, "Free-lance writers are indispensable to American print media today." You can join them if you practice the art of writing articles and essays with the finesse and discretion befitting an academician. There are at least fourscore commercial print media of the caliber of *Atlantic Monthly, Christian Science Monitor, Harper's Magazine, National Geographic Magazine, The New Yorker,* and *Smithsonian Magazine* that qualify as quasi-intellectual journals worthy of a professor's talents.

Let's say Bill Campion at Midland University has an idea for a semi-popular article on how the federal Endangered Species Act has operated both to save rare species of plants and animals from extinction and on occasion to stifle economic development in some depressed areas of the country. For ideas on where he might place such an article, he turns to the "Nature, Conservation, and Ecology" section of *Writer's Market.* There, under the magazine *Natural History,* he finds this tip:

> We lean heavily toward writers who are scientists. We favor an ecological slant in most of our pieces, but we do not generally lobby for any causes, environmental or other. The writer should have a deep knowledge of his subject, then submit original ideas in query. Acceptance more likely if accompanied by high-quality photographs .... Buy 60 mss. a year .... Length: 2,000-4,000 words. Pay $750-$1,500 plus additional for photos. Buy one-time rights.

That sounds like a promising outlet for what Bill has in mind. *Environment, The Amicus Journal, National Wildlife,* and *Sierra* are other possibilities listed, but because Bill knows that *Natural History* has an excellent reputation among academics, he opts to make it his initial target.

ORGANIZING YOUR ARTICLE/ESSAY

While the article/essay typically can vary considerably in its construction, it invariably will exhibit the application of three principles of design:

Force

Unlike the research paper, in which you save the best for the last, in the article/essay you're under an obligation to state your text, clearly and concisely, high up in your piece; not necessarily in the first sentence, as in the classic newspaper lead paragraph, but certainly on the first page or so of your MS.

Then you add force to your text by making it an integral part of a headline/beginning/ending team.

For example, this opinion piece by economist Kevin L. Kearns in a recent issue of *The Chronicle of Higher Education*:

> **The Economic Orthodoxies Offered U.S. Students Won't Prepare Them to Work in World Markets**
>
> The American economy today is being radically transformed by the trade and foreign investment patterns established by the rise of Japan, the economic integration of Europe, and the deindustrialization of the United States.
>
> Yet, in spite of the massive changes under way, much of the academic community acts as though it's business as usual. Unfortunately, they're dead wrong.
>
> * * * * *
>
> We need our best academic minds to help formulate a new national economic policy now.

No beating around the bush there. Kearns tells us what it's all about right away, and concludes on a concordant note.(10)

Another example. Let's say, anticipating the calendar you decide to do an article for *Change* on the upcoming 75th anniversary of the university extension movement (a.k.a. outreach). To lend color to your beginning you borrow a vignette from *Time* and go on from there:

> **University Extension Comes of Age**
>
> Down the wilderness trail from the Tahawus Club to North Creek in New York State's Adirondack Mountains a rattle-trap buckboard jolted through the night, skidding out of ruts, swaying past boulders and tree stumps, creaking and clattering through the silence of the forest. The night was black and misty. The horses were barely under control. The passenger sat tensed and hunched, eyes screwed up behind steel-rimmed spectacles, mouth clenched tight like a steel clamp beneath a prairie-dry mustache, his thoughts projected far out across a new century big with change. "Too fast?" the driver shouted. Theodore Roosevelt, Vice

President of the U.S. and due before dawn to become President of the U.S., rattled back like a Gatling gun: "Go ahead. ... Go on. ... Go on!"

It was in the fungible soil of Theodore Roosevelt's "Go on" era that the university extension movement first took root 75 years ago, pledged to bringing American life and American learning into fruitful partnership. Today, as extension organizations across the country plan observances, university extension faces new problems and new possibilities.

* * * * *

For setting before the American people an unfinished agenda there are many agencies — public and private, federal and local, commercial and educational. But, says Robert H. Atwell, President of the American Council on Education, "none is more objective than the university." None is better motivated than a university with an unswerving commitment to outreach. None is better equipped than a professional university extension organization.

It is university extension that again can say to America: "Go ahead. ... Go on!"

More expansive than the first example, but the headline/lead/text/ending team are definitely in evidence, lending symmetry and force.

Focus

By focus we mean, somewhere high up in your article, maybe even right at the beginning, reduce your subject to a picture a reader can visualize and identify with — a representative person or situation.

If you're describing something like new trends in first-year orientation at large universities, for instance, use plenty of national data, of course, but also focus in on the experiences of one student on one campus in one week.

Or like this:

Older Students Blend Into Campus Scene

The first semester of classes at Midland State University is about to close. Dispersed through the crowded lecture halls, or hanging tightly to seats in seminars, are students with not-so-young faces, faces that mirror experience, receding hairlines, furrowed foreheads.

More and more, the returning adult student is becoming part of the American university campus scene.

Midland's Mary Williams is typical.

* * * * *

"The university must be a tributary to a larger society, not a
sanctuary from it," says A. Bartlett Jerome, Midland President. He speaks for college presidents across the country.

Another example, a *Chronicle of Higher Education* story. Its
text:

A small but growing number of colleges are devising
programs for minority children who are still in elementary
school.

The focus:

Most afternoons, school buses pull up to Beloit College's
campus just before 4 o'clock and a passel of chattering
youngsters tumbles out ....

Note how we lent focus to this section on writing and publishing the interpretive article or essay by profiling at the outset
a newsmaking practitioner of the art.

Framework

That outline you construct as a method of work — make it
pop out at your readers. Lead them by the hand through your entire development so they never have to say, "Gee, I'm lost."

A simple device: make your main points abundantly clear —
1, 2, 3 — just as if you were highlighting a lecture on a blackboard. Another technique, used by a sociologist in an article on
the government's effect on families in a *U.S. News & World
Report* — she introduced each principal sub-topic with questions, like this:

Can two pay taxes as cheaply as one? Should Mom go to
work? Is the big, happy family out of date? Are courts
promoting family breakups? What happens to the children?
Is welfare an anti-family program? Where will the extended
family live?

No matter how clearly you think your framework shows
through, don't leave its relationships to chance. In ways both obvious and obscure, supply your readers with abundant connec-
tives that lead them surely from one section to the next; terms
like "now let's," "as we've said," "you'll remember that." Always
keep them oriented to the terrain of your article/essay — and
the "them" includes the reviewing editors, of course.

The "framework" principle has particular utility for the
professional school or extension professor in his or her public
service role as consultant to a citizen group or organization.
Let's say you're an assistant professor of agricultural economics
asked to develop a public information folder for an area
Resource Conservation and Development program in three
cooperating counties: Price, Rusk, and Taylor (Pri-Ru-Ta). Don't
put out something that looks and reads like a campus

committee report; in both structure and appearance, make it sing by building strong declarative topic statements and emphasizing them in boldface type, like so many headlines:

Conserving and Developing Resources for a Better Community:

YOUR PRI-RU-TA RC&D PROJECT

- **Informed and balanced resource planning/actions result from the RC&D approach**
- **Pri-Ru-Ta past and present measures add up to future accomplishments**
- **Sustaining RC&D leadership is local**
- **Many cooperating agencies support local commitment with technical assistance**
- **The backbone of an RC&D project is the citizen-agency review process**
- **An approved proposal can become a completed RC&D program**
- **Completed programs encourage more proposals**

If all your audience reads are the headlines, they'll at least get the gist of your message; with luck you'll intrigue them to dive down into the body of the copy.

STYLE

If you felt yourself somewhat under wraps in writing a research paper, in writing an article you can indulge in the flavor of your writing, its spirit, your feeling for the quality of words. In short, let yourself go, albeit remembering that style doesn't condense on your document like dew.

In crafting your prose, avoid the old-fashioned, the verbose, the hackneyed, the pontifical; in other words — let's face it — don't sound like a faculty committee report. Use colorful adjectives, emotional verbs, rhythm, change of pace, figures of speech that appeal to the senses. In other words, effective style is "the evidence of things not seen."

Examples:

Harvard President Abbott Lawrence Lowell waxing poetic in the early 1900s as he pictures his vision of America: "aglow with universities and colleges like a field with campfires of an army on the march."

Clark Kerr having fun with plebeian words in *The Uses of the University*: "I once said in the 1950s as Chancellor at Berkeley that the great administrative problems of the day were

sex for the students, athletics for the alumni, and parking for
the faculty; but it could better be said now that the problems
are, instead, athletics for the students who have gone "straight,"
sex for the professors with some of whom the counter-culture
still finds support, and parking for the alumni as they return for
their refresher courses."

Professor Fritz Machlup, writing in *The Chronicle of Higher
Education* about "A Recipe for a Good Graduate Department,"
starts out with — what else? — a recipe:

> Recipes are most expediently given in the pragmatic style of
> the cookbook. Here is my recipe for a good graduate depart-
> ment:
>
> "Take 12 juicy professors of different brands and ripeness
> and place them together with 50 preheated thoroughly
> selected students at different stages of preparation on the
> same floor of a building, around a fine collection of books
> and journals and well-equipped laboratories; stir them for
> five to six hours a day; allow them to boil over several times
> and keep them simmering near the boiling point. Most stu-
> dents will be well done after about four years."

But Machlup doesn't just drop his figure of speech there; he
uses it as a framework for the balance of the article, introducing
each section with a "recipe" reference:

> Now to the ingredients. Naturally I begin with good profes-
> sors. ... The second ingredient is good students. ... The next
> ingredient is the book collection and the labs. ... Now for the
> last directive in my recipe.(13)

Professor Barbara Wright, discussing in a recent *Change*
how the best and the brightest students seem to be turned off
these days from careers in college teaching, employs allusion to
construct an appealing title: "A Thousand Points of Flight: Or
Why We Need a Kinder, Gentler Academy and How to Get It."

PERSPECTIVES

Bring to every article/essay the five perspectives your
readers will bring:

- Human interest — one living, breathing person in an article is worth a shelf of statistics.

- Significance — Your readers are asking, "What's in this
  for me?" Make sure they understand.

- Timeliness — the act of happening now, or at least just
  about now.

- Geography — if your subject is local, does it have national manifestations as well? Or, if you're writing about a
  national event, is there a local angle?

- History — Does your subject have a relevant past? a promising future? Fill your readers in.

TAILORING TO FIT: USING A QUERY

In tailoring an article, you have a big advantage over tailoring a research paper: it's professional practice that you send a prospective editor a query before submitting the MS itself, a query being a letter inviting an editor to assign you a particular writing job.

You write and mail a query when you're well in command of your subject matter and its treatment but before you invest in closure. So the query system saves you a good deal of time and effort, not to mention signifying your professional know-how.

What exactly does a query contain if it's to perform its sales mission? In brief, your query should summarize or suggest (a) your subject, (b) its appeals, (c) any special lures an editor will find enticing, (d) extras, such as photographs, and (e) you — your general competence and particular qualifications.

There's no set pattern for a query. Sit down at your keyboard and talk to an editor, exhibiting your grasp of his or her needs as well as your grasp of the English language.

Just because one editor turns down your query idea won't mean the idea has no merit; send it out again, retailored. Editors don't always know what they're doing:

> Once the editors of *Reader's Digest* received a query from a biologist proposing to do an article on "what DDT may do to the delicate balance of nature besides wiping out insect pests." The editors weren't interested. Years later, with the publication of *Silent Spring*, the name of author Rachel Carson became a household word — and *RD* would have snapped up anything she offered.

After you've received a favorable response to a query and prepared an article MS for submission, insert in your package a cover sheet recapitulating the sales pitch elements you used in the query, just as a reminder to the editor what a precious commodity is about to be accepted.

WORDS TO THE WISE

We must be frank and point out again what you probably already recognize: except in some appointments in some disciplines, what appears as a precious commodity to the editor of a commercial periodical will not carry the same prestige in the eyes of your colleagues as does the appearance of a research paper in a rigidly refereed journal. From campus situation to situation, the evaluative scale varies considerably, so you'll just have to learn to sense where and when to bet your chips to your best advantage in the publishing game.

SHAKESPEARE DID IT, TOO

Somewhere along in this discourse we can hear some of you saying, "Isn't it really beneath my dignity to write for a narrow, plebeian, modern medium? If I'm going to be an outstanding publishing scholar, don't I want to write for all time — like Shakespeare, for instance?"

All right, let's take a look at Shakespeare. Nobody questions his greatness. What made him great? The very same principle of marrying message and medium that we've been talking about.

Will Shakespeare was a man with both eyes firmly focused on the box office, since the major portion of his income came from gate receipts. His competition was the bear-baiting pit, and he was always concerned to meet it — with murders, duels, battles, wrestling matches, star-crossed lovers, suicides, ghosts, witches, clowns, songs, costume parades, explosions, thunderstorms, and plain and fancy eye-gouging. By writing for Elizabethan Everyman, he wrote for you and me today.

Take another example: Lincoln's Gettysburg Address. Examine the audience: a crowd of Pennsylvania farmers and shopkeepers out in the weather, stultified by a two-hour-and-a-half address by a renowned orator of the time, whose name today is known only to a few. What did Lincoln do? He talked directly to his grass-roots audience. He used everyday, albeit lilting, language. He kept to the subject at hand. He kept it short. So his words are more remembered than those of any other president.

No, tailoring a message to fit an audience or a publication is not some cheap trick for a supermarket rack. It's a time-tested rhetorical device right out of the copybooks of literary masters.

Or, as author W. Somerset Maugham once said: "The nature of the vehicle whereby the writer approaches his public is one of the conventions he has to accept, and on the whole he can do this without any violence to his own inclinations."

THE TEXTBOOK

Writing a textbook can be a marvelously creative experience, a tough-nosed business, and a gamble.

Let's touch briefly on each of these aspects before we dive into the nitty-gritty.

First, the absolute expression of professing is writing a text. Not only do you hone your teaching materials and techniques, but you disseminate your skills and insights to a wider public.

Second, publishing a textbook takes a lot of up-front money — not yours but the publisher's. Hence, publishing means selling, and selling means marketing, in all of which you'll be expected to play a pivotal role. So if you don't have a stomach for a certain level of entrepreneurship, forget about textbook writing.

Third, even a good textbook can rate so-so reviews and meager adoptions. On the other hand, from a first-class mass-market textbook the financial returns can be staggering. Consider, too, that the academic rewards also can vary. In some departments on some campuses, the author of a successful textbook is positively venerated; in others, a 100,000-word textbook may not count for as much as a 2,000-word research paper.

A literary critic has written of the Faustian bargain facing serious thinkers who become celebrities: "the choice between careful, qualified, well-argued scholarship or submission to the popular demand for simplified, sloganized ideas, unburdened by footnotes."

But Walter Lippmann has demonstrated that it is possible to be both a popular writer and a philosopher, that day-to-day journalism and serious works can co-exist; in fact, they can be mutually reinforcing. As Lippmann himself put it:

I have lived two lives. One of books and one of newspapers. Philosophy is the context in which I write my columns. The column is the laboratory or clinic in which I test the philosophy and keep it from becoming too abstract.

Lippmann was able to fulfill his constant journalistic responsibilities while writing major philosophical books because he zealously guarded his time, putting away large blocks solely for scholarly reflections and writing. His colleague James Reston remarked that Lippmann was just about the only thoughtful man in Washington who never complained that he couldn't find the time to think.

— Alan Hirsch, *Talking Heads* (New York: St. Martin's Press, 1990), pp. 120, 125.

If you're still into writing and publishing a textbook, there's a good way to warm up if you haven't done so already — revamp one of the courses you're teaching or, better yet, develop a new course.

GETTING INTO PRACTICE: THE DEVELOPMENT PROCESS

Ordinarily as a new assistant professor you'll be teaching existing courses in the department repertory which the chair will assign, with or without consulting you.

It's not impossible, however, that sometime in the next six

years you'll have an opportunity to develop and teach a custom course of your own — and no more pleasing and challenging an assignment could come your way as a teacher. Not that teaching a standard course can't be interesting and challenging; it can, of course, particularly if you're encouraged to use your own creativity and approach. And yet constructing your own course has an added appeal, just as would designing your own home over taking one on the market.

What's more, developing a new course is ideal practice for writing a new textbook; consider the similarity as you go along.

If you've been brought into a department specifically to open up a new line of inquiry or instruction, you can be thrown into course development right away. More likely, you'll have to identify and occupy a niche that doesn't overlap exceedingly with existing courses. Perhaps it can be initially in a summer session curriculum, where innovation is often a dean's priority.

In either case the procedure is similar. You'll have to surmount in all likelihood the hurdle of a course evaluation and review committee whose mission is to monitor campus course proliferation in the interests of fiscal control and faculty norms. In essence, you'll have to prove your proposal is eminently worthwhile in its own right without impinging on the territories of other professors and/or departments while matching the mission of your college.

That's exactly what you'll have to do to convince the publisher to take on your textbook development proposal.

In either case, jump ahead in your mind's eye to the day you'll meet the first class in your new course. Draft a document that spells out exactly what you expect your students to gain, do, and accomplish — sort of a course syllabus, in other words, albeit couched in language attuned to a faculty committee or an acquisitions editor.

As you compose the document, here are some of the questions you might ask yourself:

- What level of student am I aiming at?
- What sort of background do I expect them to bring to the course?
- What do I expect them to carry away?
- So, then, what will the course content be?
- What will be its (my) purpose?
- What will I pose as student objectives?
- What will be my method of instruction?
- What text(s) or readings will I require?
- What other materials, if any, will my students need?

- What will be my schedule of instruction?
- What measures of student attainment will I employ?
- Will this course be required or optional? For whom?
- Where will it fit into the department/college/university curriculum?
- What exactly are my credentials for proposing this course?
- If I had to distill the key teaching points for this course, what would they be?

Given your particular situation, no doubt other questions will occur to you. As you face them, keep in mind your audience — your students, above all else. Not that you won't throw other factors into the equation; they're appropriate, just so your focus remains on your students.

As you'll see later on in this section on textbook writing, all we're suggesting is that you marry your concepts to your primary medium, the classroom, and then adapt them as needed to intermediate audiences. As a matter of fact, the quicker you place yourself in a framework of textbook writing, the sooner your course plan will take on a sharp sense of direction. Besides, you may very well discover you'll have to write a text anyway, particularly now that the courts have blown the whistle on assembling pseudo-texts out of fugitive photocopied materials.

To further sharpen your thinking, take a crack at drafting the handouts you'll use for one or more instructional units, or as a textbook chapter introduction. Here's a possible outline, aimed at your student audience:

UNIT NUMBER: UNIT TITLE

Your materials
Our purpose
Our scope
Your objective
Reading assignment
Lab/library assignment
Study notes
Written assignment
Points to remember

Or something like that.

Developing a new course can be as much fun as it is challenging, and it's an ideal training exercise for the main event — writing a textbook.

You don't need to be a seasoned teacher before you attempt to write a text. Indeed, a certain synergism may develop if your maturation and your manuscript proceed together. For example, the senior author (**ACS**) started drafting his first journalism text when he was an instructor. The resulting publisher's contract became part of his P&T dossier. (Incidentally, after his *Effective Feature Writing* [New York: Harper & Row, 1960] was in circulation, a 1965 Drake University poll of journalism professors and newspaper editors, to name "the ten most valuable references" for budding writers, rated *EFW* eighth. First? Strunk and White's *The Elements of Style.* Tenth? *The Collected Works of William Shakespeare.*)

UNDERSTANDING THE TEXTBOOK WORLD

Today's a good time to be thinking about textbook writing. Challenged by skyrocketing production costs, competition from computer software, and demands for better teaching, many publishers, authors, and higher education officials together are examining ways to improve the quality and status of college textbooks.

Debra E. Blum quotes Richard Greenberg, president of the Wadsworth textbook publishing company: "Publishers don't want to spend much money, students don't want to pay so much money, and many professors want to get back to the basics of pedagogy. All this can add up to a new kind of textbook that deserves a renewed kind of respect."(2)

Two new organizations are in the field: the Publishers/Higher Education Roundtable, sponsored by the American Association for Higher Education, and the Textbook Authors Association.

You can profit from this heightened attention if you know the territory:

- As campuses re-examine their faculty reward systems, the acclaim attached to textbook writing can change with the venue. At research institutions, the heavy emphasis placed on productive scholarship tends to give textbook writing comparatively low status, but on a growing number of campuses textbook writing enhances authors' credentials under the teaching aspect of criteria for merit raises and promotions. While significant introductory textbooks may not be coming out of frontline research universities now, that leaves the door open for professors at institutions that recognize the importance of restructuring the pedagogy of a discipline. For example, historian/textbook author Robert Kelly is at UC-Santa Barbara, not Berkeley.

- The need for bigger up-front investments by publishing companies has forced editors to demand more marketing sense on the part of textbook writers. When there's so much money involved in production and promotion, publishers expect authors to be sharply attuned to audience needs and wants, not to self-gratification.

- Textbooks have to be well adapted to classroom conditions, because they face growing competition in the campus marketplace from instructional software packages, anthologies of course materials produced by photocopy stores, desktop publishing, and emerging technologies like electronic books.

- But the industry is by no means fading. The higher education textbook market saw almost $2 billion in new-book sales in 1990, up slightly from the previous year. Members of the Textbook Authors Association earned an average of $15,000 in royalties from the sale of their books. (Don't count on that much!) At most colleges, the money that professors earn from textbooks is considered their own, but some institutions take a percentage.

- Publishing companies can expect to invest anywhere from $25,000 to more than $1 million in a college textbook before printing ever begins — advances to authors, payments to proofreaders and reviewers, book design, illustrations, supplements. On the press a book can cost anywhere from $1 to $10 to produce. It may take several years to see your manuscript through to distribution — working with editors, designers, illustrators, contributors; proofreading, rewriting, obtaining permissions to quote. If there's a co-author involved, double the ante.

- The royalty rate for a college text ranges from 10% to 19% of the publisher's net receipts, equal to sales minus returns and discounts, or about 15% of the book's list price. Some costs may come out of that percentage up front: advances, artwork, copyright permissions, indexing. It's up to the author to negotiate the best contract possible. It's usually desirable to retain a knowledgeable lawyer or at least seek advice from an experienced colleague.

- Some textbook publishers invest a great deal of skill and resources in marketing. Others simply seem to shoot a lot of arrows into the air in the fond hope that when they fall to earth they'll hit adopting professors. A sound rule of thumb is to assume that what marketing strategies and actions you don't personally provide won't get done — and then be pleasantly surprised when the company knows what it's supposed to be doing. At a minimum, purchase extra books, autograph them, and send them to likely prospects around the country. You can be your own best sales rep.

Blum quotes M.L. Reedy, executive director of the Textbook Authors Association, professor emeritus at Purdue University, and author of mathematics texts: "It's time to give textbooks the respect they deserve as important instructional tools in the classroom. Writing a textbook is a big task, but a rewarding one. You're helping students to learn, and may even put a little money in your pocket — and adding to your CV."

Authors of text materials must be able to transform expert knowledge and field-specific jargon into accessible and understandable formats. In other words, they must not only know their field, they must also know their audience. ...

Text materials ... represent creation and academic innovation at the intersection of curriculum / teaching and research .... Their authors act as mediators between research and the application of that research in the educational enterprise. ...

Good text materials represent a creative synthesis and analysis. They point in new directions. ...

Effective text materials that embody current knowledge as well as innovative presentation often function efficiently as a means of faculty development. ... In fact, the most effective means of working toward change in college and university classrooms may well be through the medium of text materials.

— L. Kathy Heilenman, associate professor of French, University of Iowa, "Text Authoring as Academic Work," *The Department Chair*, Spring 1991, pp. 12-13.

THE TEXTBOOK DEVELOPMENT/WRITING PROCESS
Know Your Course Requirements

So you're unhappy with the textbook options for one of the courses you're teaching. What exactly is the matter with them from your viewpoint? Their pedantic or sophomoric style? Their surfeit or lack of substance? In what ways would your approach, your supplementary materials, your teaching points be better?

Know Your Market

Is the course you're zeroing in on unique to your campus, or is it pretty much universal? Is it a catalog artifact or does it have a future?

Know Yourself

Are you on top of your concept? Can you really handle the whole project? Do you have the time to spare from teaching, research, service, other writing, family, friends, recreation? How about logistical support? Should you seek a collaborator to share the work and broaden the market?

Draw Up a Brief Synopsis

Those are all tough questions. If they sound like many of those posed earlier in regard to a research paper or article, you're right. The players and their lines are basically the same; it's only the play and its setting that are different.

So what do you do now? Well, remember how your first step in writing a paper or article was to reduce your subject to a nub? Do the same thing now, only in a more expansive form.

When your textbook appears, its jacket or back cover will carry a summary/sales pitch. Sooner or later your publisher will ask you to draft one. **Write it now.** Nothing will so rivet your mind to the task at hand; nothing will so keep you on track through months of labor. You may somewhat alter it later, of course, but don't postpone putting down at least an initial draft.

To illustrate, here's what the trade calls "the blurb" for Robert Kelly's two-volume introductory American history text, *The Shaping of the American Past:*

> The first textbook to be built around the "new political history," THE SHAPING OF THE AMERICAN PAST by Robert Kelly, noted comparative historian, reveals how the great controversies which have shaken each era in the past are explained not simply by the conflict of economic interests and the struggle of political ideologies, but the ranging of ethnic group against ethnic group, the members of one religious faith against those of another, even life style against life style. Exploring these cultural roots makes the story come alive, for we learn to see in the past the same volcanic energies at work which have made our own time so tumultuous.
>
> The main stream of Volume I deals with the classic themes in American history: the founding of settlement and the sweep of population across the continent; the evolution of the society, its ways of life and its institutions; the great events and crises through which the nation passed, from the Revolution through Reconstruction. Volume II narrates such themes as the rise of America as a world power; the growing complexity of its society through industrialization,

urbanization, and immigration; the rise of a powerful national government, from Theodore Roosevelt to the modern
presidencies. Especially close attention is paid to the years
from 1960.

THE SHAPING OF THE AMERICAN PAST is an engaging
book to read. A new synthesis, based on the latest scholarship, it bears the stamp of single authorship, continuity of
interpretation, and coherence in structure.(11)

If modesty deters you from injecting adjectival superlatives,
OK; Madison Avenue word merchants will insert them for you.
But don't leave it to them to capture the essence of your text.
You need that crutch now as a strong prop to lean on while you
navigate the avenues and side-streets of MS construction.

THE PROSPECTUS STAGE

After you've expanded a good deal on your synopsis with
plenty of perspiration and paper, you're ready to write a prospectus (a fancy name for a fancy query).

Publishers tend to think of textbooks as resolutions of six
primary issues: content, elements, approach, market, competition, and author. To sell your textbook idea to a potential publisher, you must clearly delineate how you propose to satisfy
each of these issues.

Content

A draft table of contents will best suggest to the publisher
your resolution of content. At a minimum you'll need a list of
chapters with a two- or three-sentence explanation of what you
propose to cover in each one. Better yet would be that list accompanied by full-scale section titles and subheads.

Approach

Your prospectus will also describe to a publisher your approach. A history textbook, for example, may exemplify a social
approach, an economic approach, a political approach. A mathematics text may involve a rigorous approach, an applied approach, a conceptual approach. A biology text may be built
around a cellular approach, an organismal approach, an ecological approach. Your publisher will want to know your ideological
and pedagogical leanings; in other words, your approach. Naturally you'll want to explain why your approach is appropriate,
timely, significant, different.

Sample chapters are not essential to sell your idea but
there's nothing like one or two to demonstrate your scintillating
style and your command of those variables. What's more, sample chapters demonstrate that you can do more than generate
good ideas; you can actually carry them out. A cautious publisher is always more content to explore your potential when he or

she has at hand a sample of the goods. (N.B.: A sample chapter need not be Chapter 1 — often the hardest to write.)

Elements

By "elements" a publisher means primarily the pedagogical features you intend to infuse into the exposition. Describe these compellingly in your prospectus. Different academic fields are accustomed to different standard features: in mathematics, elements comprise examples, exercises, and definition and theorem boxes; in business, elements comprise principles, problems, and cases; and so on. But the standard features, while customary and required, must not be your only features. Features are often the "handles" the publisher uses to promote a book.

Subtle content differences among texts, while important to teachers, are usually too technical for sales reps to discern or promote. Features, on the other hand, are grist for the rep's mill. The extent to which you and your publisher devise superlative features may well be the extent to which your book is a sales success. Not just because these features probably make your book a better learning tool, but because they excite the sales force charged with exciting the market. (If all this sounds hard-boiled, we told you so.) Historical notes, interviews, group activities, sidebar highlights, summary grids, challenging problems, photo essays, marginal notes — these and many other element options can constitute innovative, unique features that will set your book apart, pique a publisher's interest, and stimulate adoptions.

For example, a potent selling point in the prospectus for *Interpreting Public Issues* was the authors' promise that all examples of news analysis and case studies of in-depth reporting would be taken, not from the likes of *The New York Times* or *The Washington Post*, but from representative small-city dailies around the country, where fresh mass communication grads habitually find their first jobs. As the publisher told the authors, "Stick to this concept. It's a good drawing card because it's a fresh twist to the requisite examples and because it's meaningful and useful to students. Fresh and useful is a winning combination in any market."

Market

If you've picked a likely publisher, the acquisitions editor probably will have a pretty good idea about market potential, but he or she will still want to know your assessment. Describe in your prospectus the course your book will fit. Is it taught at two-year or four-year colleges or both? Ivy League or state universities or both? Is it a first-year, advanced, major, or service course? How big is the market? That is, about how many students across the country take the course each year? If your market is a niche, that is, if your book can serve only a limited yet well-defined segment of the overall course market, say so. Nothing is more disheartening to a publisher than spending developmental money on your idea only to find it fits but a market niche. There's nothing wrong with writing a market-niche book; publishers sponsor them all the time, but they want to know the score up front.

Describe, too, trends in the market with which your idea is in tune. If the professional association in your field recently promulgated new curriculum recommendations, tell the publisher how your text meshes exactly with those stipulations. If an undercurrent of change is welling up in your field, tell the publisher how your text will give her or him a jump on competitors.

The more market savvy you display, the better you demonstrate your grasp of the whole undertaking.

Competition

Pick at least three texts widely used for the course your book will serve. Outline in your prospectus their generally accepted strengths and weaknesses. It's not wise to ignore or refute their strong points. Acknowledge them, but minimize them by suggesting unequivocally how the strengths of your book go one better. It's not wise either to spend paragraph after paragraph hammering away on — usually exaggerating — your competitors' weaknesses. Illustrate them, to be sure, but do so by contrasting those weaknesses with your superior advantages.

The Author (That's You!)

A publisher who is ready seriously to consider your proposal needs reassurance of your reputation and your capacity to work hard. In a single page of your prospectus, outline your achievements and standing in your field. Don't lay it on with a trowel, but don't be overly shy either. A publisher wants to hear about **you.** In your prospectus convince a publisher that you have the time, resolve, and stamina to handle a major writing task. Many first-edition texts take at least two years to write and rewrite, and another year to produce. Publishers will appreciate hearing that you might arrange a light teaching load or, better, a sabbatical. They'll want to know, too, whether you have access to word-processing equipment. If you're able and willing actually to compose on a computer, many publishers will be delighted at the prospect and will take your MS from a diskette, reducing the likelihood of typos.

AND SO TO MARKET

When do you send off your prospectus? After you're confident you can deliver on all its promises but before you go much further. Oh sure, it's possible to complete your MS before you test the waters, but that's really foolhardy. An interested publisher will likely have a good deal constructively to say about your plan, so wait for feedback before you plunge far ahead. Be prepared, though, to send a chapter or two in short order to a publisher who nibbles at your bait and wants to see more.

And now here's a big switch. Unlike the ethic governing the submission of research papers and interpretive articles, which limits you to approaching one publication at a time, in selling your textbook idea you can approach any number of publishers simultaneously — provided you are reasonably up-front about it. That's because fully evaluating a prospectus can be so time-consuming that if you submit to publishers one at a time, literally a year or several could pass before the right publisher gets a turn to see your brainchild. Publishers recognize this, so they expect you to canvass the field. A dynamite prospectus can prompt several favorable responses at about the same time, which puts you in the driver's seat.

Choosing Prospective Publishers

To whom do you send your prospectus? To publishers specializing, or at least dabbling, in your field. Who are they? Here's where we're almost tempted to say, "If you don't know, then maybe you're not ready for the writing task." To jog your market savvy, peruse the shelves of your department reference room, the campus library stacks, ads in professional journals, directories of text publishers, the sample texts that come to you.

Cruise the display concourse at your association convention. Talk to the publishers' reps there or when they come to your office to sell you their wares. (Some may even — oh, happy day! — proposition you to write a text for them.) In fact, some publishers require a sales rep's recommendation.

Be on the lookout both for the old established houses that carry great repute in your field, and for young and hungry houses eager to build their lists. If any colleagues have had publishing experience, pump them for tips about editorial support, marketing energy, royalty rates, and so on.

(Of course, your savvy can deteriorate as publishing house control, interests, and personnel change mercurially these days. So yesterday's expert can be pass tomorrow.)

Packaging Your Prospectus

Cover your prospectus with a personal letter on professional stationery in which you adapt your handy-dandy synopsis to its marketing mission. With well-chosen words, sell your sizzle as well as your steak. Mail unfolded first-class, addressed to the acquisitions editor by name. (It's worth a phone call to get it.)

Now What?

While you're waiting for publisher reactions, there are a couple of useful things you can do, besides betting on the outcome by working on another chapter or two.

Field Test. Why not use your classes as a sample market to field-test your product? Take that sample chapter and either stake your students to free copies or get your favorite local copy shop to act as publisher. Before you do, copyright. That's easy. Get the simple application form from the Copyright Office, Library of Congress, Washington DC 20559. Fill it out and return with a copy of your MS and the $10 fee. On your MS indicate "© 199_ by author."

After exposing your students to your draft chapter as supplementary reading, generate some feedback through questionnaires, focus groups, or even a pop quiz. But take any results under advisement; it's professors who adopt texts, students just buy and use them.

Anticipate Publisher Requirements. Even the most sanguine publisher is going to lean on you for help in marketing your text, so start now to compile the lists of names and addresses he or she will want: experts you know directly or indirectly who might give you the sort of favorable capsule review a publisher likes to put on book jackets and in ads; colleagues you know directly or indirectly around the country who teach a course for which your text might be most appropriate; professional organizations in the field; journal editors you know directly or indirectly who might be inclined to give you a boost; ditto for newspaper book page editors, potential writers of your foreword, and so on.

Keep Your Eyes Open. Read those same journals and newspapers regularly for breaking news and commentary that can lend timeliness and significance to your MS. (You'll want to do the same after your text comes out, looking ahead to a second edition!)

Keep Records. Start keeping detailed records of all the legitimate expenses you incur in producing your textbook. They're deductible against royalty income. There are whole books on this subject; for example: *Tax Guide for College Teachers and Other College Personnel* (College Park MD: Academic Information Service), published annually.

Keep Your Nose Clean. Don't get so ensnared in your textbook project that you neglect what the comptroller is paying you for — teaching, research, service — or what your family and friends expect in the way of time and attention.

Signing That Contract

Assuming that glorious day arrives when you have a

textbook contract in hand, break out the party hats — and consult a knowledgeable lawyer who can guide you through the fine print and help assess the rewards and constraints.

One textbook author/commentator lists such points as these to negotiate:

- How about a large advance as evidence of the publisher's commitment?
- How about a grant-in-aid to help defray expenses?
- Who pays for permissions?
- Who pays for artwork/photos?
- Is there a non-competition clause restricting your association with another publisher?
- Who will you work with after the acquisitions editor?
- Who makes the ultimate decisions on substance and style?
- How many author copies do you receive?
- Who pays for any last-minute changes in page proofs?
- Can royalty payments be spread out over X years to escape heavy taxes in any one year?
- Is the publisher on the hook for a second edition?

Once you sign on the dotted line, add "under contract" to your CV!

OBITER DICTUM

In developing this section on textbook writing and publishing, we relied significantly on a professional independent developer of textbooks for major publishing houses, Laurie Golson of Evanston IL.

Her closure to you:

> Almost any teacher can write a textbook. But it takes vision to write a good one. And by 'good' I don't mean 'big selling.' No matter what its sales outcome, a textbook that honestly reflects the vision of a determined author is a good textbook. If you're the author of such a textbook, you can be proud of its quality.

PRINCIPLES OF CONSISTENT PUBLICATION

As you know, when you come up for tenure your productive scholarship will be evaluated not only in terms of your **performance** to date but equally in terms of your **promise** in years to come. Promotion-and-tenure (P&T) committees take a dim view of one- or two-shot authors. Again, when you're up for promotion to full professor, the story will be the same. So the sooner you outline and begin a long-range publication plan as an intimate aspect of a lifelong career in academe, the surer will be your footing.

Fortunately there are a number of effective strategies you can employ to get maximum publication mileage out of every hour you spend on your scholarly pursuits.

To illustrate these strategies, the authors of this manual will share with you here some of their varied real-life experiences.

By way of background, Clay Schoenfeld (**ACS**) has a 40-year career in university administration, in a professional school, and in the social sciences. Hence his publication record spans far more time than you have as a candidate for associate professor, but that record can well suggest the options you can already begin to adapt in building a formidable dossier. Robert Magnan (**RM**), on the other hand, is a relatively recent veteran of the publish-or-perish wars in the humanities, so the strategies he employed beginning even as a graduate student are directly relevant to your needs.

At any rate, we think you can draw some useful tips from what has worked for us — and for many others.

PRESENTING PAPERS

A typical convention of a learned or professional society will be built around a series of sessions or panels on current topics selected by the program committee, which in turn will make an advance announcement of the subject matter in demand. Cast as wide a net as you can for these announcements. A paper you're working on but which isn't yet ready to submit for publication may be just what a session chair is looking for. Usually you'll be asked to submit an abstract and a CV for review. Give it your best shot. Perhaps a senior colleague can also help arrange that you be invited to make a presentation. Jump at the opportunity.

Now here's a valuable tip: **Give them something to take home.** In other words, don't go with just notes or a fragmentary script; go with manifold copies of a complete, albeit draft, MS — complete with title, author, institutional affiliation, address, phone number, and the name, date, and place of the conference. Indicate at the top of every page something like "Draft" or "Not for publication." Pass it out or make it available at the close of your presentation, so as not to distract attention from your talk itself.

That handout is not only a great business card for potential contacts; it constitutes a type of published (that is, "made public") work, so you can add it right away to your dossier and CV.

You don't have to wait, of course, for a session or panel topic announcement to show up. If you have a paper in its final stages, why not suggest to a society program chair a session topic custom-made for your subject matter? (This approach naturally requires lead-time.)

Does presentation of a draft paper at a professional conference jeopardize its eventual acceptance by a learned journal? Not usually. Journal editors are gun-shy only of research results made known to the mass media in advance of peer review. But when you submit the paper you'll want to acknowledge its prior presentation in a footnote.

One pitfall in presenting papers: P&T committees may assign different values to different sorts of presentations, as we've said before. For example, the value of a solicited work may be problematic. Sometimes colleagues rate it higher than unsolicited work, since it shows that you've established a reputation. Others give less credit, since it's only nominally refereed, and since there's the nagging suspicion the solicitors strongly encouraged, maybe helped, even collaborated. By and large, though, any sort of presentation is better than none.

Both authors inaugurated their scholarly careers presenting invited papers at their respective learned society conventions — and some of the resulting contacts bore rich fruit over the years.

NETWORKING

In the world of productive scholarship, quite as much as in most callings, contacts are the name of the game. As at that first learned society meeting, make contacts — and keep in touch. It may take time and energy to build and maintain a utilitarian network, but there are considerable benefits.

Write letters now and then to members of your dissertation committee, updating them on your activities. Correspond with fellow grad students who are now out there in areas related to yours. When you attend those conferences, take the initiative to meet kindred scholars, both new and established. It's called casting your bread upon the waters.

Keeping in touch doesn't have to be tedious. Keep a log — another use for your computer — of your professional activities, research interests, related contacts (with a summary of their activities and interests), presentations, publications, and so on. (You should be doing this anyway, as you've learned, to maintain a record for your annual reviews and your P&T dossier.) Periodically, perhaps when you're feeling temporarily burned out, write a few "update letters," customizing your "brag sheet" with personal chitchat and questions about what your colleagues are up to. A few hours from time to time can keep you active in your network. Don't ignore phone or electronic mail options, either.

You can live well on the fruits of your professional

grapevine. For example, **RM** kept in touch with several of his professors who had a professional stake in his progress as a product of theirs. When one of them got involved in compiling a book about the literary representation of aging, he invited his former student to write a chapter. A few years later the same professor asked **RM** to translate an essay for a collection. Even later, another of his former professors, in the throes of organizing a conference session, suggested that **RM** submit a proposal, which she accepted.

In some examples to come, you'll see evidence of an **ACS** network in high gear.

The moral: If you want to be a shining star, it helps to be part of a constellation.

CAPITALIZING ON CALENDAR, CONTACTS

Editors of learned journals and professional magazines alike pay attention to anniversaries in their fields as a means of breathing currency into their publications. So it's a good practice to anticipate their needs.

Knowing that April 21, 1978, would mark the 30th anniversary of the tragic early death of ecologist/author Aldo Leopold, **ACS** proposed to compose a personal tribute to the man with whom he'd had contacts as a student.

To pre-empt space in an appropriate publication, **ACS** wrote a letter of query to Les Line, editor of *Audubon Magazine* — dated a year and a half in advance of the anniversary. Impressed with the evidence of thinking ahead, Line asked to see a 5,000-word MS. The resulting article, "Aldo Leopold Remembered," came out in the April 1978 issue.

Timing is important; contacts are helpful.

MULTIPLE PAPERS FROM ONE IDEA

ACS had illustrated the Leopold MS with original color transparencies depicting scenes highlighted in Leopold's best-selling *Sand County Almanac*. When Line rejected them as "not up to par," **ACS** wrote extended captions for each one and placed the result, "Our Leopold Legacy," in a 1979 *Wisconsin Sportsman*.

That's a simple illustration of how to milk as much as possible out of a single data set. For examples of more bountiful means of developing multiple papers from one idea, read on.

The passage of the federal Wilderness Act of 1964, reserving millions of American acres "where the earth and its community of life are untrammeled by man, where man himself is a visitor who does not remain," reserved as well a fruitful field of research for scholars in a dozen disciplines. By 1974 their studies cried out for analysis, consolidation, and application, so a trio of social scientists in USDA Forest Service research stations allied with universities set out to develop the first book-length treatise devoted exclusively to the philosophical, biological, social, and political dimensions of wilderness management.

For the chapter on wildlife management in wilderness, one of the three, John Hendee, enlisted the assistance of **ACS**, then an adjunct member of a department of wildlife ecology faculty. (Building on a chance acquaintance at a professional conference when they were both neophytes a score years before, Hendee and **ACS** had become professional collaborators and personal friends. Hendee is now Dean of the College of Forestry, Wildlife, and Range Sciences at the University of Idaho.) Their first draft resulted in "Wilderness Management for Wildlife: Philosophy, Objectives, Guidelines," a paper published in the 1976 *Transactions of the North American Wildlife and Natural Resources Conference*.

After the eventuating chapter on "Wildlife in Wilderness" in *Wilderness Management* came out in 1977, the two co-authors realized they had compiled enough material for a separate book, so they found a publisher for *Wildlife Management in Wilderness* in 1978. Over the next 18 months, spin-off reports and articles included: "Who's Minding the Wilderness Store?" in *The Journal of Soil and Water Conservation*, "Wilderness and Wildlife" in *National Wildlife*, "Managing Wildlife in Forest Wilderness" in *American Forests*, "Wildlife Management in Park Wilderness" in *National Parks and Conservation Magazine*, "Let's Keep Wilderness Wild" in *Outdoor Life*, and "Wilderness Wildlife Management Conflicts" in *Western Wildlands*. (Matching their credentials to the standards of the various publications, the co-authors alternated as senior author.)

The moral: Without pandering to popularization, it's perfectly possible to get multiple respectable mileage out of a single set of data, while more broadly disseminating your message to peers and public alike. You'll note also that the time-span for this exercise was well within the constraints imposed on tenure candidates.

Another example:

Growing out of their part-time roles in university administration, **ACS** and colleague Theodore Shannon were importuned by the Center for Applied Research in Education to write an introductory text, *University Extension*, as part of a series for graduate students in higher education administration. Their deadline: six months. They met it. The co-authors then realized that some of their chapters, properly focused and condensed, had the makings of journal articles. The result:

"Whither Goest the CES?" in *Journal of Cooperative Extension*, "Factors Critical to Extension Success," in *The NUEA Spectator*, "The Professor and University Extension," in *The Journal of Higher Education*, "University Extension and Public Relations," in *College and University Journal*, "Emerging Patterns in University General Extension," in *The Educational Record*, "Evaluating University Extension," in *Adult Education*, "Azimuths for University Adult Education," in *Adult Leadership*, and "Extension's Continuing Education Model," in *The Journal of Alternative Higher Education*. (Each paper, of course, indicated the source, and the textbook publishers were delighted with the free advertising!)

The time-span for this exercise: two years.

Generating multiple papers from one central theme must, obviously, be guided by integrity, not just finesse. Each paper must represent a **substantial,** independent contribution in its own right, not just a cosmetic change in phrasing. Further, each target journal must be viewed by both its editors and its readers as being non-competitive with all other publications in substance, style, thrust, and audience.

Violate these strictures and you'll merit a charge like this one from Sharon Boots, managing editor of *Analytical Chemistry*:

> This publish-or-perish business is getting out of hand. ...
> I regularly receive papers that have been submitted elsewhere under different titles or with only minor changes. ...
> I call it "salami science." People slice up their research results into 'least publishable units' so they can get several papers out of work that rightfully merits one.

Engage in one or two escapades like that and your name is mud in the profession, and rightfully so.

SPLITTING YOUR DATA

In the late 1970s, anticipating the upcoming 10th anniversary of Earth Day in April 1980, **ACS** posed a question: "Was E-Day a passing fad or is the environmental movement a permanent fixture on the American landscape?" With the aid of his academic, media, and environmental networks, he began to assemble data and opinions from:

1. Twenty former undergraduate E-Day leaders on 15 representative campuses.

2. A dozen of the original young staff members of Environmental Action, the E-Day headquarters organization in Washington DC.

3. Another dozen former environmental activists, now relatively high up in the Washington environmental establishment.

4. "Big name" leaders of veteran and new environmental societies.

5. Student environmental clubs active on 22 campuses.

6. Environmental reporters for 40 daily U.S. newspapers, and editors of 27 old and new magazines carrying environmental materials.

7. Directors of 60 environmental studies programs in colleges and universities.

8. A dozen eminent opinion leaders in the U.S., Canada, Britain, and Germany.

9. Heads of member schools in the Association for Education in Journalism.

10. An extensive literature search.

Once all the disparate data were in hand, he put together a tome. He should have known better. It was long on length, short on focus — and "bounced" from three journals. Whereupon **ACS** took the obvious remedial action: he split his data, did considerably more research and cogitation, sought some collaborators, and developed a number of discrete papers tailored to the demands of various editors.

The results: these publications prepared in the time-span 1978-1982:

From Sources 1, 2, and 3: "Student Eco-Activists Revisited: Long-Term Correlates of Earth Day," in *The Journal of Voluntary Action Research;* "Earth Day Leaders Revisited: Where Are They Now?" in *Environment.*

From Source 6: "Ecological Conscience in the Newsroom," in *Journalism Quarterly;* "Assessing the Environmental Reportage of the Daily Press," in *The Environmental Professional.*

From Sources 3, 4, 5, and 8: "Environmentalism: Fad or Fixture After 10 Years?" in *American Forests;* "Environmentalism: Over the Hill or Coming of Age?" in *Not Man Apart.*

From Source 7: *Environmental Education in Action: Case Studies of Environmental Studies Programs in Colleges and Universities,* ERIC/SMEAC, The Ohio State University.

From Sources 6 and 10: "American Magazines and the Environmental Movement: Symbiotic Relationship, 1966-1975," in *Journalism Quarterly;* "Media Roles in a Social Movement: An Ideology Diffusion Model," in *Journal of Communication;* "Pitfalls and Possibilities in Environmental Communication: A Review of the Research Literature," in *Environmental Education and Information.*

From Sources 6, 8, and 10: "Constructing a Social Problem: The Press and the Environment," in *Social Problems;* "The Press and NEPA: The Case of the Missing Agenda," in *Journalism Quarterly.*

From Sources 6, 7, and 9: "Environmental Communication Programs Come of Age," in *Journalism Educator;*

"Environmental Impact: University Programs in Journalism,"
in *The Journal of Environmental Education.*
From Sources 4, 6, 7, 8, and 9: "Educating the Public: The
Media and the Environment," in *The Environmentalist;* "Environmental Communication as Education," in *Facets and
Faces of Environmental Education*, New Jersey School of Conservation.

All of these were in print between 1979 and 1983.

We trust you'll recognize the *programmatic* nature of this re-
search/publication record — variations on a central theme. But,
as you might imagine, not everyone in academia will agree with
the "multiplier" approach. For example, this from a reviewer:

> I would never recommend that a new assistant professor
> spend time preparing different versions of the same data
> set for different outlets and levels of readers. He or she
> should use the same time more wisely working on more sub-
> missions to scholarly journals. Only full professors seem to
> have the luxury of trying to reach wider audiences!"

A moral: While splitting your data can be a very effective
strategy, it's no short cut. Along with it goes research, compilation, submission, rejection, submission, rejection, remedial
work, submission again.

Obviously there are professional hazards to be assiduously
avoided if you propose to split your data. To quote Professor
Camille Paglia (this time she's right on):

> The publish-or-perish tyranny has led the profession to be-
> come obsessed with quantity over quality .... Burger King
> now rules the campus. ... Right now, young academics are
> caught in a bind that pits scholarly integrity against eco-
> nomic self-interest, particularly if they are responsible for
> children. ... Rushing people into print right after grad school
> just leads to portentous fakery, which nobody reads anyhow.

> Maynard Mack was already saying in 1969 to my graduate
> seminar at Yale that "95% of what is published in any given
> year should be ritually burned." The pressure on shaky
> novices to sound important and authoritative makes for
> guano mountains of dull rubbish.(15)

We're not recommending any such frantic proliferation, of
course.

SAILING ON CROSS-CURRENTS

A prime strategy for generating multiple papers calls for
practicing peripheral vision by bringing into your sights conferences and journals not directly in your discipline but not unrelated to your scholarly interests.

When **RM** was a graduate student in medieval French literature, the subject of his dissertation was "Aspects of Senescence

in the Work of Eustache Deschamps," a lesser-known 14th-century writer. In diligently scanning department bulletin boards, he found out about a conference organized around the theme, "The Meanings of Old Age," sponsored by the Missouri Gerontology Institute. Drawing on his research, **RM** prepared a paper and made a presentation on medieval attitudes toward aging and sexuality.

The conference exposed **RM** as well to other work being done on the literary representation of aging — valuable data for his Ph.D. thesis. The Institute published his paper in its conference proceedings and Hunter College published an abstract in its newsletter. **RM** had found an academic cross-current, sailed along on a minimum of time and energy — and added to his CV a presentation, a published paper, and a citation.

At another conference **RM** found posted on a bulletin board some information about *Ars Lyrica*, a journal dedicated to the relationships of words and music through the ages. Several poems by his medieval Frenchman not germane to **RM**'s dissertation provided material for a presentation at a subsequent conference — and forthcoming publication in *Ars Lyrica*.

When he found a proposal for a conference session on images of the apocalypse in medieval literature, and for another session on the *Book of Psalms* in medieval literature, **RM** considered what Deschamps had written in those two veins and prepared two presentations for the conference. In doing so, he gained entry into circles of scholars interested in tangential religious matters.

So don't wear blinders that obscure all but the publishing outlets in your little corner of the world. Are there associations or journals outside your specific area that might be interested in some aspect of your work? Is there a conference topic that touches your interests in some way? As you read articles and books in furthering your research, note references to unfamiliar journals and association publications. When you scan bulletin boards, consider whether you have anything to offer conferences or essay collections outside your usual purview.

There's a quadruple bonus to "working the neighborhood": presentations and papers outside your primary focus provide wider recognition of your scholarship, an opportunity for contacts off your beaten path, **and** proof for your colleagues that you aren't a one-trick pony.

A frequent P&T committee question: "Is the candidate continuing to develop beyond the thrust of his Ph.D. thesis?" Presentations, publications, and reference scholars in diverse areas can provide cogent evidence of scholarly development — especially valuable at an institution where the ultimate P&T

committee is all-campus and multidisciplinary.

ORGANIZING A CONFERENCE/PROCEEDINGS

You don't have to wait for a fitting symposium announcement to show up on a bulletin board; you can use your network
to plant and water a seed. While organizing a custom conference
is always possible, it's much easier to project a session that rides
piggy-back on an annual convention.

To help stimulate research and policy formulation at that
point where the wildlife sciences and the social sciences impinge, Professor John Hendee and **ACS** formed a network of
kindred scholars around the country — a People/Natural Resources Research Consortium. Then they persuaded the program
chair of the 38th North American Wildlife and Natural Resources Conference to schedule two technical sessions in the genre.
The resulting papers were published in the Conference *Proceedings* under the general title "Human Behavior Aspects of Wildlife Management."

When a concurrent new North American Wildlife Policy concluded that "our most neglected and crucial research needs are
those concerning human social behavior," Hendee and **ACS**
drew on the assembled papers and others to edit what in effect
was an interim text for resource management grad students,
*Human Dimensions in Wildlife Programs: Reports of Recent In-
vestigations*, published by the Washington DC Wildlife Management Institute.

If you think that only scholars with track records can organize a conference and/or edit a collection of papers, think
again.

Beginning when he was a graduate student, **RM** used his
research on Eustache Deschamps, that 14th-century French
writer, as the basis for several presentations at the annual International Congress on Medieval Studies — one in 1982, one in
1985, and two in 1987. Because Deschamps is considered a
minor figure, **RM** labored in relative obscurity. But his presentations nonetheless caught the attention of a few other young
scholars interested in Deschamps. One of them then decided to
organize a conference for which **RM** prepared a presentation.
The other raised the possibility of founding a Deschamps
society. (All it takes is a letterhead.)

Although organizing an entire conference involves a lot of
work — especially if you aren't well-known — and may lack
some P&T clout, it may be worth your while, as we've said, to
propose sessions in conjunction with an established conference
and/or to create a special-interest network of scholars in your
particular area. There is indeed strength in numbers. Sessions
can lead to opportunities to publish a collection of articles

(perhaps with you as the editor). A society offers you a chance of serving as an officer, in addition to prominence as a founding member.

Remain ever vigilant for the knock of opportunity. A few years ago a colleague of **RM** was asked to help organize a symposium session. Although she was busy, she recognized that the activity would put her in contact with some major figures in her field, so she grabbed the opportunity. The benefits of networking and session inception are well worth the investment in time and energy.

FOUNDING A JOURNAL

As scholars open up ever more discrete fields of research, new journals multiply like wire hangers in a closet. It's not so difficult as you might think to participate in founding one.

In the early 1960s, before the term "environmental" had entered the higher ed lexicon, scattered cadres of scholars and their graduate students in an array of disciplines were beginning to try to identify the scope and depth of what would become, if not a new field, at least a redefined field of investigation and instruction. At the time, however, editors of existing journals, unaware of the coming wave, were uniform in their rejection of manuscripts with an environmental cast, not recognizing that sometimes a topic can be so prescient and important that research methodology and conclusions are secondary.

Frustrated by their consistent inability to break into print, those cadres of professors simply created their own custom journals, using a variety of backers with venture capital.

For example, botanists started *The Ecologist;* nuclear scientists, *Environment;* sanitarians, *Environment Action Bulletin;* psychologists, *Environment and Behavior;* lawyers, *Environmental Affairs;* urban and regional planners, *Environmental Comment;* engineers, *Environmental Science and Technology;* mass communicators and educators, *The Journal of Environmental Education;* librarians, *Environmental Abstracts;* and so on.

By 1974 a directory of journals open to environmental papers listed 27 that had not existed 10 years before. Some were to disappear as established journals began to welcome environmental submissions; others today are among "most cited" publications.

The moral is clear: if you're at the growing edge of an as yet unconsolidated field, identify fellow pioneers, locate an angel, and start your own journal.

Let's use the inception of *The Journal of Environmental Education* as a case study in how to go about it:

The *JEE* was actually the brainchild of two University of Wisconsin-Madison grad students, Keith Stamm in agricultural journalism (now professor of mass communication, University of Washington) and Robert Roth in curriculum and instruction (now assistant director, School of Natural Resources, The Ohio State University). They sold the concept to **ACS**, who then undertook to follow these procedures recommended by a publisher of multiple journals:

> 1. Draft an initial prospectus to use in lining up an editorial board well dispersed in terms of geography, discipline, and institution.

> 2. Prepare a "for instance" first-issue table of contents, plus a sample paper.

> 3. Make a thorough analysis of the width and depth of potential subscribers.

> 4. Prepare a first-year budget, preferably starting out with a quarterly.

> 5. Now put together the same type of detailed proposal you use to market a textbook idea.

> 6. Send the proposal to likely sources of funding. Your graduate school may maintain a kitty of funds as start-up money to encourage new journals. So may your campus press. Your learned or professional society may help. Then there are commercial publishing houses that make it their business to support a stable of journals exploring frontiers of scholarship, from Heldref Publications in Washington DC to Sage Publications in Beverly Hills CA.

In the case of the *JEE*, a local "angel" appeared in the form of the president of Dembar Educational Research Services, Inc., a Madison WI publisher of educational research journals and monographs. With a $5,000 stake and a well-conceived subscription campaign, the *JEE* came out in fall 1969 and broke even by the end of its first year.

Today the *JEE* is **the** journal in its multidisciplinary field, now a Heldref publication, with Roth and Stamm among its editors, and with a 3,000-plus circulation.

Incidentally, selecting outstanding papers from early journal issues, the editors put together two collections published in hard cover by Dembar: *Outlines of Environmental Education* and *Interpreting Public Issues. JEE* personnel also participated in energizing the North American Association for Environmental Education, which recently saluted **ACS** for "tireless, dedicated, creative service." (What some of its members really meant was, "We made tenure, thanks to the outlet you provided for our research papers that didn't fit anywhere else.")

A final word: Your first couple of issues are your "show windows," your very best advertisements. Invest plenty of time and attention on them. Go for quality rather than quantity. Better to start out printing 32 top-notch pages than 64 second-rate. If you begin accepting almost every MS that comes in over the transom, you'll quickly gain a reputation as an "easy mark" and you'll have a tough time ever raising your pecking order rating.

As an alternative, in advance openly solicit contributions from "name" people in the field. It's the rare scholar or practitioner who won't have a conference paper in a drawer, ready to go. The first issues of the *JEE* were so distinguished it took some time to get up to that speed again. In the meantime, the *JEE* was collecting citations in other journals and compliments from readers — establishing its prestige quickly.

It must be admitted, of course, that *The Journal of Environmental Education* caught a wave, its inception coinciding by a few months with the arrival of the National Environmental Protection Act, the Environmental Protection Agency, the National Environmental Education Act, and Earth Day. You might not be so lucky.

No less a personage than Amitai Etzione, University Professor at George Washington University, is having trouble launching a journal, *The Responsive Community: Rights and Responsibilities*. Says Etzione:

> If you're thinking of starting a quarterly publication, lie down until the urge goes away. I did not; I am still standing, but barely. The economic, social, and intellectual curve balls that I have had to field in the past I would not wish on my least favorite people.
>
> ... You need deep pockets to start a publication .... Besides needing money to get started, we needed writers .... Our biggest challenge, however, has been to keep our voice clear enough so that it adds to the intellectual give and take and avoids the labeling applied by extremists on either side of various issues ....
>
> Despite such frustrations and the realization that starting a new quarterly is a sure way to make enemies and lose friends *en masse* as well as being a fabulous way to lose all your money and more in a hurry, our experience has been exhilarating. We seem to have reached a lot of people.(6)

One reviewer remonstrates: "This is all absolute *craziness* — that an assistant professor found a journal. Even if he or she can find the time, it will be viewed as a 'vanity press.' "

CO-AUTHORING, COLLABORATING

As you've seen, sharing your time and talent can open up publishing opportunities to you that would otherwise be denied, as well as professional and personal relationships. By hitching your wagon to a star, you can ride along on a mentor's reputation. Sometimes you've got to use a crutch before you can walk

alone. Of course, it's not unknown that a junior professor can
wind up doing a senior's work. So just make sure that you're not
a beast of burden — and divorce yourself once you get a feel for
the road.

To what extent should you share authorship on publications,
and how will academic decision-makers evaluate your multiple-
author research papers?

Professors Alan E. Bayer and John C. Smart present quantitative and qualitative evidence to suggest that:

- The practice has grown exponentially since World War
  II, until it represents the majority of work in many
  fields.
- The greatest degree of collaboration tends to occur in the
  "hard" sciences.
- Particularly in the humanities is there a markedly lower
  rate of collaborative scholarship.
- Collaborative scholarship can result in a better product,
  or at least in a higher rate of acceptance by more prestigious research journals.
- There seems to be a career path leading from single
  authorship to multiple authorship and back again.
- No uniformity exists among the disciplines with respect
  to who goes first, senior or junior author(s).
- A scholar who publishes almost exclusively as sole
  author may be negatively characterized as an uncoopera-
  tive "loner" and one who does not adequately provide a
  mentor role for graduate students. Some evaluators, indeed, may view participation in co-authorship as a form
  of collegiality that should be rewarded.
- Those who publish principally as co-authors may be
  questioned for their ability to fulfill independently all
  the tasks expected of publishing professors. Collaboration can be costly for junior faculty, whose evaluators
  want to see at least some independent publications.

As you can see, you'll just have to feel your way in regard to
the issue of multiple-author papers. There's no consensus out
there.(1)

The real question is, how will your review panel rate multiple-author papers versus single authorships? It's probably safe
to say the latter will usually outweigh the former. So it's well to
be judicious in investing in collaborative projects. On the other
hand, dual authorship is better than none.

A computer-conferencing program could be a boon to joint
authors of scholarly papers or texts. Apple Macintosh Group

Technologies' "Aspects" lets as many as 16 people work together at their own computers, writing and editing the same document simultaneously. When one person makes a change, it appears immediately on all other computer screens.

MARK TWAIN SAID IT

> To give birth to an idea — to discover a great thought, an intellectual nugget, right under the dust of a field that many a brain plow has gone over before. To find a new planet, to invent a new hinge, to find the way to make lightning carry your messages. To be the **first** — that is the idea. To do something, say something, see something, before **anybody** else — these are the things that confer a pleasure compared with which all other pleasures are tame and commonplace, other ecstasies cheap and trivial.

That was in 1869, in *Innocents Abroad*. Today he might well add, "But it doesn't count unless you publish."

References

1. Bayer, Alan E., and John C. Smart, "Career Publication Patterns and Collaborative Research Styles in American Academic Science," *The Journal of Higher Education*, November/December 1991, pp. 613-636.
2. Blum, Debra E., "Authors, Publishers Seek to Raise Quality and Status of the College Textbook," *The Chronicle of Higher Education*, July 31, 1991, pp. A 11-12.
3. Boice, Robert, *Professors as Writers* (Stillwater OK: New Forums, 1990).
4. Carnegie Foundation for the Advancement of Teaching, *Trendlines*, "The Payoff for Publication Leaders," *Change*, March/April 1991, pp. 27-30.
5. Coughlin, Ellen K., "U. Presses Ponder Their Fate," *The Chronicle of Higher Education*, July 10, 1991, p. A 5.
6. Etzione, Amitai, "The Slings and Errors of a New Publication," *The Chronicle of Higher Education*, Sept. 11, 1991, pp. B 3-4.
7. Frasca, Ralph, "The Importance of Writing Well," University of Iowa *Graduate Journal*, pp. 1-3.
8. Fulton, Tara, unpublished paper in the Loyola University of Chicago Library, 1991.
9. Jarvis, Donald K., *Junior Faculty Development* (New York: Modern Language Association of America, 1991).
10. Kearns, Kevin L., "The Economic Orthodoxies Offered U.S. Students Won't Prepare Them to Work in World Markets," *The Chronicle of Higher Education*, March 27, 1991, pp. B 1-3.
11. Kelley, Robert, *The Shaping of the American Past* (Englewood Cliffs NJ: Prentice-Hall, 1975).
12. Leopold, Aldo, "The State of the Profession," *The Journal of Wildlife Management*, November 1940, p. 346.
13. Machlup, Fritz, "Recipe for a Good Graduate Department," quoted in Robert J. Griffin *et al.*, *Interpreting Public Issues* (Ames: Iowa State University Press, 1991), p. 126.
14. Magner, Denise K., "Using Latin and History, Beloit College Aims to Instill Desire for Higher Education in Low Income Children," *The Chronicle of Higher Education*, March 27, 1991, pp. A31-32.

15. Paglia, Camille, *Opinion*, "Academe Has to Recover Its Spiritual Roots and Overthrow the Ossified Political Establishment of Invested Self-Interest," *The Chronicle of Higher Education*, May 8, 1991, pp. B 1-2.

16. Swan, Judith, and George G. Gopen, "The Science of Scientific Writing," *American Scientist*, November/December 1990, pp. 550-558.

17. Watkins, Beverly T., *Portrait*, "An Outsider Pierces Veil of 'Math Anxiety' and 'Science Avoidance,'" *The Chronicle of Higher Education*, April 17, 1991, p. A 13.

18. Weisheit, Ralph E., and Robert M. Regoli, "Ranking Journals," *Scholarly Publishing*, July 1984, pp. 312-335.

19. Zanna, Mark P., and John M. Darley, Eds., *The Compleat Academic* (New York: Random House, 1986).

VII

PRESENTING YOUR CREDENTIALS FOR THE ULTIMATE DECISION

Now comes the final race: surmounting the hurdles in the all-bets-off steeplechase to tenure. No matter what the odds the campus bookies have quoted, you can still win or lose, depending on how you traverse the final course.

Initially we had titled this chapter "Packaging the Product for Sale," but our reviewers thought that a little too "commercial," so we changed it. Yet that first-draft heading may actually be more accurate. While no assistant professor makes tenure on marketing strategies alone, you certainly could miss the mark if you don't package your wares properly.

The substance and style in which your department frames your P&T portfolio can indeed represent either a compelling consumer-oriented "package" or a humdrum CV shorn of required documentation and conviction. Like it or not, at this stage of the game you're a "product" — not a living, breathing human being but an entity your reviewers can assess only from a bundle of inanimate papers. And you're certainly up "for sale" to various echelons of judges as either a hot item or a dud.

But never fear. We're about to lead you over and through the fences, ponds, and sand traps of that Queen's Cup steeplechase finale to tenure.

CONTINUOUS PREPARATION

Your warm-up for the final starting gun you obviously should have begun and continued from the moment you reported to the campus course:

- Constantly refreshing your CV.
- Cataloging annual faculty activity reports.
- Amassing and distributing a supply of your published papers and citations.
- Preserving copies of your better sets of student evaluations.
- Preparing excerpts of published reviews and/or citations of your work, with sources indicated. (Your files may have a published citations index.)
- Accomplishing in good heart your varied responsibilities for varied echelons.
- Responding to requests from the campus instructional development office for copies of your most imaginative syllabi.

- Energizing new departures in disciplinary research and synthesis.
- Performing institutional service chores with a will and a way.
- Making yourself available to the campus outreach dean.
- Befriending colleagues, students, and staff alike as a gentleperson and scholar.
- Listening carefully to suggestions from periodic review panels.
- Picking likely role models.
- Assimilating the realities of pragmatic career politics.
- Applying appropriate suggestions from the previous six chapters in this manual in order to help you join a community of professors making themselves as useful as possible.
- All in all, striving to merit an evaluation on the order of that once bestowed by a London newspaper on a young MP named Winston Churchill: "A portentous amalgam of genius and plod."

There's a continual opportunity as well to practice a little discreet personal public relations:

- Cultivating key contacts.
- Supplying the campus news service with items.
- Contributing to news note pages of professional journals.
- Circulating offprints of research papers and citations.
- Distributing reports of any committees you've chaired.
- Responding to queries from local news media.
- Presenting to strategic colleagues autographed copies of any books or monographs you've authored or co-authored.
- Apprising the chair of any awards or grants.
- In general, making yourself as visible as valuable.

Personal PR can be overdone, of course, but without it you may become a routine serial number and your record just another personnel file.

In the final analysis, of course, the best public relations is not publicity but performance. And it is here that you can profit from one of history's great performers: "I am easily satisfied — with the very best."(2)

PICKING A MODEL

Despite their former association with the University of Wisconsin-Madison, the authors make no apologies in suggesting that you might well use as a model for preparing and presenting your own promotion-to-tenure documents the instructions provided by that institution to assistant professors and their department chairs in similar circumstances.

In its stature as an institution, in its faculty quality-control mechanism, and in the completeness and clarity of its *Form of Recommendations for Appointment or Promotion to a Tenured Position* (in this case, in its faculty division of the social studies), UW-Madison can serve admirably.

THE INSTITUTION

When the first national ranking of institutions of higher education was assayed in 1906, 15 made the list. In order: Harvard, Columbia, Chicago, Cornell, Johns Hopkins, California-Berkeley, Yale, Michigan, MIT, Wisconsin-Madison, Pennsylvania, Stanford, Princeton, Minnesota, and Ohio State. Of those original 15, nine have remained consistently in the top 10. In alphabetical order: Cal-Berkeley, Chicago, Harvard, Michigan, MIT, Princeton, Stanford, UW-Madison, and Yale — by any standard, a remarkable record of sustained academic achievement.

Clark Kerr, Emeritus President of the University of California, wrote in the May/June 1991 *Change* that all but one of those nine institutions enjoy some form of geographic, economic, or cultural endowment. The one university to rise above what Kerr calls its "natural level" is Madison: "Madison rose and stays above both its general geographical location and the economic resources of its state — a great historic feat of self-levitation."

So, their football and basketball records notwithstanding, they must do a great many things right at UW-Madison. One is the university's faculty quality-control mechanism under which every single assistant professor up for tenure — regardless of his or her department, school, college, interdisciplinary home, sex, race, creed, color, previous condition of servitude, or the clout of a dean — must run the gauntlet of one of four faculty-elected all-university divisional executive committees (biological sciences, humanities, physical sciences, and social studies) before the recommendation can go forward to the top administration, which, in its wisdom, can conceivably do some more screening before sending an annual list on to the Regents. (A school or college dean can overrule a divisional committee, but only at his or her own risk.)

Very few other institutions have such a daunting system of faculty self-governance, evaluation, and credentialing. Hence the standards and forms used in recommendations for promotion to tenure at Madison carry a certain quiet credential of their own.

Nor is it insignificant that for more than a decade the chief executive officers of America's three largest and most influential higher education associations have been UW-Madison staff products: Robert Atwell of ACE, Robert Clodius of NASULGC, and Allan Ostar of AASCU.

THE COMMITTEE CHAIR

Few people in academia today are so familiar with the multi-variate ethos of the American professoriate as John A. Ross. Oregon rancher and Army medical corpsman turned scholar of the theory and practice of mass communication with an emphasis on the role of the media in public environmental policy formulation, Ross is professor and former chair of the department of agricultural journalism, College of Agricultural and Life Sciences, the University of Wisconsin-Madison. His advisees today are staffing news media, government bureaus, conservation organizations, and college faculties around the country.

In addition, Ross has served as assistant to the dean, associate director of the Institute of Environmental Studies, executive director of PROFS (the PAC of the university faculty), member of the executive committee of the University faculty senate, and chair of the social sciences divisional committee.

It was as divisional committee chair that Ross revised and polished the University's "Statement of Criteria and Evidence for Recommendations Regarding Tenure" and devised a new 1990 "Form of Recommendation for Appointment or Promotion to a Tenure Position" — all to reflect more aptly the diverse qualifications and expectations that can characterize faculty in a "multiversity."

As Professor Ross confides:

> It wasn't too difficult to work out the criteria, but it certainly was not easy during my three years on the committee to deal with specific cases .... But then I realized that you can, on a case-by-case basis, judge quality work. Rigor is rigor! To assume otherwise is not fair.

> It seems to me the key is to have people in the quality-control structure who understand and appreciate the varied responsibilities to which faculty members in a trivium-oriented institution can be assigned. Not all professors understand, and you'll never finish the job of internal education. But I'm convinced you can recruit good people and promote them, even in a climate of a very high, single standard of academic excellence.

The Ross sense of the fitness of things academic and his feeling for the quality of words inform and inspire the UW-Madison P&T form that follows.

THE FORM

FORM OF RECOMMENDATION
FOR APPOINTMENT OR PROMOTION
TO A TENURED POSITION

FACULTY DIVISION OF THE SOCIAL STUDIES
UNIVERSITY OF WISCONSIN-MADISON

September 1990

Tenure appointments are governed by Chapter 4, "The Faculty Divisions," and Chapter 7, "Faculty Appointments," of the Faculty Policies and Procedures; the procedures of the relevant school or college; and the attached "Statement of Criteria and Evidence for Recommendations regarding Tenure, Division of the Social Studies."

If the candidate's proposed tenure appointment is to be divided among several departments, each department's executive committee must make an affirmative recommendation (see Ch. 7.02 of Faculty Policies and Procedures). In such circumstances, the chair of the department that is principal sponsor of the recommendation is responsible for preparation of the supporting material described below.

Each recommendation for appointment or promotion to a tenured position must include:

I.   A letter of transmittal from the appropriate dean or a statement indicating that the dean has given approval for requesting the advice of the Divisional Committee.

II.   A covering letter from the chair of the sponsoring department. The letter should include:

A.

A statement indicating the nature of the proposed appointment including the percent of time devoted to extension activities, if applicable. If past and/or proposed appointments are divided among several departments, indicate the nature of the arrangement and the fraction of appointment in each department.

B.

The number of eligible voters in the departmental executive committee during the semester of the tenure decision and the exact vote, including absences or abstentions. (If appropriate, explanation of absences or abstentions should be given.) In the case of divided appointments, the Divisional Committee requires a letter from the chair of each department providing the information for that executive committee.

C.

The number of years of probationary service the candidate will have completed at the end of the current academic year.

D.

A departmental evaluation of the candidate's <u>research,</u> <u>teaching</u>, and <u>service</u>, which should include factual and judgmental statements about each area. The evaluation should address the candidate's blend of research, teaching, service attainments, and anticipated contributions to the future development of the department, as well as the tenure standards applied in comparable departments elsewhere. It should review the factors entering into the department's judgment in relation to the Divisional Committee's "Statement of Criteria." The use of superlatives without analysis of the work is not helpful.

In the case of divided appointments, provide a summary of the contribution of the candidate to the relevant other departments. If the recommendation is to be made on the basis of an exceptional case, extensive documentation and justification are expected.

III.   <u>Curriculum Vitae</u> with entries corresponding to the list below:

— Name;
— Formal Education;
— Title of Thesis;
— Positions Held (list chronologically with no time period unaccounted for);
— Special Honors and Awards;
— Research and Publications: Proper bibliographical form should be followed, <u>listing the names of coauthors in sequence</u> <u>as published</u>, and paging. Names of journals should be given in full. These groupings may be useful: books and monographs; research and other scholarly papers; minor publications and book reviews. <u>Those that are peer-reviewed should be indicated by an</u>

<u>asterisk</u>. Publications not based on work performed as an assistant professor at UW-Madison should be identified. Extension publications should also be separately identified. Number each publication in the vita and identify each publication submitted with that number. (Use small self-stick tags for marking each publication with its number.)
— Research and Publications in Progress;
— Research Support (source, dates, and amount);
— Teaching (principal areas and experience);
— Service (public, university, and professional).
IV. Documentation of Research Output.
The Divisional Committee Requires:

A. Two copies of each of the candidate's significant professional publications. (These will be returned to the department.) The chair of the department should also select two research publications that are considered most representative of the candidate's work and forward <u>20 copies</u> of each for distribution to the entire Divisional Committee. For extension candidates, one of these documents should be illustrative of typical extension documents meant for use by the unit's clients.

B. For co-authored publications give the full reference including the names of all coauthors and an indication of what role the candidate has played in the research and writing. Each candidate is to be asked to estimate his or her contributions in percentage terms to any jointly authored publication including the following data: (a) percent contribution to conceptualization, (b) percent contribution to methodology and data analysis, and (c) percent contribution to writing.

C. For publications that are peer-reviewed, the department chair should provide an evaluation of the quality and standing of the publication outlet. For non-refereed publications, evaluation of the work's research and scholarly merit should be solicited from recognized authorities in the field. Please also distinguish peer-reviewed articles from non-peer-reviewed pieces clearly on the candidate's curriculum vitae. When possible please include the acceptance rate of the various journals. This information may be available from the Memorial Library reference department if you do not have ready access to it. For extension publications, also indicate for each publication outlet, any specialized nonacademic audiences for which it is designed and its influence on public policy and welfare.

D. Evidence of acceptance for publications "in press" or "accepted for publication."

E. As evidence of the candidate's stature in the field, letters of evaluation from distinguished scholars should be solicited by the departmental executive committee. At least five letters of evaluation of the scholarly activities must be provided by authorities in the candidate's own field, including at least four letters from outside the University of Wisconsin-Madison. In most cases more than eight (8) letters is excessive. Extension candidates should also include letters from recognized extension leaders and professional experts in the candidate's field. Peer and client evaluations are also to be included. Provide a sample copy of the letter sent to distinguished scholars that requests their evaluation; the letter should include a request for general comments about the candidate's several contributions and a request to explain how the evaluator knows the candidate. A list of all persons solicited for letters should be provided, indicating their affiliation and their stature in the field. A statement should also be included in the document acknowledging that all letters received have been submitted; if not, the reasons should be specified. The chair should identify any relationship (major professor, previous colleague, etc.) the evaluator may have with the candidate.

F. Each candidate is to prepare a succinct statement on his or her future research and teaching plans, say, over the next five years. This should not be more than three pages.

V. Documentation of Teaching.
The Divisional Committee requires:

A. A chronology covering all of the candidate's teaching experience at the University of Wisconsin-Madison, and other teaching to the extent possible. Teaching at other institutions must be chronicled and course evaluations provided. For classroom teaching, list each course by course number and title, and indicate its enrollment and whether undergraduate or graduate. For other teaching situations, off campus or nontraditional, be specific about the type of situation, duration, level, and audience or participants. This chronology should include a list of graduate students supervised.

B. Evidence of the candidate's general abilities as a teacher. <u>Assessment of teaching performance requires several kinds of evidence</u>. Most evidence of teaching performance can be placed in one of the following six categories:

1. Surveys of student opinion. Such surveys are most useful if they have been prepared by departments for general and anonymous administration, using carefully selected questions that have proven useful in the particular teaching situation. <u>Comparative information for other faculty and similar courses or teaching situations is necessary</u>.

When the mean values for student evaluations are provided to document an individual's teaching, please provide the standard deviations as well. In every case, include information comparing the candidate's evaluations to those of others in the same department. If such comparative information is not available, please so indicate. Student evaluations are useful. Peer reviews, if available, may also be submitted together with other materials such as course syllabi. Contextual factors the department has found important (size of class, difficulties of material, preparation of students, etc.) should be noted.

2. Assessment by workshop participants, trainees, teaching assistants, or others. Such evidence should summarize systematically, rather than simply quoting a few laudatory comments.

3. Assessment by colleagues.

4. Course outlines, bibliographies, scripts, and other teaching materials. Selected examples should be accompanied by an evaluation by colleagues or other experts.

5.   Record of student advising, consultations, and research supervision. Some candidates for promotion to tenure, and most candidates for appointment to tenure, will have a record of such service as major professor to graduate students. The subsequent performance of these students and advisees may provide useful evidence of the capabilities of a candidate.

6.   Development of courses, programs, and teaching materials. Special consideration should be given to documentation of attempts at new or improved teaching methods and materials, and to evaluation of their effectiveness.

C.   For extension candidates, description of up to three significant extension programs in which the candidate made a major contribution. Use the following format:

1.   Identify the problem, the clientele, and the needs assessment procedure.

2.   Outline the objectives.

3.   Provide details on the method of instruction and delivery, innovative teaching methods, materials, aids or approaches, and client evaluation of the program's effectiveness.

4.   Document the significance of the program and its relevance to the social problems in the state and nation, and its potential or demonstrated impact on public policy and welfare.

VI.   Documentation of Service.

To be relevant in tenure decisions, service activities must clearly involve a high level of skill in communicating and applying the knowledge of one's professional competence. Documentation of service should highlight individual efforts that are especially significant. The discussion should identify the nature of the tasks performed and the particular responsibilities of the candidate. When service is a major aspect of a candidate's responsibilities, letters should be solicited from authorities in the field evaluating the impact of the service and its importance to the university.

Evidence of public service may include:

A.   Consultations to the community and significant advisory work with government, business, or industry.

B.   Outreach program planning and development.

C.   Membership on committees and boards.

D.   Public lectures and presentations.

E   Participation in radio, television, and ETN programs.

F.   Service in official positions of public organizations or agencies.

G.   Publications for nonprofessionals.

H.   Testifying at public hearings.

I   Preparation of reports.

J.   On-site visits.

K.   The development of exemplary materials.

Evidence of university service may include:

A.   Major committee assignments in the department or the university.

B.   Chair or associate chair of a department or dean or associate dean of a school or college.

C.   Coordinator of statewide outreach programs.

D.   Special administrative assignments in a department, college, or university.

Evidence of professional service may include:

A.   Membership on state, regional, or national review panels, study sections, councils, etc.

B.   Membership on editorial boards of professional journals or other reviewing or editing activities.

C.   Office of national or international scientific, professional, and educational organizations.

D.   Leadership in the development of continuing professional education for personnel in the field.

VII. Presentation of the Case.

No useful purpose is served by the receipt of complex and expensively packaged tenure materials. The following specific suggestions are to be followed in assembling tenure proposals.

A.   Number all pages of the document in consecutive order. Copy documents on both sides of the page, where possible, for handling ease.

B.   Include a table of contents.

C.   A simple metal clamp may be used to contain the document.

D.   Plastic dividers with tabs are unnecessary. A colored sheet of paper with a heading identifying each section is sufficient.

E.　Do <u>not</u> use "Accopress" or 3-ring binders or any other bulky cover.

F.　Do not use expandable "accordion" files except when necessary to contain publications.

G.　When publications or other materials (such as manuals, tapes, or irreplaceable items) are sent in limited number for reviewers, please list these items on a separate sheet for special handling.

H.　Prepare <u>20 copies</u> of the tenure document (including 2 selected publications).

I.　Copies must be submitted at least <u>three weeks before</u> the divisional committee meeting.

J.　Questions about tenure documentation should be directed to the divisional committee office.

K.　If documentation is incomplete, delays in committee review may ensue.

Weighing the Evidence

A recommendation for promotion or appointment with tenure should identify the candidate's relative balance of responsibilities and accomplishments in research, teaching, and service. Demonstrated excellence in at least two of these areas is normally required. Occasionally a tenure recommendation may be generated for a candidate, other than one who has primarily extension responsibilities, whose efforts and abilities are not well balanced among research, teaching, and service. Such recommendations are welcomed where the candidate is clearly exceptional in either teaching or research, not inadequate in the other, and where the overall balance within the candidate's department will not be adversely affected. Where a recommendation is made primarily on an exceptional record in either research or teaching, the evidence must show clearly that the candidate is one of the very best in his or her field, and that the candidate's special competence or talents will bring added distinction and visibility or otherwise be of special value to the department. Where a recommendation is based primarily on teaching, the impact of the candidate's contributions should extend beyond the university; there should be evidence that the candidate has contributed creatively to teaching in the field. Unusual rapport with students in important, but not by itself sufficient to support a case for tenure based primarily on teaching. Significant public service contributions may strengthen a case for tenure but, except in the case of faculty with budgeted extension/outreach responsibilities, cannot be the primary basis for a tenure recommendation.

A tenure recommendation may be made on the basis of significant outreach activities for a candidate with primarily extension/outreach responsibilities. In such cases the evidence must show that the candidate is recognized both within and outside the university in his or her field, and has made significant contributions to outreach through an appropriate balance of teaching, research, and public service. The Executive Committee recognizes that translation and dissemination of research results through teaching and service are the most important responsibilities of a faculty member with primarily extension responsibilities.

If a tenure recommendation is based on administrative service as the major activity of the candidate at the present time, or where tenure is sought for an administrative appointment from the outside, evidence of excellence in either teaching or research (with adequacy in the other) must also be presented to demonstrate the candidate's ability to fill a teaching and/or research function when his or her administrative activities come to an end.

A ROSS OBITER DICTUM:

"Regarding the presentation to a divisional committee at Madison, under Faculty Rules and Regulations it is the responsibility of a departmental executive committee to prepare the documents and make the case for promotion to tenure. In practice, obviously, the candidate does a lot of the work. However, in my experience, the strongest presentations are the ones where a subcommittee of the department executive committee does the homework to make the case. The most impressive cases I reviewed, assuming academic competence, were the ones where there was a *synthesis* of the candidate's work within the context of its importance to the field. In other words, the best proposals were interpretations of the science, with 'generalizations.' This is precisely what we try to teach science writers."

A WORD OF CAUTION

It probably isn't necessary to tell you this, but we'll do it anyway: the promotion-to-tenure form we've exposed you to is a "for instance" only. Even though it's employed by one of the more distinguished institutions of higher education in the country, it's not to be followed slavishly in any cases other than in the social studies at UW-Madison.

For example, your institution may have its own recommended form, in which case by all means follow that. Lacking such guidance, remember that UW-Madison is a "multiversity," so its policies and procedures — and resulting forms — are not

exactly applicable at a teaching-oriented college, a graduate research institute, or an outreach-bent urban university.

Nonetheless, we think it worthwhile that you examine the
UW-Madison form. If nothing else, it seems to establish certain
parameters of scope and evidence. And it certainly is explicit in
terms of mechanical instructions — which again may or may not
be relevant to your situation. (For instance, *your* P&T committee
may be impressed by a portfolio tied up in ribbons, so to speak.)

The bottom line: the UW-Madison P&T form is at least a
starting point you and your department chair can use to spark
discussions and detective work on how to best present you as a
compelling candidate for tenure.

At the moment, no topic is more important in your life!

---

*The tenure system is a nearly unique employment
relationship with faculty. In essence, the tenure arrangement is a long-term contract of employment, often as long
as 35 years. It is an arrangement that provides job security
for the faculty member without any regular performance appraisal as a condition of continued employment. Such a
contract is far removed from the conventional employer-
employee relationship in corporate America.*

*The job security provided by the tenure contract, and
the accompanying autonomy over the nature of one's
work, confers on faculty academic freedom, which is the
defining characteristic of the higher education desired by
a free society.*

*The uniqueness of the tenure relationship between
employer and employee in academia is further enhanced
by the governance responsibilities exercised by faculty as
an implicit part of the relationship. Tenured faculty function normally as partners sharing control of a common
enterprise. This is vastly different from the hierarchical
flow of power and control over employees in other work
conditions. ... The contribution that academic freedom
makes to the quality of higher education, and to American society, makes such an arrangement into a sensible
one for academic institutions.*

— *The Commission on College Retirement, Pension and
Retirement Policies in Colleges and Universities* (San
Francisco: Jossey-Bass, 1990), p. 283.

LOOKING AHEAD TO TENURE

You propose to join a great and noble American reality and

an even more challenging American dream — higher education.

America's colleges and universities are a many-splen-dored thing:

- Two-year community colleges contribute egalitarian postsecondary opportunities.

- Four-year colleges offer undergraduate experiences that countless alumni/alumnae look back upon with unusual warmth and appreciation.

- Graduate research universities attract outstanding students from every corner of the earth.

- Professional schools are revered at home and emulated abroad.

- The fruits of libraries and laboratories — the quality of scholarship — are universally admired.

- Outreach services carry light and learning throughout commonwealths.

But we haven't hit our potential yet.

THE FUTURE, UNIVERSITIES, AND YOU

- Are our institutions doing enough to surmount the tensions that affect our ability to maintain a growing, competitive economy while providing adequate security and opportunity for all citizens?

- Are they contributing sufficiently to help society enjoy efficient corporate management, technological progress, competent government, effective public schools, a sustainable environment, and the conquest of poverty with its attendant afflictions of crime, drug abuse, alcoholism, and illiteracy?

- Are our institutions of higher education doing enough to build in their students, faculty, and administrators a stronger sense of civic responsibility, ethical awareness, and concern for the interests of others?

If you agree that the answer to those questions, posed by Harvard Emeritus President Derek Bok in his *Universities and the Future of America,* (1) is at least a qualified "No," then you and your colleagues have your work cut out for you.

Tenure, remember, is not so much a reward for past performance as it is a wager that a past record is clear promise of greater distinction. As a land-grant dean once advised his college P&T committee:

"In granting tenure, institutions should be like bankers lending money — they should require collateral. The collateral should be the most precisely measured potentiality possible."

REALITIES AND MYTHS

Richard M. Millard, longtime academic leader and author of *Today's Myths and Tomorrow's Realities*, (3) says higher education faculty face four key challenges — **realities:**

- Meet changing conditions,
- Provide contexts that make possible life-span learning,
- Meet social requirements of adequate advanced education for minorities and the economically disadvantaged and,
- Help the country meet increasing challenges of international competitiveness.

To accomplish these goals, to face realities, Millard holds there are seven key areas in which it's imperative that academicians modify certain key assumptions — **myths:**

1. The academy's "sacred cows" — the normative character of the past, the nature of college students, the peripheral role of older students, and the focus on "the university" as the primary vehicle for higher education.

2. "Turf wars" — emphasis on institutional autonomy, and opposition to state-level coordination and planning.

3. Curriculum — confining and even arbitrary traditions about the relationship between the arts and sciences and professional and occupational education.

4. Quality — how really to measure it, and what does and does not undermine it.

5. Access — the role of remedial education.

6. The information society — the explosive development of educational technology as a "threat" to the sanctity of the classroom, job security, and quality control of long-distance learning.

7. Relationships between business and industry and the academy — the concern that such liaisons will dilute institutional integrity.

Whether you think Millard's realities and myths are perennial or transient, enervating or inspiring, real or imaginary, worth confronting or disposable, they'll be on your agenda for discussion as a tenured professor in any venue. At least your academic life won't be dull — unless you make it so.

MARCHING BREAST FORWARD

We don't know of a better way to wrap up this manual than to send you off with a paraphrase of Stanford professor of public service John W. Gardner's address at Stanford's 100th commencement ceremonies in June 1991:

If and when you settle into a tenured career, you cannot

write off the danger of complacency, boredom, growing
rigidity, imprisonment in your own comfortable habits and
opinions.

If you are conscious of the danger of going to seed, you can
take countervailing measures:

Keep your curiosity, your sense of wonder. Discover new
things. Care. Risk. Reach out.

The test will be whether in confusion and clash of interests,
distracting conflicts, and cross-purposes, temptations to self-
indulgence and self-exoneration, you have the strength of
purpose, the guts, the conviction, the spiritual staying
power to build a future worthy of your past.

And, in case your struggle for tenure left wounds — to you
and to others — heed this paraphrase of a Winston Churchill
benediction:

We must turn our backs on past traumas. We cannot afford
to drag forward across the years the tensions which have
sprung from the injuries of the past.

The story is told about Marshall Lyautey just after he assumed control of French territories in North Africa. Surveying
the barren sweep of the veldt around him, he turned to his aide
and said, "We must plant trees."

"But sir," the aide responded, "in this climate it will take a
hundred years for a tree to grow to full height."

. "In that case," Lyautey replied, "we have no time to waste.
We must begin this afternoon."

References

1. Bok, Derek, *Universities and the Future of America* (Durham NC: Duke University Press, 1990), p. 3.
2. Churchill, Winston, quoted in Richard Hough, *Winston and Clementine* (New York: Bantam Books, 1990), p. 113.
3. Millard, Richard M., *Today's Myths and Tomorrow's Realities: Overcoming Obstacles to Academic Leadership in the 21st Century* (San Francisco: Jossey-Bass, 1991), pp. 6-8.

APPENDIX: WHAT DO I DO IF DON'T MAKE TENURE?

> *Denial of tenure ... is necessarily a traumatic experience. But it is a simple fact of university life that not every appointee to the rank of assistant professor, even one who may possess some degree of qualification, can be given tenure. ... To award tenure to marginally qualified candidates would block the road to advancement for more highly qualified prospects who may be coming down the tenure track in the future and seriously impair a university's quest for excellence.*

— Judge Henry J. Friendly, *Lieberman v. Gant*, 630 F.2d 60 (2d Cir., 1980)

Theoretically, nobody should ever run a full six-year obstacle course and then involuntarily fail to make tenure. A whole series of events should transpire to prevent such a thing:

- The candidate's Ph.D. regimen should have been sufficiently rigorous to provide ideal training for an assistant professorship.

- A search and screen committee should have accomplished its task so thoroughly that the chosen candidate was a sure bet for tenure.

- Department, campus, and domestic support systems were in place and functioning effectively.

- The candidate herself or himself quickly grasped and strove to meet institutional expectations in regard to teaching, research, and service.

- Individual mentors and collective review committees offered constructive suggestions — or clear warnings.

- In either case, the messages were sufficiently precise that the candidate need have no doubts about a likely course of events.

- In response, the candidate either voluntarily picked up the cadence to ensure a favorable final evaluation or opted to seek success elsewhere.

- P&T panels were of one mind about the caliber of candidate desired and the fit of the candidate in question.

But this isn't an ideal world, so assistant professors do indeed at times fail to pass muster, often perhaps because the perception it takes to read the writing on the wall is the very perception they lack — and they play out the string to no avail.

FOUR ALTERNATIVES

What if *you* don't win the big prize? That's a tough question — one that's probably darkened your bright hopes on occasion.

First of all, it's not the end of the world. Remember that. Life goes on.

Keep calm. Above all, avoid saying or doing anything that you might later regret. Sure, it's only human to feel disappointed, even rejected or maybe betrayed, and to strike out, to lose your cool.

So just try to relax. Maybe get away somewhere, if only for a weekend, to let loose. Then collect your thoughts and feelings and plan your next step.

If you don't make tenure, you have basically four options:

- Try, try again.
- Check out legal avenues.
- Pull out the most recent job list and a good map.
- Build a career in another profession.

The decision depends on your situation in the department and division, your CV, your personal circumstances, and your state of mind.

OPTION 1: TAKE ANOTHER SHOT

This is your most likely option (a) if you went up for tenure before your clock ran out, (b) if there's no tenure-or-out ultimatum in your department or division, (c) if you were turned down by your colleagues in the department in a close vote, (d) if vacancies are about to occur in the department, or (e) if the negative decision came at the dean's level, especially if for financial reasons.

Consider also the possible effects of our changing times. If the predictions of some higher education experts are accurate and if the national economy improves, the '90s will be a time of faculty shortages.

The signs are there. Nationally, the number of Ph.D.s awarded in education and the humanities has dropped 14% since 1979, and 3% in the social sciences. While doctorates awarded in the natural and physical sciences have increased, the number going to U.S. citizens has declined since 1979. Furthermore, many of those Ph.D.s leave academia. The Association of American Universities reports that half of all doctorates now seek employment in the outside world, with the percentages higher in physical sciences (67%) and engineering (70%).

Given the emerging and predicted trends, it might pay to keep abreast of developments at your institution, noting any difficulties in recruiting and retaining faculty in your area. If you decide to try again, your chances may improve within the year — even if you foolishly do nothing to improve your CV.

Meet with your mentor and/or advisory committee to discuss the reasons behind the setback. If it's a question of presentations and publications, then you know what you have to do and how much time you have to do it. (So get going, already!) If the decision was financial, keep working — and cross your fingers for an improvement in the fiscal environment your next time up. But if you lost out because of your teaching or service, differences of personality and/or politics, or similar problems, face it: it's unlikely that you can improve your chances at tenure within a year.

You might also consider switching from the tenure track to a parallel line, such as academic staff.

One of the junior author's former colleagues, who joined the faculty of a small, private institution, was recently denied tenure. Unable to continue along the tenure track, she moved into a quasi-permanent academic staff teaching position. It may well have been a case of *felix culpa*, since she's now able to devote her energy to teaching, free of any expectations to "publish or perish."

Another colleague went through a similar shift. After her negative tenure vote, she was appointed to head the campus center responsible for training teaching assistants, where she can now pursue her primary interest — teaching — and work on a textbook with a major publisher.

OPTION 2: FILE AN APPEAL

If you feel that you were unjustly denied tenure, whether through some technicality or misunderstanding or because of discrimination (yes, even in the enlightened '90s!), then you may seek justice through prescribed channels. Since these differ from institution to institution, find documentation on the appropriate procedures and consult with your mentor or other ally.

If your blackball occurred at the all-campus level, it's possible that the decision could be overturned through the intercession of a distressed department chair and a feisty dean.

If a straightforward appeal, a grievance, or similar action is out of the question, you might want to invest in outside legal counsel. There are some precedents for obtaining remedial compensation through court decisions or out-of-court settlements. Although almost all tenure lawsuits have been "lost causes," according to one attorney in higher education, some courts have lately shown less reluctance to get involved in academic matters and less reverence for campus personnel procedures.

With those points in mind, review the following legal decisions:

Procedural Matters

- In *Davis v. Oregon State University*, 591 F.2d. 493 (9th Cir. 1978), a written tenure policy carried more weight than a chair's oral promise that the plaintiff would receive tenure "as a matter of course." The disappointed faculty member lost out.

- In *McLendon v. Morton*, 249 S.E. 2d 919 (W. Va. 1978), a West Virginia court ruled a professor denied tenure had been deprived of a "property interest" and minimal due process rights. It held that institutions must give faculty members notice and an opportunity for a hearing before the final decision to deny tenure.

- In *LaVerne v. University of Texas System*, 611 F.Supp. 66 (S.D. Tex. 1985), the court ruled that if a university has published procedures governing tenure, a professor can't base a claim to tenure outside those procedures. The moral: know the rules — and don't count on making it outside those rules.

- In *Levi v. University of Texas*, 840 F.2d 277 (5th Cir. 1988), the court allowed a university to deny tenure because the professor's grading policies were deemed too lenient. Although grading policies weren't considered in the tenure decisions of other faculty, the court ruled that there was a rational link between the grading policy and the legitimate goal of maintaining a certain level of instructional quality. Remember: academic freedom protects you — but there are limits.

Since the key to a successful lawsuit is in obtaining evidence, the 1990 U.S. Supreme Court ruling in *University of Pennsylvania v. Equal Employment Opportunity Commission*, 110 S.Ct. 577, is a landmark decision. Declaring that Title VII of the Civil Rights Act applies to higher education, the Court opened faculty review files for a professor who claimed discrimination in her negative tenure decision.

This decision affirmed the decisions rendered in a series of tenure cases, including *In Re Dinnan*, 661 F.2d 426 (11th Cir. 1981), *EEOC v. University of Notre Dame du Lac*, 715 F.2d 331 (7th Cir. 1983), *EEOC v. Franklin and Marshall*, 775 F.2d 110 (3rd Cir. 1985), and *Gray v. Board of Higher Education of City of New York*, 92 F.R.D. 87 (S.D.N.Y. 1981), *rev'd*, 692 F.2d 901 (2d Cir. 1982). As Justice Harry Blackmun expressed the Supreme Court decision:

The costs associated with racial and sexual discrimination
in institutions of higher learning are very substantial. Few
would deny that ferreting out this kind of invidious discrimination is a great if not compelling governmental interest. ... If there is a 'smoking gun' to be found that demonstrates discrimination in tenure decisions, it is likely to be
tucked away in peer review files.

The ruling in *University of Pennsylvania v. EEOC* should
allow faculty greater means to bring legal action under Title VII
of the Civil Rights Act of 1964 and the Equal Pay Act (both
passed in 1972), through the Equal Employment Opportunity
Commission, and Title IX of the Education Amendments of 1972
(as amended in 1974, 1976, and 1987), through the Office for
Civil Rights, U.S. Department of Education.

Discrimination Cases

Between 1970 and 1984, federal courts considered 42 char-
ges of discrimination in tenure decisions. The results? As George
R. LaNoue and Barbara A. Lee put it in *Academics in Court: The
Consequences of Faculty Discrimination Litigation* (Ann Arbor:
University of Michigan Press, 1987):

One can speculate that where academic plaintiffs have
raised procedural/jurisdictional issues that were part of the
mainstream of civil rights law, they have been relatively
successful. But where they have raised claims that touched
the distinctive nature of the academic personnel process,
judges have been reluctant to intervene. (pp. 30-31)

A brief guide to litigation in this area is *Court Challenges to
Tenure, Promotion, and Retention Decisions* by Peter Seldin
(Kansas State University IDEA paper #12).

If you believe that you're the victim of sex discrimination,
you should consult an article by S.L. Schoenfeld and P.A. Zirkel
in the *Journal of Law and Education* (Fall 1989), "Sex Discrimination in Higher Education Employment: An Empirical
Analysis of the Case Law." The authors reviewed 10 years of sex
discrimination cases against colleges and universities. The
claims covered salary, hiring, promotion, denial of tenure, and
termination. The authors found that the plaintiff was successful
in only 20% of the cases.

Professional Help

You may not be alone in your tenure battle. For information
and support you might turn to the American Association of
University Professors (1012 14th St., NW, Suite 500, Washington, DC 20005; Ph: 202/737-5900). This association has long
been fighting for academic freedom and fair treatment of faculty,
chronicling the results in its bulletin, *Academe*.

Warning: Involving the courts is a very difficult and chancy

route. The odds are against you, since courts tend to avoid inter-
vening in "academic matters." And even if you win, you'll probably lose. Faculty and the dean are unlikely to accept you as a
colleague if you bring the court into their academic world. If you
succeed in winning tenure the hard way, that's only the first half
of the battle. You may feel great pressure to go elsewhere to continue your career — and probably without the benefit of letters
of recommendation. And wherever you go, you'll bear the stigma
of a "troublemaker."

---

*No one wins and most people lose when the univer-
sity and individuals resort to litigation. The right to
litigate is invaluable. ... The reality is generally a loss.*
— Irving J. Spitzberg, Jr., former General Secretary, American
Association of University Professors

Sure, there are some happy endings. Connie Rae Kunda was
denied tenure at Muhlenberg College (PA) in 1974. Her case —
Kunda v. Muhlenberg College, 463 F.Supp. 294 (E.D. Pa. 1978),
aff'd, 621 F.2d 532 (3d Cir. 1980) — was finally resolved in 1980,
as the courts awarded her "conditional tenure." Most of the faculty were pleased with the decision. Kunda continued along her
career path, receiving her promotion to full professor in 1987.

But then there are plaintiffs like Marcia Lieberman. After
losing her tenure discrimination suit against the University of
Connecticut — *Lieberman v. Gant*, 474 F.Supp. 848 (D. Conn.,
1979), *aff'd,* 630 F.2d 60 (2d Cir. 1980) — she was very disappointed and abandoned her attempt to obtain a full-time teaching position. The results of 10 years of litigation, with five
judges, 23 attorneys, the Connecticut Women's Educational and
Legal Fund, the AAUP, and dozens of faculty and administrators? Lieberman described herself as financially ruined, without
a career, in poor health, and at risk of marital problems.

OPTION 3: SEARCH FOR GREENER PASTURES

Consider what you have to offer higher education. If you lost
out on tenure because your scholarship wasn't up to departmental, divisional, or institutional expectations, check out your possibilities with another institution that places less emphasis on
scholarship, especially if you're stronger in teaching and service.
If, on the other hand, you've got impressive presentations and
publications, but lower grades for teaching, or you don't fit into
the political or social climate, maybe you can find a niche where
scholarly productivity is the primary criterion.

Sure, it would be great if every new Ph.D. found the perfect job right away and then stayed there happily ever after. But we all know that life doesn't work that way. (Just ask all those "gypsy scholars" out there!) And remember: if there are faculty shortages as predicted, higher education may become more of a "seller's market" in the '90s.

You may decide that it's worthwhile to enlarge or shift your area of specialization somewhat. Is there a glut of faculty in your field? Are branches developing? If you're alert to trends, you can add some new arrows to your quiver.

So, try to be open to seeking your fame and fortune in another venue. It's always difficult to pull up the stakes, fold the tents, say goodbye to friends and neighbors, and hit the road. It can be particularly difficult to move, of course, if you have a family with strong ties to the area. (Have you considered staying home with Option 4?) But it's not unusual for faculty to move about within the academic world — and the best way is with a healthy optimism, a sense of adventure — and a portfolio of letters of recommendation, however temperate.

Over the last 10 years the junior author (RM) has collected stories of interesting faculty career paths. Several may serve as examples of good moves:

- D.T. was an assistant prof shared between a language department and the department of instructional development at a large state university. At tenure time, both departments voted in his favor, but neither pushed his case at a higher level, primarily because his chief interest was teaching and his dossier was long on presentations but short on publications. The university offered to move him to academic staff, but he preferred to take an academic staff position elsewhere, at a smaller, topnotch research institution. Several years later, he packed his bags once again, to move to a midsize university with an emphasis on teaching. He's now happily chair of the language department.

- A.C. landed a job at a prestigious, small state college, where she was assured that teaching was top priority. When the college shifted its emphasis toward more research and publication, she failed to receive tenure. She filed an appeal and shopped around. The college reversed its decision about the time she received an offer from a small, religious school, where she'd have an opportunity to work in a department with an innovative teaching program. She seized the opportunity to move to a better academic climate.

- J.P. failed to make tenure at a small, private, and

prestigious college. Her husband, in the same department, decided to look elsewhere before he came up for tenure. J.P. expressed an interest in studying law, so they found a major university with an opening for him and a good law school for her. Several years later, he received tenure and she was beginning her second career, as an attorney.

Not every story will have a happy ending. But these faculty and others like them have taken their unfavorable tenure decisions positively, as an indication that they didn't really fit their environments. So they found opportunities to develop their potential and pursue their interests elsewhere, at more suitable institutions, among colleagues who appreciate what they have to offer higher education. It wasn't easy, but it was worth it.

OPTION 4: BUILD ANOTHER CAREER

It's not too late to change career directions. (Sometimes a negative tenure decision can be a blessing in disguise!) Just take some time to assess your talents and interests, using such instruments as the Strong-Campbell Interest Inventory and the Myers-Briggs Type Indicator. Then explore career possibilities along those lines.

If you've shown talent in research, you may want to try the corporate sector or the government, or to go into private consulting. If you enjoy teaching and are reasonably good at working with people, consider a career in training, social services (private or public), or personnel/human resources.

Some former faculty have fashioned distinguished ex-campus careers.

Consider Paul Wellstone, for example. He was once a political science prof at Carleton College. His department voted unanimously in 1974 against offering him tenure. Outside evaluators subsequently recommended that the decision be reversed. Although he finally received tenure, it wasn't enough, so he put his knowledge of political science into practice. Wellstone now represents Minnesota in the U.S. Senate ("Under the Senate's Skin," Lynn Rosellini, *U.S. News & World Report*, June 24, 1991, pp. 33-34).

Or take this case:

In 1967, a professor's son with a Trinity B.A., an Oxford M.A. in philosophy, and a Princeton Ph.D. in political science (thesis: "Beyond the Reach of Majorities: Closed Questions in the Open Society") landed a teaching position at Michigan State. After an unhappy year he moved on to the University of Toronto. The fit was no better there, so he spun off as a speechwriter and jack-of-all-trades for a U.S. Senator in Washington. Today you know him as Pulitzer Prize-winning *Newsweek*, ABC, book, and syndicated commentator George Will. Like Walter Lippmann before him, Will "chose the role of helping produce public sense in the community rather than pursuing truth in individual solitude in the academy." You can see him every Sunday on "This Week with David Brinkley" or hear him deliver a campus lecture. Perhaps in due time he'll write his own ticket as Ronald Reagan Professor of Political Economy at a prestigious university (or as coach of a struggling college baseball team.)

A generation earlier, another Oxford graduate had joined a college faculty, only likewise to find the environment something less than hospitable, particularly after he married one of his students, something that simply wasn't done at Mills College at the time. World War II and his Davidson College ROTC commission rescued Dean Rusk and sent him to the CBI Theater on the staff of General Stillwell. After V-J Day he never returned to academia. We next know him as President Kennedy's choice for Secretary of State in 1961.

But it isn't only in *Who's Who* that you find examples of faculty expatriates "making it on the outside." From his personal acquaintants, the senior author (**ACS**) can cite random instances of representative assistant professors who broke rank into successful professional careers:

- Gene Kroupa was an accomplished "numbers cruncher" who didn't hit it off with colleagues in a department of journalism. He's now president of Gene Kroupa and Associates, a market research and analysis firm in Madison WI.

- Earl Braly returned safely from the Korean Conflict to internecine warfare in an English department. Before he could be fatally wounded, he left for a long and lucrative hitch in public relations with various organizations in Washington DC.

- Richard Heilman never felt entirely at home in a department of wildlife management. He was recently retired as a senior biologist from the U.S. Fish and Wildlife Service.

- Carol Holmes got caught in an interdisciplinary environmental studies institute without a safe departmental haven of her own. She's now head of environmental education programs for a large metropolitan K-12 school system.

- Douglas Jones failed to make tenure in a school of mass communication. You may recognize his name: he's the freelance author of the celebrated book (and movie)

> *The Court Martial of George Armstrong Custer* and
> other self-illustrated novels of Army life in the Old West.

- Martha Jones-Van Dyke never felt actually harassed as
  a token woman in an all-male department of electrical
  and computer engineering, but a certain discomfort
  translated into slow research progress. When Zenith
  recruited both her and her husband with great enthusiasm, she left the campus quietly to become a data systems team chief.

Almost any senior faculty member can cite similar illustrations of the point that not making tenure doesn't have to be the
end of the line.

Career-Change Guides

There are plenty of career guides out there, including some
specifically for people embarking on career changes:

Baldwin, Roger, Louis Brakeman, Russell Edgerton, Janet Hagberg, and Thomas
   Mahar, *Expanding Faculty Options: Career Development Projects at Colleges
   and Universities*. Washington DC: American Association for Higher Education,
   1981.

Bolles, Richard N., *The Three Boxes of Life and How to Get Out of Them: An Introduction to Life/Work Planning*. Berkeley CA: Ten Speed Press, 1981.

Bolles, Richard N., *What Color Is Your Parachute?* Berkeley CA: Ten Speed Press,
   1989.

Crystal, John C., and Richard N. Bolles, *Where Do I Go From Here With My Life? A
   Very Systematic, Practical, and Effective Life/Work Planning Manual for Stu-
   dents, Instructors, Counselors, Career Seekers, and Career Changes*. Berkeley
   CA: Ten Speed Press, 1974.

Furniss, W. Todd, *Reshaping Faculty Careers*. Washington DC: American Council
   on Education, 1989.

Kennedy, Joyce Lain, and Darryl Laramore, *Joyce Lain Kennedy's Career Book*. Lin-
   colnwood IL: National Textbook, 1988.

Metzger, Walter P., et al., *Tenure*. Washington DC: American Association for Higher
   Education, 1979.

Reilly, K.P., and S.S. Murdich, *Teaching and Beyond: Nonacademic Programs for
   Ph.D.'s*. Albany: State University of New York Press, 1984.

You may even get some valuable advice and assistance from
the career placement center on your campus. Take tests to determine your abilities and interests: you might be surprised at
what you learn about yourself. Consult with "headhunters."

Pursue your education. Take courses in areas tangential or
totally apart from your areas of specialization. Try workshops
and short courses at a community college. Use your network of
contacts: talk with colleagues, friends, relatives, and neighbors
to explore possibilities. Be alert to ideas and interests that
might develop into career opportunities.

Above all, keep an open mind and be confident in your education and abilities. Good luck!

ABOUT THE AUTHORS

A. CLAY SCHOENFELD (a.k.a. Clarence A., Clay) holds degrees from the University of Wisconsin-Madison and two armed forces colleges. He is a University of Wisconsin-Madison emeritus professor of journalism and mass communication, emeritus affiliate professor of wildlife ecology/environmental studies, and emeritus dean of inter-college programs/special students/summer sessions.

The founding executive editor of *The Journal of Environmental Education,* he is the author, co-author, or editor of 27 books and innumerable research papers and articles in the fields of higher education administration, wildlife conservation, and mass communication, his latest being *Interpreting Public Issues* (Ames: Iowa State University Press, 1991).

Past president of four higher education associations, Schoenfeld has taught from Arizona State to Alaska and continues to be a consultant to colleges and universities from Maine to Hawaii, as well as to state and federal natural resource management agencies. Before being retired as an Army colonel after rising from private, he served as Commandant of the Wisconsin USAR School and as Reserve Deputy Chief of Public Affairs in the Pentagon.

Schoenfeld is now Contributing Editor of Magna Publication's national monthly newsletter for deans and department chairs, *Academic Leader.*

ROBERT MAGNAN earned a B.A. in English (with teaching certificate) and an M.A. in French at Michigan State University, and a Ph.D. in French (minor: medieval studies) at Indiana University. He taught for 13 years at MSU, IU, and the University of Wisconsin-Madison, with short stints at the Université des Sciences Humaines (Strasbourg, France) and Beloit College (WI).

As a graduate student and faculty assistant, Magnan edited a graduate journal, presented papers at scholarly conferences, published articles in journals and books, translated articles and poetry for publication, collaborated in designing a multidisciplinary course, edited scholarly papers for colleagues, and helped develop language textbooks.

Magnan is currently Senior Editor, Magna Publications. In his work with Magna, he has edited *147 Tips for Teaching Professors* (1989) and *First Steps to Excellence in College Teaching* (1990), and collaborated on *Classroom Communication: Collected Readings for Effective Discussion and Communication* (1989), *Teaching College: Collected Readings for the New Instructor* (1989), and *Building Diversity: Recruitment and Retention in the '90s* (1990).

What They're Saying About *Mentor in a Manual*

Grounded in reality, with life-like examples, this book will serve both as a new professor's guide to getting tenured and as an insider's view of how universities really run.
—Dean **John C. Hendee**, *College of Forestry, Wildlife, and Range Sciences, University of Idaho.*

This manual will be equally useful for faculty at small liberal arts colleges as well as for those in larger, more research-oriented universities.
Eminently readable, realistic, engaging, worthwhile.
—*Assistant Professor* **Ann McElaney-Johnson**, *French, Ripon College.*

I'm impressed with the organization, the thoroughness, the clarity of the writing. An accurate, down-to-earth presentation of information that is available only piecemeal to new faculty members. An outstanding job.
—*Emeritus Professor* **Dayle Molen**, *Journalism, University of California-Fresno.*

The best thing that could result from this ambitious book would be for deans, department chairs, tenured professors, and assistant professors to engage in round-robin oral reading, to start a continuing dialogue on goals and expectations.
—*Professor* **Mavis Donahue**, *College of Education, University of Illinois at Chicago.*

Honest, straightforward, clear, authoritative, representative, well-written, concise — to be used in concert with local mentoring.
—*Professor* **John Disinger**, *School of Natural Resources, Ohio State University.*

The mechanics of the manual are fine. It reads great; the reader is able to keep up with and anticipate the material. One can get promoted to tenure without this manual, of course, but it provides some crucial material that one might not get anywhere else.
—*Professor* **Robert F. Meier**, *Chair, Sociology, Iowa State University.*

Assistant professors will benefit from reading this book
[which] transcends the "cookbook" genre in its
consideration of such issues as professionalism.
The specific practical advice and recommended resources
are the manual's greatest strengths.
— *Associate Professor* **Penny Morgan**, *Forest Resources, University of Idaho.*

A glorious catalog of ideas, perspectives, sources, and
structure for the aspiring professor. Everyone should set
aside a few hours every week to read and reflect on the
guidance and wisdom of the mentoring authors.
— *Dean* **Harland Samson**, *Inter-College Programs, University of Wisconsin-Madison.*

The chapters on teaching and publishing alone are
essential reading for all professors,
tenured and untenured.
— *Professor* **Robert J. Griffin**, *Director, Center for Mass Media Research, Marquette University, Milwaukee WI.*

Assistant professors have needed a guide like this for a
long time — and now they have it.
— *Dean* **William Feyerharm**, *College of Arts and Sciences, Kansas State University.*

I'm especially pleased with the way the authors meet,
with understanding and finesse, the particular needs of
extension personnel.
— *Emeritus Professor* **James Bell**, *Agricultural Economics, Virginia Polytechnic Institute and State University.*

This guide to how to get promoted to tenure succeeds
admirably, tenaciously, and with a minimum of cant.
— *President Emeritus* **Allan W. Ostar**, *American Association of State Colleges and Universities.*

I can think of no one better suited or equipped to offer
such guidance to those entering or contemplating the
academic profession.
— **Robert M. O'Neil**, *Founding Director, The Thomas Jefferson Center for the Protection of Free Expression, University of Virginia.*